Georgetown Journal
of International Affairs

SUMMER/FALL 2013, VOLUME XIV, NUMBER 2

Georgetown Journal

of International Affairs

To become a sponsor, contact Victoria Moroney, Director of Development,
Edmund A. Walsh School of Foreign Service, Georgetown University
ICC 301, 3700 O Street, Washington, DC 20007
Telephone (202) 687-1461 / Email: gjia@georgetown.edu

Notice to Contributors

Articles submitted to the *Georgetown Journal of International Affairs* must be original, must not draw substantially from articles previously published by the author, and must not be simultaneously submitted to any other publication. Articles should be around 3,000 words in length. Manuscripts must be typewritten and double-spaced in Microsoft™ Word® format, with margins of at least one inch. Authors should follow the *Chicago Manual of Style, 15th ed.* Articles may be submitted by e-mail (gjia@georgetown.edu) or by U.S. mail; those sent by U.S. mail must include both a soft copy on a compact disc and a hard copy. Full names of authors, a two-sentence biography, and contact information including addresses with zip codes, telephone numbers, facsimile numbers, and e-mail addresses must accompany each submission. The *Georgetown Journal of International Affairs* will consider all manuscripts submitted, but assumes no obligation regarding publication. All material submitted is returnable at the discretion of the *Georgetown Journal of International Affairs.*

The *Georgetown Journal of International Affairs* (ISSN 1526-0054; ISBN 0-9824354-2-8) is published two times a year by the Edmund A. Walsh School of Foreign Service, Georgetown University, 301 Intercultural Center, Washington, DC 20057. Periodicals postage paid at Washington, DC. Annual subscriptions are payable by check or money order. Domestic: $16.00; foreign: $24.00; Canada: $18.00; institutions: $40.00.

GEORGETOWN JOURNAL OF INTERNATIONAL AFFAIRS, SUBSCRIPTIONS
EDMUND A. WALSH SCHOOL OF FOREIGN SERVICE
301 INTERCULTURAL CENTER
WASHINGTON, DC 20057
PHONE (202) 687-1661
FACSIMILE (202) 687-1431
e-mail: gjia@georgetown.edu
http://journal.georgetown.edu

The views expressed in the articles in the *Georgetown Journal of International Affairs* do not necessarily represent those of the *Georgetown Journal of International Affairs*, the editors and staff of the *Georgetown Journal of International Affairs*, the Edmund A. Walsh School of Foreign Service, or Georgetown University. The *Georgetown Journal of International Affairs*, editors and staff of the *Georgetown Journal of International Affairs*, the Edmund A. Walsh School of Foreign Service, and Georgetown University bear no responsibility for the views expressed in the following pages.

In 1950 six nations created the European Coal and Steel Community, laying the foundations for what would later become the European Union. Since then many other regions have integrated and the number of regional organizations has proliferated. In Africa alone there are several, and often countries are members of multiple organizations. Regional organizations are key actors in tackling tough problems, such as protecting human rights, preventing and resolving conflict, strengthening regional cooperation, and promoting economic growth.

The purpose of this issue's Forum, consisting of five articles, is to provide readers with a theoretical and practical overview of key aspects of regional integration and regional organizations. The first two articles provide a theoretical discussion on regional integration, while the following three articles present case studies on regional organizations – the Shanghai Cooperation Organization, the Arctic Council, and ASEAN. These pieces are summarized in Piero Graglia's introduction.

Other contributions to this issue include articles about self-defense groups in Mexico, reconstruction efforts in Afghanistan after the 2014 withdrawal, the Chinese middle class, and Scotland's referendum on independence. The issue also features interviews with Ambassador Joseph D. Stafford III on his experience in the U.S. Embassy in Tehran during the hostage crisis, Professor Joseph S. Nye on American leadership, and Ambassador-at-Large Melanne Verveer on global women's issues. In selecting the topics for this issue we have reached beyond the headlines in an effort to explore tough and persistent global problems.

We are proud to end our tenure as Editors-in-Chief with an issue that looks to the future. We are grateful to Dean Jennifer Windsor and Allyson Goodwin for their invaluable advice and support as well as to our dedicated team of editors for their tireless work on this issue of the *Georgetown Journal of International Affairs.*

Nora McGann   William Handel

Science&Technology Politics&Diploma
cy **Culture&Society** Business&Economi
cs Law&Ethics Conflict&Security Boo
ks **Science&Technology** Politics&Diplom
acy Culture&Society Business&Econom
ics Law&Ethics **Conflict&Security**
Books Science&Technology Politics&Dip
lomacy Culture&Society Business&Econ
omics **Law&Ethics** Conflict&Security Sc
ience&Technology **Politics&Diplomacy**
Culture&Society Business&Economics
Law&Ethics Conflict&Security Bo
oks **Business&Economics** Politics&Diplo
macy Culture&Society Business&Econ

Georgetown Journal

of International Affairs

Each Section. Every Issue. One Journal.
for more information or to subscribe
visit http://journal.georgetown.edu or email gjia@georgetown.edu

now featuring bi-weekly short essays, commentaries and analyses online

Forum

GEORGETOWN JOURNAL OF INTERNATIONAL AFFAIRS

The Integration of Regions

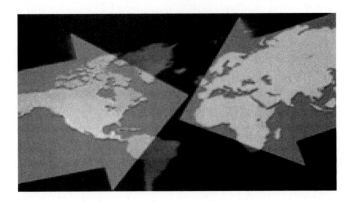

Regional integration and regional organizations are two sides of the same coin although at times stamped with different metals. Regional organizations are often characterized by different levels of integration, and an integrated region can present itself in various ways with regards to security integration, environmental protection integration, and economic and trade integration. In other words, we lack a reference system or scale to determine the "extension" (as a logic theorist would say) of the integration process. The reason is that between the Westphalian Nation-State willing to collaborate with its neighbors and a complete federal union, we can find several models and historical examples of political and economic integration, sectorial or functional, military or trade-oriented.

In this crowded context, it is meritorious to devote this *Journal*'s Forum to such an important matter that characterizes contemporary international relations (in the wider sense of the noun "relations").

First I must confess that I felt a sense of embarrassment reading the punctual remarks made by Fredrik Söderbaum in his article about *Rethinking Regions and Regionalism*. His point that there are two major methodological problems when dealing with regionalism - parochialism and the failure to conceptualize regional space - deserves careful consideration and a sort of *mea culpa* by the historians of the European Integration process (or, as the French say, "construction").

Of course, like many other European colleagues, I grew up professionally and culturally within that parochialism that is the subject of Söderbaum's complaint. Too often scholars of the European integration process have regarded the European experience as a universal point of arrival. This is an attitude very similar to that of the theorists of the centrality of the Nation-State in the nineteenth century. The Nation-State was then considered the point of arrival of every significant social and institutional experience. Similarly, in a sense, the process of European integration has erroneously become the benchmark of any other process of integration, even when a comparison is hardly possible.

The solution proposed by Söderbaum - to increase comparative studies of different regional integration experiences - is an interesting point of discussion. However, the question arises whether there are enough instruments, tools, and sensibilities to make sense and to give meaning to such comparisons. To compare means to examine similar objects, or at least things belonging to the same order, or species. I do not think it can be considered parochialism to sustain that a European exceptionalism exists in the field of regional integration, similarly to an American exceptionalism in the field of International Relations. There exists no other example of regional integration that spans from the sectorial beginning of economic integration (the European Steel and Coal Community in 1950-1952) to the prefederal result of the common currency and the creation of a central bank not controlled by any national power. It is a situation that is, perhaps, at the base of the present crisis of credibility for the future of the Union, but one that certainly needs to evolve into "something" different in both the institutional and political domain. Whether this evolution goes in the direction of further deepening or pulling back the level of integration is an open-ended question. In the meanwhile, I think that if it is pretentious to force the rest of the regional integration phenomena to observe the rules and to conform to the EU characteristics, an alternate subtle kind of parochialism would be to sustain that the EU is a typical kind of regional integration similar to those that are analyzed in this issue.

This problem is the subject, in some ways, of Luk Van Langenhove's article, *The Unity and Diversity in Regional Integration Studies* and is, in some ways, complementary to Söderbaum's piece. These are two contributions that I will likely use next September for my first year students in my courses on the *History of European Integration* to fight the cultural and academic tendency to affirm the European teleology of the "victorious future" of the European Union. Van Langenhove's view regarding the "social construction" of regional integration helps to go beyond the idea of regional integration based solely upon intergovernmental initiatives and will. Such a view can help overcome any constraints imposed by sectorial studies and enrich the study of how political movements, intellectual elites, political and social forces, and trade unions, promote - or hinder - regional integration processes.

These two contributions prepare the reader for the subsequent essays that are centered on regional integration case studies of great interest.

Klaus Dodds presents the case of the *Arctic Council as Regional Body* that reveals the centrality of the issue of the exploitation of the Arctic's resources against the problem of the actors – the Arctic States – that want to maintain their security and sovereignty prerogatives. The Arctic Council (AC) is a very young organization (created in 1996) and brought together not only the Arctic States but also observers states such as Germany, the United Kingdom, China, Japan, India, and South Korea. The AC, in its development and in its dynamics, represents the limits of an organization that essentially lacks the power to intervene as well as the ability to pressure its members to conform to certain behaviors. In an area so crucial to the future of the Arctic environment as the exploitation of natural resources, the AC can surely serve as a forum for discussions. For the time being, however, it lacks the tools necessary to do anything more than give recommendations. Dodds recounts the short history of the AC and shows that there are two major problems within this institution itself: institutional evolution and membership. Both are issues that can paralyze or reduce the influence and the activity of the AC. The AC may perhaps serve to avoid a next cold war in the Arctic but, at the moment, it still seems short of supranational powers. And this is a matter which is a primary question for an international organization. That is, whether the organization is able to assert its authority and its decisions over Member States.

The second case study presented is by Stephen Blank on the *Shanghai Cooperation Organization (SCO)*. This is a very strange animal in the family of International Organizations. The Shanghai Cooperation Organization was created on China's initiative in 2001, involving Russia and other states resulting from the dissolution of the

USSR in 1991. This organization was founded with the aim of increasing the overall level of security in the Asian region, which is particularly delicate. However, as it is clear from Blank's article, the SCO has never actually succeeded in clarifying what it is. One problem is that China and Russia believe that the SCO has different goals, and this is, of course, a major argument in the context of the Eurasian relations. Russia, for instance, can play a decisive role in ensuring security in the area. For this reason Russia has tried to transform the SCO, which has a weak institutional structure, into a formal military alliance. This attempt, however, has been thwarted by China. For its part China sees the SCO as a commercial organization that can help guarantee Chinese penetration in the Eurasian area. Likewise, this perspective has been opposed by Russia, which has tried to halt China's commercial initiatives. With this diversity of positions, it is quite clear that the SCO can evolve only with better relations between the two main players. This opens an interesting discussion on the possible cross-fertilization between military and economic domains that "ambiguous" organizations, such as the SCO, can play until it is clear what their real, and accepted, function is.

Last but not least Mathew Davies introduces us to ASEAN in the field of the Human Rights protection, in his article *The ASEAN Synthesis*. In particular Davies analyzes the process of the elaboration and the definition of the ASEAN Human Rights Declaration (AHRD). According to Davies there are two orders of problems at the base of the AHRD negotiations: at times a bitter debate between progressive and traditionalist members to define the extent of the AHRD in the cultural and social context of South-East Asia; the influence of the old-style principle of non-intervention while still trying to define ways and instruments to make the Human Rights protection effective. This is a contribution of great interest to deal with the problem of a set of values – the human rights as intended in the Western cultural and political tradition – that are declined in some diverse ways out of the Western hemisphere, thus presenting the necessity to cope with complexity.

As you finish reading this challenging panoply of articles you feel that you have also been introduced to a wide presentation that goes beyond the limits of the Eurocentric mantra of one regional integration model (that sometimes has been declined in a Euro-U.S. special-relationship refrain). In this issue, in fact, both methodological reflections and concrete examples are analyzed, thus offering different views of the variety of regional integration organizations. It would be interesting to continue to analyze this important and central topic for the future evolution of international relations, devoting some attention to other examples as well. For instance the role played (or not played) by the Arab League in the Middle East conflicts (historical and recent) or the ECOWAS-CEDEAO and MERCOSUR economic nature and political ambitions. Of course there is always room to do so in a future issue, and this *Journal* would be a great place for such a dialogue.

Piero S. Graglia is associate professor of political history at Milan State University (Italy); he was a Fulbright Italian visiting professor at Georgetown University in 2012.

Georgetown Journal

of International Affairs

religion & power *to...*
Espionage
Exposed

- - - tackling the issues that shape our world - -

CALL FOR
PAPERS

The *Georgetown Journal of International Affairs* is accepting submissions for the Winter/Spring 2014 issue. The submission deadline is 15 August 2013. Articles must be about 3,000 words in length. They should have the intellectual vigor to meet the highest scholarly standard, but should be written with the clarity to attract a broad audience. For submission details please refer to our website: http://journal.georgetown.edu/submissions/

Rethinking Regions and Regionalism

Fredrik Söderbaum

Over the last two decades there has been a veritable explosion of research and policy discussion on regional integration and regionalism all over the world. Some of the most influential thinkers in the field emphasize that regions and regionalism are now central to global politics. For instance, Peter Katzenstein rejects the "purportedly stubborn persistence of the nation-state or the inevitable march of globalization," arguing that we are approaching a "world of regions."[1] Similarly, Amitav Acharya examines the "emerging regional architecture of world politics,"[2] whereas Barry Buzan and Ole Weaver speak about a "global order of strong regions."[3] "Regions are now everywhere across the globe and are increasingly fundamental to the functioning of all aspects of world affairs from trade to conflict management, and can even be said to now constitute world order," Rick Fawn writes.[4]

While there is a strong tendency in both policy and academia to acknowledge the importance of regions and regionalism, the approach of different academic specializations varies considerably, and regionalism/regional integration means different things to different people in different contexts. Such diversity could be productive. However,

Fredrik Söderbaum is an associate professor in the School of Global Studies (SGS) at the University of Gothenburg in Sweden. He is also an associate senior research fellow at the United Nations University Institute on Comparative Regional Integration Studies (UNU-CRIS), Bruges, Belgium. Most of his publications are on the topic of regions and regionalism, African politics, and the EU's external relations.

the prevailing diversity is a sign of both weakness and fragmentation. We are witnessing a general lack of dialogue among academic disciplines and regional specializations (European integration, Latin American, Asian, and African regionalism) as well as theoretical traditions (rationalism, institutionalism, constructivism, critical and postmodern approaches). There is also thematic fragmentation in the sense that various forms of regionalism, such as economic, security, and environmental regionalism,

of a methodological perspective that acknowledges the social construction of regions by both state and non-state actors. Regarding the second problem, it is argued that Eurocentrism and parochialism are two sides of the same coin, and that comparative regionalism constitutes part of the solution.

Rethinking regional space. Historically the study of regions and regional integration has focused heavily on sovereignty transfer and political unification within inter-state regional organi-

The prevailing diversity is a sign of both weakness and fragmentation.

are only rarely related to one another. Such fragmentation undermines further generation of cumulative knowledge as well as theoretical innovation. It also leads to unproductive contestations, among both academics and policy makers, about the meaning of regionalism, its causes and effects, how it should be studied, what to compare and how, and not least, what are the costs and benefits of regionalism and regional integration.

The aforementioned divisions in the field are exacerbated by two interlocking (but largely overlooked) methodological problems: the failure to conceptualize regional space and the problem of parochialism. The purpose of this article is to try to contribute to a rethinking of these two problems in the study of regions and regionalism. Regarding the first problem, the prevailing emphasis on inter-state regional organizations is criticized in favor

zations. This is seen in countless studies on the European Union (EU) and other state-led regional frameworks, such as the African Union (AU), the Association of Southeast Asian Nations (ASEAN), the Economic Community of West African States (ECOWAS), the North American Free Trade Agreement (NAFTA), the Southern African Development Community (SADC), and the Southern Common Market (Mercosur). This focus on inter-state or supranational organizations stems from the fact that many scholars in the field have concentrated on determining what types of regions are the most functional, instrumental, and efficient to rule or govern. Regions have usually been taken as pre-given, defined in advance of research, and seen as particular inter-state or policy-driven frameworks.

Classical theories of regional integration and cooperation, such as functionalism and neofunctionalism, appreciated liberal-pluralist assumptions such as the need for cordial relations between states and non-state actors to promote commerce. But these early perspectives were subordinated to the analysis of what "states" did in the pursuit of their so-called "interests" as well as the consequences of state-society relations for supranational and intergovernmental regional organizations. This preference for regional organizations continues to be dominant in the field, even if the debate is nowadays usually framed in terms of "institutional design."[5] Moreover, the policy debate is plagued by idealism about the benefits of regional organizations and

with voluntarism and make room for cultural factors and the pooling or splitting of identities as determinants for action.

From this point of view, the puzzle is to understand and explain the process through which regions are coming into existence and being consolidated—their "becoming" so to speak—rather than a particular set of activities and flows within a pre-given, regional framework. In fact, regional organizations can be seen as surface phenomena produced by the underlying logic of regionalization and region-building. This does not mean that scholars should cease focusing on regional organizations and "institutional

The policy debate is plagued by idealism about the benefits of regional organizations and more or less naïve assumptions about what they can achieve.

more or less naïve assumptions about what they can achieve.

This article offers an alternative, societal understanding of regional space, the way regions are socially constructed, and for what reason. From this perspective, there are no "natural" or "given" regions (or regional organizations), but these are made and unmade—intentionally or unintentionally, endogenously or exogenously—by collective human action and identity formation. In other words, regions are not structurally or exogenously given, but socially constructed by historically contingent interactions. Constructivists replace determinism

design," only that the overwhelming dominance of this focus has prevented alternative answers to how and why regions are formed and who are the region-builders.

The heavy emphasis on state and global levels in mainstream international theory leads to a weak, even superficial, conceptualization of "regional space." Therefore, when the "taken for granted" national scale/space is problematized, then other spaces and scales necessarily receive more recognition. It needs to be emphasized that the rejection of "methodological nationalism" is not equivalent to ignoring the state or national scale/space. On the contrary, "states," "countries," and interstate organizations are crucial objects of analysis, and it is important to continue to study them, however defined. The point is that the political and institutional landscape is being fundamentally transformed and needs to be rethought in terms of more complex, multilevel political structures, in which the state is "unbundled," reor-

seeks to describe this multidimensional process of regionalization in terms of levels of "regionness"[6]: the process whereby a geographical area is transformed from a passive object to an active subject, capable of articulating transnational interests. Regionness means that a region can be "more or less" a region, and the level of regionness can increase or decrease. The

The socially constructed nature of regions implies that they are politically contested, and there are nearly always a multitude of strategies and ideas about a particular region which merge, mingle, and clash.

ganized, and assumes different functions and where non-state actors are also contributing at various levels and scales. The methodological issue is to transcend the Western conceptions of the unitary and Westphalian state inherent in mainstream theorizing— be it neo-realist, institutionalist, or liberal theory. In doing so, the view offered here emphasizes critical assessment of state-society complexes in the formation of regions and opens up a broader understanding of what characterizes regionalism and regionalization in various parts of the world and globally.

When different processes of regionalization in various fields and at various levels intensify and converge within the same geographical area, the cohesiveness and thereby the distinctiveness of the region-in-the-making increases. The new regionalism approach (NRA)

socially constructed nature of regions implies that they are politically contested, and there are nearly always a multitude of strategies and ideas about a particular region which merge, mingle, and clash. Furthermore, since regions are political and social projects, devised by human (state and non-state) actors in order to protect or transform existing structures, they may fail, just like other social projects. Hence, regions can be disrupted from within and without, sometimes by the same forces that build them up.

It is relevant to illustrate how the various agencies of market, state, society, and external actors can play out in a specific regional context—namely, Southern Africa.[7] For more than a century, myriad private economic actors—such as mining houses, settlers, large and small farmers, trading companies, small scale traders, investors, capitalists, ethnic trading and business networks—have been deeply involved in the multidimensional construction of "Southern Africa." One important form of regionalization is constructed around large South African corporations and capital interests in the formal economy. Partnerships between South African corporations and governments in the region are particularly evident.

Southern Africa is simultaneously shaped through its informal economy, in which cross-border activities arise for a variety of reasons. They can be informal and petty survival strategies, organized business strategies, criminal strategies, strategies for opting out of the formal economy, or they may simply arise as a consequence of regional concentration of economic interests and geographical circumstances. Some arise for socio-cultural and historical reasons, while others are based on tax and tariff evasion.

State actors may tie into the formal and informal economies in different ways. The "project of market integration" draws attention to overlapping state-led strategies to advance African economic integration on different scales (continental, regional, and micro-regional) and ties well into the South African business expansion in the formal economy mentioned above. Many of these state-led regionalist strategies gain strength through EU support as well as support from the International Financial Institutions (IFIs), G8, and donor nations.

State actors are also involved in a variety of other regionalization strategies, driven by other motives and leading to different spatial demarcations.

"Regime-boosting regionalism" draws attention to the discursive strategies of political elites in weak states who seek to strengthen a regime's official status, official sovereignty, image, and legitimacy—for example, rhetorical/symbolic regionalism where implementation of agreed policies is not the primary purpose. Regime-boosting may be a goal in itself, but it may also be closely related to "shadow regionalism," which refers to an informal mode of regional interaction, whereby public office-holders utilize their position in order to engage in informal and illegal market activities. This strategy is thus built upon a clandestine form of informal economy. Regime-boosting regionalism and shadow regionalism may be connected in that the former provides a façade behind which the latter is allowed to prosper.[8]

Finally, there exists a wide range of heterogeneous civil society activities in Southern Africa. Although civil society actors may have weak capacity compared to state and formal market actors, they still shape and influence region-building in important ways. In general, civil society is divided over how to relate to state-led regionalization projects. There is a tendency for service providers and "partners" to be favorable towards state-led regionalism whereas "resistors" and radical civil society actors are critical of the "establishment" and reject laissez-faire policies forged on principles of open regionalism and free trade. Many of these NGOs promote alternative forms of regionalism. Increasingly, the donor community tends to support a variety of regional civil society actors, further increasing the pluralism of region-building strategies.

There is no doubt a pressing need for theoretically informed and comparative studies about the agency of state, market, and civil society actors and how these actors come together in order to construct and de-construct regions. As discussed in the next section, however, different forms of parochialism undermine the comparative study of regions and regionalism.

Rethinking parochialism. After World War II the study of regionalism, especially the early debate on "regional integration," was dominated by an empirical focus on Europe. During the era of such early regionalism, European integration theories were developed for and from the European experience and then more or less re-applied or exported around the world (even if neofunctionalists were conscious of their own Eurocentrism and performed rigorous comparisons). Too often the European Community (EC) was seen and advocated as *the* model, and other looser and informal modes of regionalism were, wherever they appeared, characterized as "weaker" or "failed," with no "regional integration" according to the dominating definition. To be fair, there are good reasons why these notions have developed, but the fundamental problem is that such generalizations continue to plague both academic and policy discussions about regionalism.

The Eurocentric bias lies in the ways that underlying assumptions and understandings about the nature of regionalism (which most often stem from a *particular* reading of European integration) condition percep-

tions about how regionalism does and should look in other parts of the world. Heavy emphasis is placed on the economic and political trajectory of the EC/EU. Several realist/intergovernmental and liberal/institutionalist approaches belong to this perspective, and often these theories are dominated by a concern to explain deviations from the "standard" European case. Other modes of regionalism/regional integration are, where they appear, characterized as loose and informal (such as Asia) or failed (such as Africa), reflecting "a teleological prejudice informed by the assumption that 'progress' in regional organisation is defined in terms of EU-style institutionalisation." Indeed, as Hurrell asserts, "the study of comparative regionalism has been hindered by so-called theories of regionalism which turn out to be little more than the translation of a particular set of European experiences into a more abstract theoretical language."[11]

In this context it also bears mentioning that the policy debate about regionalism in the developing world is to a large extent plagued by Europe-centered beliefs and assumptions about what these regional organizations can and should achieve. As noted above, policy makers are heavily focused on supporting regional organization in Europe's image. This is seen, for instance, in that most multi-purpose regional organizations in the rest of the world follow the EC/EU's institutional design (for example, SADC, ECOWAS, AU, Mercosur, and ASEAN). But there are still no persuasive scientific arguments why other regions would or should follow the historical integration path of the EC/EU or its institutional structure.

Whereas the mainstream literature on regionalism (especially in international relations) has favored generalizations from the case of the EU when building theories, the tendency has been the reverse in the more critical and radical literature on regional integration in the developing world. Many of these scholars and policy analysts have tried to avoid and challenge Eurocentrism, and numerous innovative attempts to develop a regional approach specifically aimed at the developing world (or particular regions) have evolved from this work.[12] These scholars and policy makers believe that regional integration is or can be tailor-made to suit specific national and regional realities and contexts. However, large parts of this scholarship (and policy) tend to mirror the Eurocentric view by taking the EU as an "anti-model" and celebrating the differences in theory and practice between regionalism in Europe and in the developing world. According to Warleigh-Lack and Rosamond, many of these scholars have even made a caricature of the EU or of classical regional integration theory—especially neofunctionalism, which is claimed to be misunderstood—which has resulted in a failure to learn from both its successes and its failures, giving rise to unnecessary fragmentation within the research field.[13] Indeed, many of the radical/critical scholars have deliberately decided not to engage with European integration theory and practice, which may be seen as "inverted Eurocentrism," perhaps even as a different form of parochialism.

The fragmentation in the study and practice of regional integration (including the failure to engage with the European case) is tightly connected to the exaggeration of regional specialization. At least empirically, most scholars specialize in a particular region, which they will often consider "special" or "unique" (parochialism), and the regional context is considered extremely important. To be fair, some of the best research in the study of regionalism is case studies or studies situated in debates within a particular region. Detailed case studies of regionalism are certainly necessary; they identify historical and contextual specificities and allow for a detailed and intensive analysis of a single case (according to mono-, multi-, or interdisciplinary studies). The disadvantage of case studies and exaggerated regional specialization is, however, that a single case is a weak base for creating new generalizations or invalidating existing generalizations.[14] In other words, although there are exceptions, regional specialists rarely contribute to a larger comparative debate or the testing or development of general theories and frameworks. The existing fragmentation prevents scholars from recognizing that they are often dealing with similar phenomena albeit using different terminologies and conceptualizations. As a result, there is a weak *systematic* debate on the fundamentals of comparative research. Deep contestations exist regarding what to compare, how to compare, and even why to compare at all.

One of the main arguments of this article is that parochialism must be transcended and there is a need for a more integrated comparative debate about regional integration.[15] How to manage Eurocentrism is fundamental in this regard. The view offered here is that a more advanced debate about comparative regionalism will not be reached through simply celebrating differences between European integration and regionalism in the rest of the world, but rather by going beyond *dominant interpretations* of European integration (or the n=1), and drawing more broadly upon alternative theories that draw attention to aspects of European integration that are more comparable to other regions.[16] This is only possible if the case of Europe is *integrated* within a larger discourse of comparative regionalism, built around general concepts and theories, while still showing cultural and contextual

Africa is often tied to, on the one hand, the supposedly specific characteristics of the African state-society complex, and to Africa's particular insertion in the global order on the other. Yet the role of procedures, symbols, "summitry," and other discursive practices of regionalism in Asia, Europe, and North and Latin America suggests a very large potential for intriguing comparison and theory development. For example, there seems to be a strong sense of regime-boosting within ASEAN, backed by the tradition of non-intervention. There is also little doubt that regime-boosting has been important historically in Europe. Here the position is quite interesting as some states have used Europe to legitimate their regimes (mirroring the African

The role of procedures, symbols, 'summitry,' and other discursive practices of regionalism in Asia, Europe, and North and Latin America suggests a very large potential for intriguing comparison and theory development.

sensitivity.[17]

Although informal regionalism is not totally absent in EU studies, the intense link between formal and informal regionalism is one important contribution of both African and Asian regionalism to broader comparative integration studies. These cases show that one can, for instance, speak of relevant and truly regional dynamics and patterns that are not *per se* mirrored by formal regional efforts and projects.

The regime-boosting regionalism in

pattern) but others have used Euro-skepticism for similar aims. In short, this may be a phenomenon of democracies or of a well-developed region, but regardless it may provide an interesting basis for comparison.

As already noted, many scholars and policy makers tend to be overly optimistic about the potential of state-led regional cooperation and regional integration, and therefore fail to ask critical questions about for whom and for what purpose regional activities are carried out. The concept of "shadow regionalism," derived from the African context, captures regional dynamics that, while keeping up universalistic appearances, mostly serve to uphold parallel and often informally institutionalized patterns of enrichment for a select group of stakeholders and their peers. However, patron-client relationships, corruption, and informal politics are certainly not unique to Africa; there is considerable scope to learn from this kind of research in order to undertake comparative research.

Conclusion. Classical regional integration in the 1950s and 1960s was often shaped in accordance with the bipolar Cold War power structure. It was primarily driven through state-led policy frameworks and usually had specific objectives and content, often resulting in a focus on free trade arrangements and regional security alliances. Contemporary regionalism from the mid-1980s has to a large extent emerged in response to globalization. In contradistinction to classical "regional integration," which primarily took shape in Europe, contemporary regionalism is a more global but also more pluralistic phenomenon. The problem is that contemporary theorizing and conceptualization often fails to acknowledge the multiplicity and fluidity of regions and tends to repeat some old mistakes,

especially Eurocentrism and the tendency to treat regions as interstate regional frameworks. Fortunately, the "constructivist turn" and an increasing number of sophisticated case studies, especially of Asian and African regionalism, have spurred an interest in soft institutionalism and informal regionalism; yet regional space and regional agency are still poorly conceptualized and understood.

This article underlines that all regions are socially constructed and hence politically contested. Emphasis is placed upon how political actors perceive and interpret the idea of a region and notions of "regionness." From this perspective, there are no "natural" regions; all regions are, at least potentially, heterogeneous with unclear territorial margins. These processes look different in different regional contexts, but there is little doubt about the need to further develop comparative regionalism. The main problem is that Eurocentrism and parochialism prevent a deeper understanding of what is particular and universal in various regions around the world. Therefore, European integration theory must be integrated within a larger and more general discourse of comparative regionalism, which is built around general concepts and theories but still culturally sensitive.

NOTES

1 Peter J. Katzenstein, *A World of Regions: Asia and Europe in the American Imperium* (Ithaca, New York: Cornell University Press, 2005), i.

2 Amitav Acharya, "The Emerging Regional Architecture of World Politics," *World Politics* 59, no. 4 (July 2007): 629-652.

3 Barry Buzan and Ole Weaver, *Regions and Powers: The Structure of International Security* (Cambridge: Cambridge University Press, 2003), 20.

4 Rick Fawn, "Regions and Their Study: Where from, What for and Where to?" *Review of International Studies* vol. 35 (2009): 5-35.

5 Amitav Acharya and Alastair Johnston, eds., *Crafting Cooperation. Regional International Institutions in Comparative Perspective* (London: Oxford University Press, 2007); Edward D. Mansfield and Helen V. Milner, eds., The Political Economy of Regionalism (New York: Colombia University Press, 1997).

6 Björn Hettne and Fredrik Söderbaum, "Theorising the Rise of Regionness," *New Political Economy* 5, no. 3 (2000): 457-74. For detailed accounts of the NRA, see Björn Hettne, Andras Inotai, and Osvaldo Sunkel, eds., Studies in the New Regionalism, Vol. I-V (New York: Macmillan/Palgrave, 1999-2001); Fredrik Söderbaum, *The Political Economy of Regionalism. The Case of Southern Africa* (New York: Palgrave Macmillan, 2004).

7 See Fredrik Söderbaum, *The Political Economy of Regionalism. The Case of Southern Africa* (New York: Palgrave Macmillan, 2004).

8 Also see Daniel C. Bach, ed., *Regionalisation in Africa. Integration & Disintegration* (London: James Currey, 1999).

9 For one recent attempt, see Ulrike Lorenz-Carl and Martin Rempe, eds., *Mapping Agency. Comparing Regionalisms in Africa* (Aldershot: Ashgate, 2013).

10 Shaun Breslin, Richard Higgott, and Ben Rosamond, "Regions in Comparative Perspective," in *New Regionalisms in the Global Political Economy*, S. Breslin and others, eds., (London: Routledge, 2002), 11.

11 Andrew Hurrell, "The Regional Dimension in International Relations Theory" in *The Global Politics of Regionalism. Theory and Practice*, Mary Farrell, Björn Hettne, and Luk Van Langenhove, eds., (London: Pluto Press, 2005), 39.

12 W. Andrew Axline, ed., *The Political Economy of Regional Cooperation. Comparative Case Studies* (London: Pinter Publishers, 1994); Daniel C. Bach, ed., *Regionalisation in Africa. Integration & Disintegration* (London: James Currey, 1999); Morten Bøås, Marianne H. Marchand, and Timothy M. Shaw, eds., *The Political Economy of Regions and Regionalism* (Basingstoke: Palgrave Macmillan, 2005).

13 Alex Warleigh and Ben Rosamond, "Comparative Regional Integration: Towards a Research Agenda" (Description of Workshop for the ECPR Joint Sessions, Nicosia, Cyprus, 25-30 April 2006).

14 Andrew W. Axline, "Comparative Case Studies of Regional Cooperation among Developing Countries," in *The Political Economy of Regional Cooperation. Comparative Case Studies*, Andrew W. Axline, ed., (London: Pinter Publishers, 1994), 15.

15 Fredrik Söderbaum, "Comparative Regionalism," in S*AGE Handbook of Comparative Politics*, Todd Landman and Neil Robinson, eds., (London: Sage Books, 2009).

16 Alex Warleigh-Lack and Ben Rosamond, "Across the EU Studies–New Regionalism Frontier: Invitation to a Dialogue," *Journal of Common Market Studies* 48, no. 4 (2010): 993-1013.

17 For some recent attempts at non-Eurocentric comparative regionalism that still includes Europe, see Alex Warleigh-Lack, Nick Robinson, and Ben Rosamond, eds., *New Regionalism and the European Union. Dialogues, Comparisons and New Research Directions* (London: Routledge, 2010); Timothy M. Shaw, J. Andrew Grant, and Scarliett Cornelissen, eds., *The Ashgate Research Companion to Regionalisms* (Aldershot: Ashgate, 2011); David Armstrong and others, eds., *Civil Society and International Governance. The role of non-state actors in global and regional regulatory frameworks* (London: Routledge).

The Unity and Diversity in Regional Integration Studies

Luk Van Langenhove

The academic study of regional integration is scattered amongst different disciplines. Political scientists have a longstanding interest in regional integration but historians, economists, lawyers, and international relations scholars have been studying regional integration as well. Often a comparative perspective is taken. Hence the development of "Comparative Regional Integration Studies" as an institutionalized academic activity aimed at performing scientifically sound comparisons of regional integration processes across the globe and across time. But as Alberta Sbragia rightly noted, the study of comparative regionalism is ill-defined and "its boundaries are certainly permeable."[1] There is indeed a lot of confusion about the study-object of the field. Take for instance Ernst Haas's classic definition of regional integration: "the study of regional integration is concerned with explaining how and why states cease to be wholly sovereign, how and why they voluntarily mingle, merge, and mix with their neighbours so as to lose the factual attributes of sovereignty while acquiring new techniques for resolving conflict between themselves."[2] Here the emphasis is on losing sovereignty. But is this the case for all forms of regional integration? What if the "integra-

Luk Van Langenhove is director of the United Nations University Institute on Comparative Regional Integration Studies (UNU-CRIS) in Bruges. He teaches at the Vrije Universiteit Brussel, the Université Libre de Bruxelles, and the College of Europe and also holds an adjunct professorship at Murdoch University in Perth.

tion" is organized on a purely inter-governmental basis? Furthermore, both the concepts of "integration" and "region" are problematic. Integration has a normative connotation as it is often implicitly regarded as a positive development (in contrast to the negative connotation of disintegration) and region is a polysemous concept that can refer to supranational, subnation-

tion has always been the position of the EU. Ever since the work of Ernst Haas in the 1960s, understanding integration became linked to understanding European integration. His neo-functionalist approach and the idea of "spill-over" (the pressures from economic integration towards further integration) became academically very popular. But Ernst Haas himself became more

All too often, the EU is pictured as a 'model' for other integration schemes. This gives the impression that the road taken by European integration is the only road possible.

al, or cross-border areas. It is therefore not always clear what the unit or object of comparison is. And on top of that, regional integration in Europe seems to obscure the field as scholars disagree on what place the EU should take in comparative regional integration studies. In recent years, many authors have pointed to these conceptual and other methodological problems.[3] This article argues that comparing different forms of regional integration is scientifically feasible, but only if a social constructivist point of view is taken. Only in this way can a general theory be developed that allows understanding of the diversity of integration processes. It also claims that it is policy-relevant to compare the European integration experiences with regional integration in the rest of the world.

The dominance of the EU. A crucial issue in the study of regional integra-

and more critical about the study of regional integration and ended up suggesting that the study of regional integration should cease to be a subject in its own right.[4] Meanwhile EU studies developed into a firmly institutionalized academic discipline, not only because it provided its own teaching that facilitated the inflow of new scholars, but probably also because the EU itself has supported the institutionalization of the discipline through financing EU study centers and chairs all over the world. Today, one can witness a general lack of communication between these EU studies and comparative regional integration studies, although the tide is slowly turning. One major problem in bridging the gap between EU studies and studying other forms of regionalism is how to deal with the uniqueness or *sui generis* aspect of the EU. This is referred to as the "N=1" problem whereby it is often wrongly assumed by positivist inspired researchers that because N=1 a scientific study is not possible.[6] This is an important issue as most of the comparative regionalism studies are focusing on comparing the EU with other forms of regionalism. All too often, the EU is pictured as a "model" for the other integration schemes. This gives the impression that the road taken by the European integration is the only road possible.[7] The trick is therefore to come up with a perspective that on the one hand allows the researcher to consider regions of all kinds, wherever they are located without being "euro-centric," but with the possibility of understanding the EU as a special case. De Lombaerde et al. have pointed out that this is perfectly feasible if one acknowledges that the study of the EU can be done from different methodological perspectives.[8] This implies that one regards the EU as comparable with *all* other integration schemes; comparable with *some* other regional integration processes; or having a number of unique aspects that makes it like *no other* regional integration scheme! So, in this view, even when acknowledging the uniqueness of the EU, there are still elements that allow for comparing the EU with other integration schemes. In order to find out those elements of relevance, one has to be as precise as possible on what to compare. This is where social constructionism comes in.

The social construction of regional integration. The philosophical school of social constructivism in the social sciences stresses that the world consists of both material and institutional facts and that both types of facts need to be studied with specific appropriated methods. Institutional facts are phenomena of the social realm that only exist by human agreement. Money is a classic example: for money to exist, humans need to agree upon treating, for instance, a piece of green paper as a dollar bill. And it requires trust that others will do the same. In one sense one can say that the dollar only exists because people believe it to exist. A major consequence of social constructivism is that it stresses the primacy of thoughts and conversations in the social realm and hence the need to study social phenomena from a discursive perspective. Social constructivism has found its way into the study of international relations and has inspired the social constructionist school that is often pictured as an alternative to the classical realist, functionalist, or liberal theories. Nevertheless, the social constructivism study of regional integration remains underdeveloped.

Advancing regional integration studies that are inspired by social constructivism can be done by acknowledging that "regional integration" is first of all a concept that is used by people in certain discursive contexts for certain purposes. Such labels can refer to different things as was pointed out by Morgan when he introduced a useful distinction between projects, processes, and products of regional integration.[9] *Projects* refer to the ideas that actors have about the benefits (or harms) of regional integration and to plans for achieving such integration. Often these ideas and plans take the form of "dreams," such as Churchill's dream of once establishing a "United States of Europe." For others the project might be just to establish a larger single market or a security community. Such ideas can be found with policy makers, academics, or civil society. The vision of regional integration in Latin America can be traced back to Simon Bolivar. The concept of the "ASEAN Way" of integration in Southeast Asia is generally attributed to the former Singaporean Minister S. Jaykuman. Dreams about a Pan-African integration were fueled by different people such as Martin Robison Delany or Kwame Nkrumah. The *processes* refer to the actual realization of

regarding supra-national interactions in a certain regional space. But it is not all talk. That talk, which one can call "integration-speak," can secondly lead to different products such as treaties or institutional arrangements. And thirdly, both the talk and the outcomes of it become elements of a historical process that will have certain effects in a region, for instance an increase in intra-regional trade or an increase in mobility.

The very essence of a social constructivist perspective on regional integration is the focus upon the primacy of ideas. Such ideas can take the form of "dreams" or projects and will always

The study of regional integration should... pay more attention to 'integration-speak,' or the storylines about regional integration that are developed in conversations between different actors.

the dreams and plans through either formal steps (such as negotiation of a regional trade agreement or adopting a treaty in parliaments) or informal actions (such as mobility of people or cross-border trade). According to Morgan, the *products* of regional integration are the actual institutions created by the processes.

Taking these distinctions seriously not only permits scholars to see three distinct areas of comparison, but also to consider regional integration as a social construction as it is in the first place a discursive label that certain actors (including individuals, interest groups, or states) put upon their ideas

involve norms. The example of European integration illustrates this: after the Second World War, a federalist movement emerged that dreamt of a "united" Europe. But this utopian dream got momentum through the 1947 Marshall Plan that linked postwar reconstruction to cooperation. The normative aspect of this was the belief that economic integration was a tool to achieve the goal of peace and security. The realization of ideas thus requires actors who have the power to start discourses that constitute an integrated region. Such actors can be opinion makers, think tanks, or lobby groups, but at the end of the day the integration needs the consent of the states involved. European integration for instance became a reality through the signing of a series of treaties from the Rome Treaty in 1957 to the 2007 Lisbon Treaty. This process is always unique and a function of the local situation.

A second characteristic of the social constructivist take is that it emphasizes that integrated regions are becoming actors themselves as they acquire autonomy to act and have some statehood properties. This has consequences for the realm of states. On the one hand, this implies that integrated regions, or more specifically the established regional organizations, can engage in discursive power relations with the states that created them. The European case clearly illustrates the problematic relationship between the sovereign member states of the EU and the powers of the latter over the former. On the other hand, the regional actor can be involved in diffusing its ideas about integration, and other actors can choose to emulate the integration projects, processes, or products. But the implementation elsewhere will again be affected by local practices and discourses.

Five strategies for advancing comparative regional integration studies. From the above perspective a social constructivist research agenda can be built, accompanied by concrete proposals on how to put these strategies into practice. Their point of departure is again the Morgan distinction between the projects, the processes, and the products of regional integration that permits scholars to see three

distinct areas of comparison.[10]

The first strategy consists of acknowledging that labeling a process as regional integration rather than as cooperation is always done in a specific discursive context. The study of regional integration should therefore pay more attention to "integration-speak," or the storylines about regional integration that are developed in discourse between different actors. One can look at how different states officially take positions about regional integration in negotiation processes, how different societal groups unfold their opinions on regional integration, and how the storylines developed by academics interact with the above forms of integration-speak. Indeed, academic theories about integration can become part of certain integration projects. The functionalist theory of integration as developed by Ernst Haas for instance became part of the "deepening" discourse of the European integration project.[11] Once a certain regional integration has become institutionalized in one way or another, it can become an actor itself and hence also develop integration-speak, up to the point that a regional organization can advance opinions that attack the states that created it. This has been labeled as the Frankenstein syndrome: the region, ultimately created by states, has acquired enough autonomy that it can turn against its creator.[12] The story of the EU is a clear example of this phenomenon: the EU member states are now obliged by the EU to keep their deficits below a certain level. The actorness and autonomy of regional organizations should therefore be a major object of study. But this is not to ignore that states play a privileged role in the process of transferring ideas and projects of regional integration into realities. Indeed, at the end of the day, it is always states that have to make the formal decisions to "integrate" some of their activities or functions with other states. Often, this is limited to negotiating and signing a free trade agreement, but sometimes it involves signing treaties that actually pool some of its sovereignty with that of other states.

The second strategy is to study regional integration through an "unpacking" of regions according to their statehood dimension.[13] This can be done in multiple ways. One perspective is to consider regional integration as a process that leads to the creation of a geographical area that is not a state but has some statehood properties, enabling it to act to a certain extent *as if* it were a state. This is in line with the views of, for instance, Hameiri and Van Langenhove who claim that regions are (discursively) defined against states.[14] Regional integration can thus be seen as a process of moving some statehood properties from neighboring states to a supra-national level. In some cases, the products of regional integration might even look very much like a fully fledged state. It makes sense, therefore, to compare regions with states. Schmitter has proposed an innovation in research design that is in line with the above thinking: "compare units at different levels of spatial or legal aggregation, provided they had similar properties and capacities with regard to the problem being studied."[15] This is of particular relevance for the study of regional integration as there are cases of regional integration that

lead to the creation of states while others do not. Think about the Zollverein that led to the German unification in 1871 or the integration that led to the birth of the United States of America. Students of regional integration usually do not look to the United States as an object of study. They should, because the U.S. Constitution of 1787 is nothing but the result of a regional integration process between newly independent states. That process was marked by a formidable clash of ideas now known as the debate on the nature of the Union. As for the product of that process, the creation of a federal state, it is worthwhile to remember that until 1929, only about 1 percent of the GDP went to the federal budget. This is about the equivalent of the budget of the EU today. But by 1953 the federal budget had risen to up to 17 percent of the GDP. So it does make sense to compare the United States to the EU! Equally, such a move allows scholars to unpack the region for analytical purposes. Since a region can be defined as a geographical area with certain statehood properties, this implies that regional integration will always be linked to certain policy domains of states because it is there that the statehood properties are acquired. According to the nature of the policy domain involved, different varieties of integration are thus possible.

Adhering to a social constructivist approach does of course not mean that one should neglect factual elements. A third strategy therefore is to take into account the situation of the states that are the elements of regional integration in a given geographical area. Not only are there potential geographical markers and geographical limits; there is also the particularity of the geographical area and the nature of the states operating in that region. States differ from each other in many ways. There are differences in cultural and value orientation. And there are the important differences between small and big states. Regional integration in Europe is therefore very different from integration in, for instance, Southeast Asia simply because of the differences in the size of the region. So the advice is: bring in geography! Not taking this into account leads to dis-

nomic and political power, from land-locked, poor, or even failed states on the one hand to superpowers with a rich colonial past on the other. And, some states are largely decentralized with federal structures, while others have a very centralized form of governance. All these variables will affect processes of regional integration, and studying these processes hence needs to take into account the social, political, and economic reality of the entities that are involved in building a region. The study of regional integration can therefore not be done without mak-

The advice is: bring in geography! Not taking this into account leads to distorted comparisons.

torted comparisons, as demonstrated by De Lombaerde et al.[16] These authors have shown that a classic indicator of economic integration such as intra-regional trade density is influenced by the size of the region: the smaller the integrated area, the larger the "rest of the world" and hence the larger the potential for trade outside the region. Using intra-regional trade as an indicator for the success of a regional trade agreement puts the EU-27 first as one of the most integrated areas of the world. Correcting the indicators for size gives, however, a totally different picture and puts other RTAs before the EU-27!

Next to the geographical differences, one also has to take into account that states have very different regimes that obviously influence the functioning of a state. States also differ in eco-

ing room for a historical perspective. The origins of regional integration in Europe for instance are clearly linked to the post-war situation in 1945 and how the Big Powers wanted to deal with the European problem. Different historical conditions shaped the efforts towards regional integration in Latin America, Southeast Asia, and Africa.

A fourth strategy is to combine the search for a general logic with understanding the differences. As mentioned above the debate about comparing regions has been blurred by two issues: the confusion about the status of the "comparative method" and the confusion about the role of the EU. The result is, as mentioned, a false debate about the *sui generis* character of the EU. If one applies the "unpacking" strategy proposed above, then one can study the EU—and for that matter any other form of regional integration—from both a nomothetic and an idiographic perspective. There are today enough regional trade agreements in the world that it makes sense to try to generate nomothetic knowledge of the processes of removing economic barriers between states. And it is equally possible to constitute a "small N" sample of regional integration schemes that deal with the common provision of public goods. Meanwhile, each regional integration scheme can and should be studied as a single case, too.

The fifth strategy is about widening the research agenda to the study of intra-regional and inter-regional processes. This is important as, unlike states, regions and regional arrangements can overlap. This has consequences for regional integration as several of such processes may occur simultaneously in a given geographical area. A lot of scholars dealing with European integration focus on the EU, but the regional integration scene in Europe is so much more diverse. Think of the Council of Europe, the Organization for Security and Cooperation in Europe, the Western European Union, Benelux, and so on. Each part of the world has a true web of regional integration schemes that partly overlap in membership and/or mandate. These overlaps show that for any geographical area, different integration projects can exist, fueled by different actors. As such it is not only possible to study the intra-regional integration dimension for each region but also compare different intra-regional integrations in Europe, Africa, Asia, or Latin America. This is an understudied field. Also, to the extent that regional integration

schemes have a global actor *télos*, they can engage in relations with other actors, states or regional organizations. In the latter case one can speak of inter-regional relations and even inter-regional integration.[17]

Conclusion. Regional integration can be studied from a comparative perspective. This article has argued that this is best done from a social constructivist point of view and has advanced a number of research strategies to take into account the unity and diversity of regional integration. The implications for comparative regionalism are that one should not focus on comparing for instance "Europe" with another region, nor on comparing regional organizations, but rather on specific governance domains, bringing in all the relevant units of governance (states and regions) that exist in a given geographical area and that have the relevant statehood properties.

One final word about comparability versus applicability. A recurring question by policy makers is to what extent the EU can be a "model of regional integration" applicable to other parts of the world. The answer is yes and no. No, if one talks about the processes of integration. In that respect each case is unique as a result of its historical and geopolitical idiosyncrasies that generate a specific and unique conversational dynamic. Yes, if one looks at the products that result out of the integration processes. As soon as they exist as regional organizations or treaties, they can be talked about and also copied elsewhere. Whether that would be advisable is another question. But diffusion happens all the time with institutional facts. Think for instance of the liberal constitutions of states; they have been copied many times by new sovereign states. The same happens with regional integration. As such regional integration can be regarded as an innovation in governance that will continue to spread around the globe.

NOTES

1 Alberta Sbragia, "Comparative Regionalism: What might it be?" *Journal for Common Market Studies* (2008): 32.

2 Ernst Haas, "The Study of Regional Integration: Reflections on the Joy and Anguish of Pretheorising," *International Organisations* 24, no. 4 (1979): 607-646.

3 See for instance Philippe De Lombaerde, Fredrik Söderbaum, Luk Van Langenhove, and Francis Baert, "The Problem of Comparison in Comparative Regionalism," *Review of International Studies* 36, no. 3 (2010): 731-53; Philippe De Lombaerde, "Comparing Regionalisms: Methodological Aspects and Considerations," in *The Ashgate Research Companion to Regionalism*, Timothy M. Shaw, J. Andrew Grant, and Scarlett Cornelissen, eds., (London: Ashgate, 2012), 31-50.

4 Ernst Haas, "The Obsolescence of Regional Integration Theory," *Institute of International Studies Research Series* (1975): 25.

5 Alex Warleigh-Lack and Luk Van Langenhove, "Rethinking EU Studies: the Contribution of Comparative Regionalism," *European Integration* 32, no. 6 (2010): 541-562.

6 For a general discussion of this problem, see J.A. Smith, Rom Harré, and Luk Van Langenhove, "Idiography and the Case-Study," in *Rethinking Psychology*, J.A. Smith, Rom Harré, and Luk Van Langenhove, eds., (London: Sage, 1995).

7 See for instance Andrew Hurrell, "One World? Many Worlds? The Place of Regions in the Study of International Society," *International Studies* 83, no. 1 (2007): 127-146.

8 Philippe De Lombaerde, Fredrik Söderbaum, Luk Van Langenhove, and Francis Baert, "The Problem of Comparison in Comparative Regionalism," *Review of International Studies* 32, no. 6 (2010): 541-62.

9 Glyn Morgan, *The Idea of a European Superstate. Public Justification and European Integration* (Princeton: Princeton University Press, 2005).

10 These research strategies are based upon Warleigh-Lack and Van Langenhove (2010).

11 For a more detailed discussion of integration-speak, see Nikki Slocum and Luk Van Langenhove, "The Meaning of Regional Integration. Introducing Positioning Theory in Regional Integration Studies," *Journal of European Integration* 26, no. 3 (2004): 227-252.

12 Luk Van Langenhove, *Building Regions. The Regionalisation of the World Order* (London: Ashgate, 2011).

13 Luk Van Langenhove, "Why we need to 'unpack' Regions to compare them more effectively," *The International Spectator* 47, no. 1 (2012): 16-29.

14 Shahar Hameiri, "Theorising Regions through Changes in Statehood: Rethinking the Theory and Method of Comparative Regionalism," *Review of International Studies* (2012); Luk Van Langenhove, "Why we need to 'unpack' Regions to compare them more effectively," *The International Spectator* 47, no. 1 (2012): 16-29.

15 Philippe C. Schmitter, "The Nature and Future of Comparative Politics," *European Political Science Review* 1, no. 1 (2009): 51.

16 Philippe De Lombaerde, Fredrik Söderbaum, Luk Van Langenhove, and Francis Baert, "The Problem of Comparison in Comparative Regionalism," *Review of International Studies* 36, no. 3 (2010): 731-53.

17 Fredrik Söderbaum and Luk Van Langenhove, *The EU as a Global Player. The Politics of Interregionalism* (London: Routledge, 2006).

Environment, Resources, and Sovereignty in the Arctic Region:
The Arctic Council as Regional Body

Klaus Dodds

The Arctic Council (AC) is an inter-governmental organization that, since its creation in 1996, has been widely recognized as one of the most progressive regional bodies in the world.[1] The membership includes the eight Arctic states (A8), six permanent participants, and observer states such as the UK and Germany. From May 2013 onwards, there are also new permanent observers including China, India, Japan, and South Korea. The European Union's candidature has been delayed and subject to further review and assessment. The Council is chaired by one of the eight Arctic states for a two year period. The current chair is Canada (2013-2015) and it will be followed by the United States (2015-2017). The permanent participants, including the Inuit Circumpolar Council, Saami Council, and Aleut International Association, enjoy full consultative status and may address the meetings of the Council. Administrative support is provided by the Indigenous Peoples Secretariat (IPS), which is based in Copenhagen.[2]

The AC lies at the heart of debates about Arctic futures. It faces two challenges – institutional evolution and membership.[3] For its supporters, the AC occupies center position in promoting an orderly and co-operative vision for the Arctic,

Klaus Dodds is Professor of Geopolitics at Royal Holloway University of London. His next book with Mark Nuttall is entitled, *Scrambles for the Poles? The Contemporary Geopolitics of the Polar Regions* to be published by Polity in 2014.

Dr. Dodds would like to thank Mary Grace Reich for assisting in this paper as well as external readers.

but there is no shortage of commentary and punditry analyzing and predicting a rather different vision for the Arctic.[4] As Paul Berkman asserted in the *New York Times*, under the heading "Preventing an Arctic Cold War," there is little room for complacency.[5] Berkman's analysis warned of Arctic and non-Arctic states being increasingly forced to confront difficult issues relating to policing, resource management, accessibility and navigability, alongside environmental protection. His suggestion at the end of the piece appeared, seemed rather odd, "[a]s the head of an Arctic superpower and a Nobel laureate, Mr. Obama should convene an international meeting with President Putin and other leaders of Arctic nations to ensure that economic development at the top of the world is not only sustainable, but peaceful."[6] Bizarrely, there is little analysis of how, and to what extent, the AC and other bodies, including the United Nations Law of the Sea (UNCLOS), are actively providing "rules of the road" (Berkman's phrase) for the Arctic region and beyond.

This piece focuses on some issues that require further attention (such as the protection of the Arctic marine environment) while acknowledging how the AC has changed in the last few years. As a regional body, it operates in a strategic environment where few specialist observers believe that military conflict or destabilizing resource speculation is likely to prevail. Nonetheless, it is a work in progress with pressing demands to address. I will discuss debates about membership status and the institutional evolution to respond to experts' concerns about disasters (which might involve a shipping or drilling accident) and ongoing climate change, including manifestations such as sea ice thinning in the Arctic Ocean.

Defining the Arctic region. Clarification of the meaning of the 'Arctic region' is necessary. Geographers tend to begin from the position that regions are socially and politically constructed, and thus multiple Arctic regions might actually exist.[7] Depending on where lines are drawn on a map (or particular themes are privileged), constructions will vary not only in terms of the spatial extent of the Arctic but also with ideas pertaining to proximity and distance. The United Kingdom, for example, defines itself as a "sub-Arctic state" and China as a "near Arctic" state.

The "marine Arctic" refers to waters north of the Bering Strait, Greenland, Svalbard, and other areas north of Euro-Asian landmass. The Barents Sea, north of Norway and western Russia, is sometimes described as "blue Arctic" because it is ice-free. There are five Arctic Ocean coastal states (Canada, Denmark/Greenland, Norway, Russia and the United States), but Iceland increasingly imagines itself as being part of that group as well. There are two other Arctic states—Finland and Sweden—without Arctic coastlines.

There are recognized (but still some disputed) maritime zones in the Arctic, including internal waters, exclusive economic zones, high seas and deep seabed. The provisions of UNCLOS apply and large parts of the Convention are acknowledged by the United States (as non-signatory) to be part of customary international law. There are four recognized high seas areas: the Barents Sea, Norwegian Sea, central Bering Sea, and central Arctic Ocean. Some regional agreements are in place such as the Fisheries Protection Zone around Svalbard. Where there are disputes (e.g. the North West Passage as an international strait), they are not in the main considered to be dangerously divisive. The maritime Arctic is a space governed by the provisions of UNCLOS, though there are areas of contention (e.g. maritime boundary delimitation in the Beaufort Sea) and concerns over implementation, especially in the field of environmental protection and resource management such as fisheries.

at a meeting in Whitehorse in October 2011. In April 2012, Canada hosted a meeting of senior military officials at Goose Bay involving other Arctic states (Denmark, Finland, Iceland, Norway, Russia, Sweden, and the United States – together with Canada making up the so-called Arctic 8). The aim of the meeting was to strengthen circumpolar relationships and specifically address areas such as search and rescue (SAR). In September 2012, the first live SAR exercise in Greenland involving the Arctic 8 (A8) occurred.[13]

Institutional strengthening, specifically through the establishment of

The main areas of interest revolve around strengthening circumpolar co-operation and developing common strategies of preparedness in the event of an oil disaster.

Recent Developments Affecting the Arctic Council. The AC is addressing the two main challenges identified earlier – institutional evolution and membership.[10] First, in terms of institutional evolution important changes are unfolding. In May 2011, the Arctic Council Ministerial Meeting adopted its first legally binding agreement involving search and rescue (SAR). The agreement established SAR areas of responsibility while acknowledging, "the delimitation of search and rescue regions is not related to and shall not prejudice the delimitation of any boundary between States or their sovereignty, sovereign rights or jurisdiction."[11] This was followed by military dialogue on SAR, which was initiated

a permanent secretariat which was implemented in 2013, and additional issue-specific negotiation complement the extension of the legally binding SAR agreement. The work of the Marine Oil Pollution Preparedness and Response (MOPPR) task force (and the member states' control who are involved with the AC task forces) is also noteworthy. Oil spill response rose in prominence following the Deep Horizon disaster in the Gulf of Mexico, alongside speculation about the mineral resource potential of the maritime Arctic (post-publication of the 2008 USGS appraisal of the Arctic region).[14] The main areas of interest revolve around strengthening circumpolar co-operation and developing common strategies of preparedness in the event of an oil disaster. The Arctic Council's Emergency Prevention, Preparedness, and Response working group has produced an Arctic guide, which identifies risks, organizational responsibilities, informational sharing, roles of indigenous peoples, and legal frame-works.[15]

The 2011 Ministerial Meeting also addressed future membership of the AC.[16] It developed a "Framework for strengthening the Arctic Council," which incorporated "criteria for admitting observers and role for their participation in the Arctic Council."[17] China, Singapore, and South Korea and various regional bodies such as the European Union are eager to be observers. Singapore, for example, submitted a request in December 2011 to be considered an observer to the Arctic Council. In January 2012, the Singapore Ministry of Foreign Affairs appointed a Special Envoy for Arctic Affairs, Ambassador Tony K. Siddique. Reasons for observer accreditation include: a desire to be represented at an important regional forum, growing scientific/resource/shipping-related interests, and existing involvement in activities such as fishing, oil and gas exploitation, insurance and tourism. Other observer bodies include inter-governmental organizations, non-governmental organizations and inter-parliamentary organizations, such as the Nordic Council of Ministers and WWF-Global Arctic Program. There are strict rules (e.g. observers are subject to review and observers have to acknowledge the sovereignty of Arctic 8) governing these current observers and the AC considered eleven new organizations/states in May 2013 - the states were accepted and the organizations were deferred/rejected.

Bids for observer status from China and the EU have been unsettling to the A8. In Canada's case, opposition to the EU was due to indigenous communities' unhappiness over trade bans on seal-based products but also a worry that ever more observer states would

Bids for observer status from China and the EU have been unsettling to the A8.

weaken the role of the permanent participants. China's growing interests in Greenland and Iceland have been monitored with interest and some commentators have expressed concern about a wider resource-strategic agenda of the country, even if there is evidence of scientific interest in sea ice thinning and Arctic-related climate change.[18] Norwegian-Chinese relations, following 2010 Nobel Prize award to dissident Liu Xiaobo, ensured that Norway was not eager to grant China observer status to the AC. This position softened in recent months in part because of fears that China might seek to create a rival Arctic network of nations. The creation of the Arctic Circle network, a multi-national grouping, might well represent a challenge to the AC. Led by the Icelandic President, Ólafur Ragnar Grímsson, this network will hold its first conference in October 2013 and appealed for a wider membership including non-Arctic states and multinationals. His speech at the New York Press Club in

April 2013 was widely reported, including his implied critique of the efficacy of the AC and general promotion of Asia's political and trading role in the Arctic.[19]

It was hoped that the May 2013 AC Ministerial Meeting in Sweden would result in the signing of a legally binding agreement over oil spill response involving the Arctic 8 and a decision on observer membership (depending on the decisions - the Arctic Circle network might include "rejected" observers). The meeting will also mark the ending of the Swedish chairmanship and the start of the Canadian leadership of the Arctic Council (2013-15). The omens may not be good. A leaked version of "Co-operation on Marine Oil Pollution Preparedness and Response in the Arctic" was condemned as inadequate by environmental organizations who noted its vague assertions regarding liabilities, minimum standards and the management of a trans-boundary leakage.[20] An earlier Chatham House report, moreover, warned that there were substantial knowledge gaps regarding oil and gas operations in the maritime Arctic region, and concern was expressed about response capacity.[21] The agreement between the Arctic 8 on oil spill response replicated other areas of agreement (e.g. knowledge sharing, encouraging best practice where established) and sidetracked difficult areas such as liability and oil response capacities, which are varied and in all likelihood under-developed. The question of the A8 agreeing on observer status was potentially more divisive and apparently settled late at night between the A8 ministers.

Mind the Gap. The AC faces pressures – Greenpeace (noting its "Save the Arctic" campaign) is lobbying for more concerted action on the protection of the Arctic marine environment. The Protection of the Arctic Marine Environment (PAME) working group of the AC is working on an "Arctic Ocean Review."[22] Its purpose is to summarize "the weaknesses and impediments" confronting the management of the Arctic marine environment and to make recommendations for what is required to ensure a "healthy and productive Arctic marine environment." Such a mandate, of course, begs a whole series of questions about what kind of national, regional and global agencies (e.g. United Nations Environment Programme (UNEP), International Maritime Organization (IMO), UK Parliament, and EU) judge such terms as "healthy" and "productive" and what measures might need to be developed to ensure the former are secured. The WWF Global campaign, for example, has argued that, "[t]he Arctic Council is now at a critical time in its evolution when its members must show accountability for implementing the recommendations flowing from the wealth of its own scientific assessments."[23] The AC does work closely with international bodies such as IMO and UNEP, so "accountability" for the Arctic marine environment is probably best thought of as a shared if contested project. The eventual report, under the auspices of PAME, is going to be a sensitive one. Co-led by AC member states (Canada, Iceland, Norway, Russia, and the United States), it was expected that details will be released at the 2013 ministerial meeting.

There will be little support for a more

treaty-based approach to the protection of the Arctic marine environment – the A8 prefer to negotiate agreements on a more incremental basis, mindful of national sovereignty/security interests. At the May 2013 AC Ministerial Meeting in Sweden, the parties signed a legally binding agreement and resolved the decision on observer membership. In 2012, the UK Parliament's Environment Protection Committee called on the UK government to demand a moratorium on oil and gas exploitation in the marine Arctic (noting the provisions of the Antarctic Environmental Protocol).[24] The UK government did not respond to that demand, mindful of both national sovereignties and the provisions of UNCLOS. It is also worth noting that AC observers such as the UK have their status reviewed in 2017.

The A8 believe there is no "governance gap." In May 2008, the five Arctic Ocean coastal states released the Ilulissat Declaration noting that there was "no need to develop a new comprehensive international legal regime to govern the Arctic Ocean." The analogy with the Antarctic Treaty was firmly rejected by the AC, and later dropped by the European Union. For one thing, sovereignty over the Antarctic remains deeply disputed, and this is not the same for the Arctic region. The Arctic Ocean coastal states were determined to remind the wider community that the Arctic region was not exceptional and governable via the provisions of UNCLOS in conjunction with other relevant maritime legal treaties.

However, discussion continues about whether the AC does need to develop a more integrated approach to the marine Arctic environment[25] in light of widely acknowledged and intensifying trends such as increased shipping, mineral resource development, SAR planning[26] and commercial fisheries' development in areas such as the central Arctic Ocean, which might become accessible and profitable if fish stocks drift due to ocean warming. To put one issue into perspective, commercial shipping along the Northern Sea Route (NSR) is increasing. In 2011 some 850,000 tons of cargo were carried, and in 2012 over 1.5 million tons were as operators seek to reduce shipping times between Europe and Asia. If sea ice thinning continues, notwithstanding seasonal fluxes, shipping experts believe that the NSR and even trans-Arctic Ocean routes will develop further.[27] While the shipping potential of the Arctic is complex, the entry of open water shipping into the Arctic Ocean will require further regulatory mechanisms concerning vessel safety standards and SAR capabilities.[28] The development of a mandatory Polar Code, spearheaded by the IMO is considered to be critical in supplementing UNCLOS and others agreements (e.g. Safety of Life at Sea (SOLAS) and Marine Pollution (MARPOL)). The Polar Code will address *inter alia* the design, construction, operation, training and SAR-related aspects of ships operating in polar waters.

Future Arctic Council Development. While there may not be consensus among all Arctic commentators about the long-term trajectory of the region, most agree that the Arctic is an important part of the increasingly inter-connected world and subject to regional/circumpolar, trans-national and global processes and structures.

The AC does face a series of future challenges relating to membership and competencies, which will have their own implications and legacies for relations between Arctic and non-Arctic stakeholders. The distinction between the two will also blur as countries such as China develop their Arctic trade, investment, and scientific portfolios.

The role and scope of the AC will be under further scrutiny. The balance between member states, permanent participants, and observers is one area. The manner in which Arctic marine and terrestrial environments are protected in the face of pressures from states and multinationals eager to imagine and act upon the Arctic as a promising energy frontier is another. There have been complaints from environmental groups

development, and the marine environment. The A8 jealously guard their national sovereignty/security interests, and sub-Arctic states, such as the UK, have been careful to acknowledge those sovereign-territorial interests. The SAR agreement and the proposed oil spill response agreement owe their existence to the collective will of the A8 and not the AC itself.

The AC's future effectiveness and legitimacy rests on recognizing the interests of the A8, as well as those of the permanent participants, while managing non-Arctic states, especially those desiring to be observers. It is a tribute to the AC that fourteen organizations and states express great interest in being observers. China, Singapore, South Korea, India, Japan, and European

The A8 jealously guard their national sovereignty/security interests, and sub-Arctic states, such as the UK, have been careful to acknowledge those sovereign-territorial interests.

in particular that the AC is not evolving fast enough and remains insufficiently rigorous when it comes to intervening in biodiversity protection and regulation of marine resource exploitation. The AC was conceived, right from the start, as an inter-governmental forum with very limited decision-making powers. Where it has enjoyed considerable influence is through its scientific assessments/reports (e.g. Arctic Marine Shipping Assessment 2009), which helped shape public understandings of climate change, shipping, northern

Union are not countries and organizations to be ignored – one cannot imagine only some being accepted and others being rejected (the EU's deferral is temporary and will lead to admission in all likelihood). The rules governing the role of observers makes it clear that their participation is limited (they have no voting rights) and that they explicitly accept, as part of the terms and conditions, the sovereignty of the A8. They are not permanent and are subject to review.

For now, the priority for the Canadian chairmanship remains northern development and the well being of communities therein. Social issues such as unemployment, suicide, and poverty are more immediate priorities for some Arctic residents and communities rather than protection of Arctic marine biodiversity. The two are not

management, and environment protection.

What will be needed, will be an arrangement where the interests, rights, obligations and even hopes and fears of the Arctic 8, the permanent participants and northern communities, and non-Arctic actors and organizations

It is in no one's interest to witness the Arctic as a space of discord. The AC cannot be complacent.

incompatible, but the AC's public commitment (under the Canadian chairmanship in particular, 2013-2015) to promote social-economic issues will be important in the light of more public attention given to the growing interest of non-Arctic actors and organizations and their extra-territorial, especially resource-related and environmental, interests. There is also a scalar tension here – reconciling issues that might be felt intensely in some Arctic communities with more regional/global interests such as shipping, science, resource

are managed in a cordial and collaborative manner. It is in no one's interest to witness the Arctic as a space of discord. The AC cannot be complacent. The creation of an Arctic Circle network demonstrates that other actors and interests are eager, as the President of Iceland noted to promote, "…an open tent or a public square."[29] While the membership is still to be resolved, their inaugural event in Iceland in October 2013 will be keenly watched.

NOTES

1 The Arctic Council was created via the 1996 Ottawa Declaration and followed an earlier initiative the Arctic Environment Protection Strategy. Details of the Declaration can be found at http://www.international.gc.ca/polar-polaire/ottdec-decott.aspx?view=d (accessed 27 March 2013).

2 The official website for the Arctic Council's Indigenous Peoples Secretariat is http://www.arctic-peoples.org (accessed 27 March 2013).

3 The wider point here is that compared to the feverish media reporting of 2007-8 warning of possible conflict in the Arctic, there are grounds for some optimism in terms of regional co-operation in the Arctic. In 2010, Norway and Russia resolved their outstanding dispute over the delimitation of the Barents Sea, and in January 2013 the Arctic Council agreed to create a permanent secretariat. In 2014, it is expected that the IMO Polar Code for Shipping will become mandatory. Progress is also being made on an Oil Spill Response Agreement.

4 For example, Richard Sale and Eugene Potapov, *The Scramble for the Arctic: Ownership, Exploitation, and Conflict in the Far North*, (London: Frances Lincoln), 2010.

5 P. Berkman, "Preventing an Arctic Cold War," 12 March 2013, *New York Times,* Internet, http://www.nytimes.com/2013/03/13/opinion/preventing-an-arctic-cold-war.html?_r=0 (accessed 27 March 2013). This drew some critical responses and one of the most astute was by H. Exner-Pirot, "The relentless myth of an Arctic Cold War," 14 March 14 2013, *Eye on the Arctic*, Internet, http://eyeonthearctic.rcinet.ca/blog/136-heather-exner-pirot/3244-the-relentless-myth-of-an-arctic-cold-war (accessed 27 March 2013).

6 P. Berkman, "Preventing and Artic Cold War."

7 K. Dodds, "A polar Mediterranean? Accessibility, resources and sovereignty," *Global Policy,* 1 (2010): 303-310.

8 In April 2013, the President of Iceland Olafur Ragnar Grimsson announced a new grouping called the 'Arctic Circle', which will hold an inaugural conference in October 2013. This network could be seen as a vehicle for Iceland to enhance its Arctic coastal state credentials.

9 The terms used to describe these high seas areas in the Arctic include "the Banana hole" in the Norwegian Sea, the "Donut hole" in the central Bering Sea, and the "Loop hole" in the Barents Sea.

10 There was consensus over the need to establish and fund a secretariat, which became operational in January 2013 onwards.

11 The Arctic Council Search and Rescue Agreement is called formally the "Agreement on Cooperation in Aeronautical and Maritime Search and Rescue in the Arctic" and signed on 12 May 2011 at Nuuk.

12 The Whitehorse meeting was framed by the Canadian hosts (Canada Command) as the first opportunity for discussing the implementation of the SAR, Internet, http://www.arctic-council.org/images/attachments/Pamphlets/FINAL_ArcticSAR_Pamphlet_4.pdf (accessed 27 March 2013).

13 The Arctic Council had no formal mandate to discuss military/security matters when it was established in 1996. However, these meetings and collaborative exercises point to a willingness on the part of the Arctic 8 to encourage dialogue amongst the militaries in areas of mutual concern such as SAR. Tensions do exist in other areas such as the Norwegian hosting of NATO countries in the context of Exercise Cold Response for example. Russia has complained about the proximity of this exercise to its northern border areas.

14 K. Bird et al., *Circum-Arctic Resource Appraisal: Estimates of Undiscovered Oil and Gas North of the Arctic Circle* (2008), Internet, http://pubs.usgs.gov/fs/2008/3049/ (accessed 27 March 2013).

15 Arctic Council EPPR, *Arctic Guide*, Internet, http://www.arctic-council.org/eppr/completed-work/oil-and-gas-products/arctic-guide/ (accessed 8 April 2013).

16 Arctic Council, "Task force on Arctic marine oil pollution preparedness and response," Internet, http://www.arctic-council.org/index.php/en/about-us/task-forces/280-oil-spill-task-force (accessed 27 March 2013).

17 Senior Arctic Officials (SAO) Report to Ministers, Nuuk, Greenland, May 2011 (Nuuk: Arctic Council).

18 L. Jakobson and J. Peng, *China's Arctic Aspirations* (Stockholm: Stockholm International Peace Research Institute, 2012).

19 "NPC Luncheon with Ólafur Grímsson," The National Press Club, 15 April 2013, Internet, http://press.org/news-multimedia/videos/npc-luncheon-%C3%B3lafur-gr%C3%ADmsson.

20 Greenpeace blogs, "Why you should know about the Arctic Council," 4 February 2013, Internet, http://greenpeaceblogs.org/2013/02/04/why-you-should-know-about-the-arctic-council/ (accessed 27 March 2013).

21 C. Emmerson and G. Lahn, *Arctic Openings: Opportunities and Risk in the High North* (London: Chatham House and Lloyds, April 2012), Internet, http://www.chathamhouse.org/publications/papers/view/182839 (accessed 8 April 2013).

22 For further information on this "Arctic Ocean review" (2009-2013), Internet, http://www.aor.is (accessed 27 March 2013).

23 WWF, "In time of rapid change, Arctic Council must strengthen environmental protection for Arctic," 20 March 2013, Internet, http://wwf.panda.org/what_we_do/where_we_work/arctic/news/?207959 (accessed 27 March 2013).

24 For further information on the UK Parliamentary report see http://www.parliament.uk/business/committees/committees-a-z/commons-select/environmental-audit-committee/inquiries/parliament-2010/protecting-the-arctic/ (accessed 27 March 2013).

25 L. Brigham, "Marine protection in the Arctic

cannot wait," Nature 478 (2011) 157.

26 One development to watch is the Arctic Security Forces roundtable, where military personnel from the Arctic 8 gather to discuss SAR and domain awareness issues. Observers such as the UK have been invited to participate.

27 L. Smith and S. Stephenson, "New Trans-Arctic shipping routes navigable by midcentury," Proceedings of the National Academy of Sciences 110 (2013): 4871-4872.

28 Ibid.

29 Paul Koring, "New Arctic Group Gives Canada New Political Competition," *The Globe and Mail,* 15 April 2013, Internet, http://www.theglobeandmail.com/news/politics/new-arctic-group-gives-canada-political-competition/article11243970/.

Making Sense of the Shanghai Cooperation Organization

Stephen Blank

Analysts have difficulty in determining exactly what the Shanghai Cooperation Organization (SCO) is, what it does, and how it functions. Founded as a collective security organization, in practice it has operated as a regulatory framework for Central Asian security. Understanding the SCO's role is a task of considerable political urgency because the United States and International Security Assistance Force (ISAF) withdrawal from Afghanistan in 2014 will decisively reshape Central Asia's political dynamics and SCO members' policies.

The SCO grew out of a Chinese initiative (hence its name) from the late 1990s that brought together all the states that had emerged from the Soviet Union in 1991 and signed bilateral border-delimiting treaties with China: Russia, Kazakhstan, Kyrgyzstan, and Tajikistan. In 2001, these states and Uzbekistan formally created the SCO. Since then it has added observer states—Mongolia, Afghanistan, India, Iran, and Pakistan—and dialogue partners—Turkey, Belarus, and Sri Lanka.

The SCO's original mandate seemingly formulated it as a collective security organization pledged to the defense of any member threatened by secession, terrorism, or

Stephen Blank is Professor of Russian National Security Studies at the Strategic Studies Institute of the U.S. Army War College in Pennsylvania, where he has been a professor since 1989. An expert on Soviet/ Russian military and foreign policy and international security in Eurasia, he has published over 800 articles and monographs, published or edited fifteen books, and testified frequently before Congress. Dr. Blank is also a consultant for the Gerson Lehrmann Group.

The views expressed here do not represent those of the U.S. Army, Defense Department, or the U.S. Government.

extremism—for example, from Islamic militancy.[1] This pre-9/11 threat listing reflected the fact that each member confronted restive Muslim minorities within its own borders. That threat may indeed be what brought them together since China's concern for its territorial integrity in Xinjiang drives its overall Central Asian policy.[2] Thus, the SCO's original charter and mandate formally debarred Central Asian states from helping Uyghur Muslim citizens fight the repression of their Uyghur kinsmen in China. Likewise, the charter formally precludes Russian or Chinese assistance to disaffected minorities in one or more Central Asian states should they launch an insurgency.

In practice the SCO has refrained from defense activities and followed an idiosyncratic, even elusive, path; it is an organization that is supposed to be promoting its members' secu-

effectiveness.

Therefore, this essay argues that the SCO is not primarily a security organization. Rather, it provides a platform and regulatory framework for Central Asian nations to engage and cope with China's rise and with Sino-Russian efforts to dominate the area. As such, it is attractive to small nations and neighboring powers but problematic for Russia and the United States. Analyzing the SCO's lack of genuine security provision, its membership expansion considerations, and Russia's decline in power will help clarify the organization's current and future roles.

Security Matters and the SCO's Actual Functions. As a security provider, the SCO differs from European institutions. Despite spawning a substantial bureaucratic apparatus, the SCO has done little to provide genuine security, unlike the EU and NATO's

In practice the SCO has refrained from defense activities and followed an indiosyncratic, even elusive, path.

rity, yet it is difficult to see what, if anything, it actually does. Officially published accounts are of little help in assessing the SCO since they confine themselves to high-flown, vague language and are short on specifics. We see from members' actual behavior that they primarily rely on bilateral ties with Washington, Beijing, or Moscow, or on other multilateral formations like the Russian-organized Collective Security Treaty Organization (CSTO), itself an organization of questionable

highly visible actions and benefits. Multiple examples illustrate how, in security matters, the SCO has been absent more than it has been present. It has played virtually no role in the war in Afghanistan, even though Central Asian states and Russia have provided routes for the Northern Distribution Network (NDN) that supplies U.S. and ISAF forces, and have made investments in Afghanistan's electricity and road infrastructure.[3] In the crisis stemming from the anti-

Uzbek pogrom in Osh, Kyrgyzstan, in 2010, the SCO was also absent. It has been totally silent regarding the severe Central Asian rivalries over water-use issues. Likewise, the SCO failed to act in the Uzbek uprising and ensuing massacre in Andijan in 2005 or in any of Kyrgyzstan's revolutions.

What is the SCO's purpose, then? Russia and China, its two principal members, have openly disagreed on this question. China blocked Russian efforts to convert the SCO into a military alliance and Russia blocked Chinese efforts to convert the organization into a trade bloc.[4] To complicate matters, Russia has created alternate institutions, including the CSTO military alliance with all of the SCO's members except China (though Uzbekistan withdrew in 2012) and a Customs Union as part of its larger Eurasian Economic Community (EURASEC). The latter project clearly aims to challenge China's commercial preeminence in Central Asia, and Kazakh analyst Marat Laumulin called it a "significant step forward in limiting China's expansion." For its part, China has generally dealt bilaterally with Central Asian states in making energy, infrastructure, trade, and border deals.

Thus, despite frequent Sino-Russian invocations of multilateralism in Central Asia, multilateralism appears more in rhetoric than in practice. As Richard Weitz writes, "[t]he SCO governments regularly express dissatisfaction with the slow pace of economic collaboration. Thus far, SCO members have allocated limited resources to these collective multilateral economic initiatives, constraining their potential. The SCO institutions lack independent sources of funding, and instead must rely on the money provided by the individual member states for each project. By world standards, none of the other SCO economic mechanisms could be considered 'serious' instruments."[6]

Therefore, the SCO's main functions are to be found elsewhere. Namely, as a diplomatic forum where Russia and China can regulate their relations in Central Asia and where Central Asian leaders can individually and collectively make their voices heard or, if necessary, engage in mediation on current disputes. Obviously this is not the original charter's intention, but it is logical that the SCO has evolved into an organization whose apparent primary purpose is to provide an acceptable regulatory framework for China's rising power and status in Central Asia. At the same time, for Moscow and Beijing another key purpose of the SCO is to organize and articulate regional support for the ouster of American bases from Central Asia, particularly the base at Manas, Kyrgyzstan, and to prevent the formation of any kind of American-led security organization there. A third clear purpose of the SCO is to provide a forum for expressing its members' virtually unanimous opinion that Washington should not interfere in their domestic arrangements. In other words, it functions as an organization of mutual protection to grant small Central Asian states the international legitimacy they so desperately lack and crave. All the members support the continuation of the status quo and reject calls from external parties like Washington on behalf of democratic ideals. Russia and

China provide both diplomatic support and ideological cover for local regimes, allowing them to uphold the status quo with some sense that key players will back them up. Thus in 2005 Moscow and Beijing fully supported Uzbekistan's brutal repression of the uprising at Andijan while the U.S. State Department condemned it.[7] The SCO also stabilizes Central Asian governments' domestic situation by institutionalizing a forum where great-power rivalries are visible but moderated, and where smaller nations can collectively demand resources from those great powers. After the SCO summit in 2005, China loaned $900

independence of Abkhazia and South Ossetia from Georgia. More recently China collaborated with Uzbekistan to thwart Russian efforts to intervene in Kyrgyzstan's domestic crises in 2010.[9] China did so to prevent Russia from obtaining a precedent using Article 51 of the UN charter and the right to protect ethnic kinsmen in another country from being applied to Central Asia. That precedent could be used to devastating effect against both Central Asian and Chinese governments. While those principles defending states' territorial integrity are enshrined in the SCO charter, Russia's actions show that they are more often observed or

If membership confers presence and real status, it allows states like Turkey and India to upgrade their effective influence in Central Asia.

million to local governments, and in 2009 offered them $10 billion while local governments now have a real voice in SCO decisions. China even offered them another $10 billion in 2012.[8] In this fashion the SCO allows its smaller members to mitigate the dual threat of internal unrest and great-power domination.

Given the rise of China and the forthcoming U.S. withdrawal from Afghanistan, we will probably see increasing Chinese efforts to form partnerships with one or more Central Asian states to advance its own interests, or block Russian interests. China worked with other SCO members in 2008 to oppose Russia's support for the

honored in the breach rather than the occurrence. Should future crises erupt within one or more member states or between any two members, it will be an important test for this organization. In all likelihood, the gap between the SCO's formal by-laws and its effective functioning will probably grow over time.

Membership Issues. Given the increasingly visible Sino-Russian rivalry in Central Asia, why do other states seek to join the SCO? In a word, influence. If membership confers presence and real status, it allows states like Turkey and India to upgrade their effective influence in Central Asia. Meanwhile, the observers Iran, Pakistan, and India have all sought membership. Iran was rebuffed since no state wants to assume a posture of support or a requirement, even implicit, to help defend Iran against potential attack over its nuclear program. Moreover, throughout Central Asia generally there is a healthy suspicion of Iran's objectives, particularly in Uzbekistan.

Meanwhile, India and Pakistan believe that they must play a bigger role in Central Asia by becoming full members of the SCO. Yet their efforts have failed because they have come up against the Sino-Russian rivalry. Moscow supported India and Beijing supported Pakistan, reflecting each major power's "alliance network." Yet over the course of 2011-12 Moscow announced a change of heart over Pakistan's full membership application, no doubt as part of its concurrent effort to improve ties with Pakistan in anticipation of the U.S. withdrawal from Afghanistan. Russia's change of heart may have also reflected a possibly growing Chinese influence over Russian policy, yet it neither softened Beijing's opposition to Indian membership nor fostered a true breakthrough in Russo-Pakistani relations.[10]

India's failure to gain full SCO membership represents part of its larger failure to make headway in Central Asia.[11] Undoubtedly, one major reason for its unsuccessful attempt to fully join the SCO is China's unrelenting determination to keep India firmly boxed into South Asia, and even challenge it there.[12] China sees India as not just an obstacle in its own right, but as a U.S. stalking horse.[13] The United States supports an expanded Indian role in Central Asia, and the American presence vastly enlarges the political, economic, and military space available to India. Absent that U.S. role (and despite Russian support), it is likely that China and Pakistan would succeed in checking India's ability to project meaningful economic or military power into the region, including its ability to negotiate contracts for energy supplies. India needs a partner to be effective in Central Asia, while China does not, and China intends to exploit that advantage for as long as possible. Certainly China has far outpaced India to date throughout the region, despite India's rising wealth and power.[14]

Not only has Turkey indicated that it wants to expand its role from being a dialogue partner of the SCO to being an observer, but Prime Minister Recep Tayyip Erdogan indicated in January 2013 that Turkey seeks full membership in the SCO. Erdogan's announcement openly revealed his (if not his government's) frustration with the EU's dilatory approach to Turkey's application for membership. In addition, Turkish membership in the SCO would have other goals and impacts, along with several interesting ramifications.[15] It would clearly demonstrate Turkey's determination to play a major investment role in Central Asia, particularly for gaining access to the region's gas. It could perhaps even signify a return to pan-Turkish visions in Turkish foreign policy.[16] Turkey recently led an effort with Azerbaijan, Mongolia, and Kazakhstan to set up a gendarmerie organization to strengthen ties among these governments' paramilitary forces and ensure security.[27] Third, SCO membership could reinforce the Islamist imperatives in Turkey's domestic policy that continue to obstruct democratization.[18] Fourth, although all the members of the SCO reject Turkish pretensions to leadership in Central Asia and its official Islamism, Central Asian states would certainly welcome more Turkish investment, while Beijing and Moscow might regard Turkey's application as another encouraging sign of the weakening of the West.

Turkey's application promises to further complicate the Sino-Russian rivalry. China would certainly welcome Turkey's commitment to the three principles of fighting terrorism, secession, and extremism—as that commitment would force Turkey to reduce if not terminate support for Uyghur nationalists—but it is unlikely that Russia would welcome Turkey, another economically vibrant and ideologically fortified Muslim rival, in Central Asia. While China has cautiously suggested a favorable response to Turkey's request for full membership (as of this writing), Russia has remained silent.[19] Turkey's move might also furnish China with another excuse for delaying India's bid even as Russia must deal with another rival.[20] Thus, perhaps inadvertently, Turkey's move highlights Russia's dilemmas vis-à-vis the SCO and, more broadly, China in Central Asia.

The Russian Dilemma. Russia knows it is losing ground to China in Central Asia, particularly commercially, and it has begun to take steps to overcome that loss, such as participating in EURASEC. Russian analysts already claim that "the interaction

with China within SCO only weakens Russia's position in the long run."[21] Maria Teploukhova of Russia's PIR Center writes that bilateral dialogue and military exercises are sufficient, making the SCO unnecessary for further interaction, and that "attempts to compete with China within the SCO are also doomed to failure, since for China the SCO is a matter of foreign strategy and for Russia it is a matter of prestige. Therefore, Moscow either has to agree to the position of second player (as it does now), or to spend much of its resources on real rivalry. Cooperation between the SCO and the Collective Security Treaty Organization helps to improve the position of Russia, but again the overall context implies that the structure is more oriented towards Central Asia than the Russian Far East."[22]

China's economic power grew so much in 2009 that Russia had to accept China's investments in Central Asia as a positive phenomenon. Deputy Foreign Minister Sergei Ryabkov actually praised Chinese investment in Central Asia for its "transparency."[23] Ryabkov further claimed, "We believe that our friends and partners in Central Asia are appropriately meeting the situation and solving the task facing them in the sphere of economic and social development using the opportunities that present themselves as a result of cooperation with China. Hence this can only be welcomed."[24]

Given the consistent paranoia of Moscow's elite toward any gain by China or the United States in Central Asia, Ryabkov's statement marked a profound change in rhetoric (if not policy) and a major concession to China. As a 2007 report of the Russian-Chinese Business Council observed, "[b]eing a member of the SCO, China views other members of the organization as promising markets. It is China that wishes to be the engine behind the trade and economic cooperation within the framework of the SCO...China's intentions to form [a] so-called economic space within the SCO are well known."[25]

Consequently in Central Asia, "China has steadily advanced, commercially speaking, into Central Asia. It is now second to Russia as a trading

merely an anti-American maneuver but is intended to keep China, who has previously expressed an interest in bases there, out. And this rivalry will undoubtedly continue or even grow in intensity as the United States winds down its military presence in Afghanistan. Indeed, one recent report flatly argued that Russia is "increasingly distrustful of the SCO and China's intentions."[28] Nevertheless, given Russian anti-Americanism and emphasis on military force, the Russian government has hitherto tolerated China's rising commercial, economic, and energy

While Russia aspires to be the principal security provider in Central Asia, it is quite unlikely that it can play a hegemonic role there.

partner for Central Asia, and its volume of trade with the three Central Asian states it borders is already equal to that of Russia. China is also actively seeking to obtain oil and gas directly from the region, bypassing Russian territory and challenging one of Russia's core strategic goals, monopoly control of energy flows in Eurasia. China is already linked to oil fields in Kazakhstan's Caspian region and to gas fields in Turkmenistan by pipelines completed in 2009."[26]

Clearly one of the goals of Putin's customs union is to divert Central Asian economies away from China by coercing them into a partnership with Moscow against Beijing's economic power. Moscow's quest for military bases in Central Asia is also not

profile as long as it did not spill over into issues of providing military security.[29] China is all too happy to saddle Russia with that burden, thus following the same free-riding security policy it follows elsewhere, for example in arms control.[30]

However, Russia's role may be changing. In addition to the Customs Union and EURASEC, which are the cornerstones of its foreign policy, Russia has been proposing numerous economic initiatives and pledging billions of dollars to improve its economic engagement with Central Asia. It has made such pledges before, of course, but they often went unfulfilled, conspicuously unlike Chinese pledges.[31] Now Moscow is moving quickly to entrench its economic and military presence in Tajikistan and Kyrgyzstan and to sign a new security treaty with Kazakhstan while expanding the Customs Union and EURASEC to include Kyrgyzstan, Uzbekistan, and Tajikistan.[32] However one interprets these developments, they certainly look like a declaration of intent to compete with China (and the United States) for hegemony in Central Asia.

While Russia aspires to be the principal security provider in Central Asia, it is quite unlikely that it can play a hegemonic role there. It must contend with an already deteriorating situation in Afghanistan, which Russia expects to become increasingly unstable as the United States leaves. It must also contend with increased Chinese economic power, growing U.S. and Indian economic presence, Uzbekistan's increasing defiance in the CSTO, demands for ever more support from Tajikistan and Kyrgyzstan, and an ever more self-confident Kazakhstan. Russia clearly has no real or effective answer to China's strategic network of pipelines, infrastructure investments, and loans and is attempting to play the role of security provider and manager. However, Russia is increasingly unable to afford that role and project effective and sustainable military power into the area. While none of them will discuss publicly the notion of Russia being in decline due to its political sensitivity, Chinese analysts long ago argued that Russia cannot unilaterally cope with Central Asia's plethora of real and potential security challenges.

Zhao Huasheng, the Director, Center for Russia and Central Asia Studies, Center for Shanghai Cooperation Organization Studies, at Fudan University in Shanghai, wrote in 2004 that issues like terrorism, drugs, and the links between drug running and the Taliban were problems beyond Russia's effective unilateral ability to cope with either in the short- or long-term perspective. Moreover, other regional organizations could not fight these challenges either. Only the SCO could combat terrorists, extremists, separatists, and drug trafficking. Zhao embellished upon the idea of China's free riding, explaining in sophisticated fashion that China concedes to Russia a leadership position in Central Asia, with its attendant headaches, as long as Russia recognizes that it needs China's influence to exercise legitimate authority there. Specifically, he wrote that

After the collapse of the Soviet Union, Russia has continued to influence this area but its ability to control Central Asia is waning. To varying extents, the countries of Central Asia wish to be independent from Russia. In the long run, Russia's control over Central Asia is worrisome. The Shanghai Cooperation Organization links the Central Asian countries and remains attractive for this reason. Therefore, the SCO may be conducive to the exertion of Russian influence and domination. In particular, Russia may cement its broad and general existence in this region with the help of China's influence and the Central Asia's confidence in China. The newly-born SCO has the potential to develop into the most influential regional organization of this part of the world. Joining the SCO is an important way for Russia to take part in Asian affairs, otherwise Russia's potential is greatly diminished.[33]

If he accurately captured China's thinking and Russia's reality, then the SCO could well resemble Asian security organizations even more than it presently does. As we have seen recently in the Asian Regional Forum (ARF) and ASEAN there are open rivalries and strong differences that are either publicly voiced or hidden behind a veil of decorous formalities. Unless Russia finds a way to compete economically with China, it may ultimately function not only as the gendarme of Eurasian autocracy but also as the gendarme responsible for safeguarding China's investments. Russia clearly does not wish to play that role, given the ever greater difficulties of holding distant provinces in thrall. When Russia's decline becomes clear to all the interested onlookers in and around Central Asia, then we will have a real test of just how viable and enduring a security organization like the SCO really is.

NOTES

1 See, for example, "'Shanghai Five' Change Turns China in a New Strategic Direction," *Kyodo*, 18 June 2001, retrieved from Lexis-Nexis; Robert A. Karniol, "Shanghai Five in Major Revamp," *Jane's Defence Weekly*, 27 June 2001, 5; Bates Gill, "Shanghai Five: An Attempt to Counter US Influence in Asia?" *Newsweek Korea*, May 2001; Ariel Cohen, "The Dragon Looks West: China and the Shanghai Cooperation Organization" (Testimony before the U.S.-China Commission, Washington, D.C., 3 August 2006); Jefferson E. Turner, "Shanghai Cooperation Organization: Paper Tiger or Regional Powerhouse" (Thesis presented to the U.S. Naval Postgraduate School, Monterey, CA, 2006); Claire Bigg, "Shanghai Cooperation Organization Mulls Expansion," Radio Free Europe/Radio Liberty, 30 May 2006.

2 There is a substantial literature on this point. For example, see Hassan H. Karrar, *The New Silk Road Diplomacy: China's Central Asian Foreign Policy since the Cold War* (Vancouver: University of British Columbia Press, 2009).

3 Ibid.; Stephen Blank, "Central Asian Perspectives on Afghanistan After the U.S. Withdrawal" (Central Asia Program, George Washington University, Afghanistan Regional Forum, No. 2, November 2012).

4 "China Denies Possibility of SCO Evolving into Military Bloc," 6 June 2012, Internet, http://english.cri.cn/6909/2012/06/06/3124s704187.htm.

5 "Customs Union to Limit Chinese Expansion in Post-Soviet Area-Kazakh Expert," *Interfax-Kazakhstan Online,* in Russian, 18 February 2011, FBIS SOV, 18 February 2011; Mikhail Rostovskiy, "How Should We Live With Lukashenka?" Moskovskii Komsomolets online, in Russian, 2 March 2011, FBIS SOV, 2 March 2011.

6 Richard Weitz, "Is the SCO Coming to LIfe," *Central Asia Caucasus Analyst*, 8 August 2012.

7 Alyson J. K. Bailes and others, "The Shanghai Cooperation Organization," SIPRI Policy Paper No. 17 (Stockholm: SIPRI, 2007) and the sources cited there.

8 Alexander Shustov, "China Strengthens Position in Central Asia," *Russia Beyond the Headlines*, 16 July 2012, Internet, http://rbth.asia/articles/2012/06/28/china_strengthens_position_in_central_asia_15652.html.

9 Stephen Blank and Younkyoo Kim, "China's Hour in Central Asia? Recent Chinese Policies in Central Asia," forthcoming *Journal of Contemporary China.*

10 "Russia Endorses Full SCO membership for Pakistan," 7 November 2011, Internet, http://dawn.com/2011/11/07/russia-endorses-full-sco-membership-for-pakistan/.

11 Emilian Kavalski, *India and Central Asia: The Mythmaking and International Relations of a Rising Power* (London and New York: I.B. Tauris Publishers, 2010).

12 Malik Mohan, *China and India: Great Power Rivals* (Boulder: First Forum Press, 2011), 305-308.

13 Stephen Blank, "How Durable and Sustainable is Indo-American Cooperation in South and Central Asia?" (Paper presented to the SSI-Dickinson College Conference Cross-Sector Collaboration to Promote Sustainable Development, Carlisle, PA, 13 March 2013).

14 Kavalski; Marlene Laruelle and Sebastien Peyrouse, eds., *Mapping Central Asia: Indian Perceptions and Strategies,* (Farnham, Surrey, England: Ashgate, 2011); S. Enders Wimbush, "Great Games in Central Asia," in *Strategic Asia 2011-12: Asia Responds to Its Rising Powers,* Ashley Tellis, Travis Tanner, and Jessica Keogh, eds., (Seattle and Washington, D.C.: National Bureau of Asian Research, 2011), 259-282.

15 Istanbul, *Today's Zaman Online,* in English, 28 January 2013, FBIS SOV, 28 January 2013; "Turkey Considers Joining Shanghai Cooperation Organization," Jane's Intelligence Weekly, 30 January 2013, Internet, https://janes.ihs.com.

16 "Is Turkey Seeking to Revive Pan-Turkism," *Today's Zaman,* 9 February 2013, Internet, www.todayszaman.com.

17 Ibid.

18 *FBIS SOV,* 28 January 2013; Daniel Pipes, "Is Turkey Leaving the West?" *The Washington Times,* 6 February 2013, Internet, www.danielpipes.org/12526/turkey-shanghai-five-sco.

19 "China Welcomes Turkish Bid for SCO Membership," *Today's Zaman,* 1 February 2013, Internet, www.todayszaman.com.

20 "Turkey Seeks SCO Membership," 28 July 2012, Internet, http://blogs.rediff.com (date accessed: 9 February 2013).

21 Maria Teploukhova, "Russia and International Organizations in the Asia-Pacific: Agenda for the Russian Far East," *Security Index* XVI, no. 2 (2010): 83.

22 Ibid.

23 Open Source Center, OSC Feature, Russia, OSC Analysis, "Russian Officials Laud Ties With China; Observers Express Concerns," *FBIS SOV,* 20 July 2009.

24 Ibid.

25 Moscow, *Interfax,* in English, 15 November 2007, FBIS SOV, 15 November 2007.

26 Thomas Graham, "The Sources of Russia's Insecurity," *Survival* LII, no. 1 (2010): 65.

27 Vladimir Mukhin, "Poslednaya Nabrosok na Iuge," *Nezavisimaya Gazeta,* 8 August 2005.

28 International Crisis Group, *China's Central Asia Problem,* Crisis Group Asia Report No. 244 (27 February 2013): 21.

29 Dmitri Trenin, "Russia," in *Is a Regional Strategy Viable in Afghanistan,* Ashley Tellis and Aroop Mukharji, eds., (Washington, D.C.: Carnegie Endowment for International Peace, Introduction by Jessica T. Matthews, 2010), 77.

30 Banning Garrett and Bonnie S. Glaser, "Chinese Perspectives on Nuclear Arms Control," *International Security* XX, no. 3 (Winter 1995-96): 43-78; Jing-Dong Yuan, "No More Free Ride: China and Nuclear Disarmament" (Paper presented to the Annual Convention of the International Studies Association, New Orleans, 17-20 February 2010).

31 Sergei Blagov, "Russia Eyes Stronger Economic Engagement with Central Asia," *Eurasia Daily Monitor*, 8 February 2013.

32 Moscow, *Interfax*, in Russian, FBIS SOV, 15 April 2013.

33 Zhao Huasheng, "Security Building in Central Asia and the Shanghai Cooperation Organization," in *Slavic Eurasia's Integration into the World Economy and Community* (Sapporo: Slavic Research Center, Hokkaido, 2004), 286.

Georgetown Journal

of International Affairs

religion& power *to...*

Espionage Exposed

- - tackling the issues that shape our world - -

CALL FOR PAPERS

The *Georgetown Journal of International Affairs* is accepting submissions for the Winter/Spring 2014 issue. The submission deadline is 15 August 2013. Articles must be about 3,000 words in length. They should have the intellectual vigor to meet the highest scholarly standard, but should be written with the clarity to attract a broad audience. For submission details please refer to our website: http://journal.georgetown.edu/submissions/

The ASEAN Synthesis:
*Human rights, Non-Intervention, and the
ASEAN Human Rights Declaration*

Mathew Davies

The ASEAN Human Rights Declaration (AHRD) has been welcomed as the most impressive commitment to protecting human rights within ASEAN ever created. At the same time, others
have criticized it as fatally flawed, creating no meaningful regional oversight of human rights.[1] In this article I argue that this
range of reactions is explicable by understanding the Declaration as embodying what I term the "ASEAN synthesis" between
progressive and traditionalist positions held by member states.
Since 1997 the progressives have lobbied for substantial reform
of ASEAN, including a commitment to human rights. The traditionalists, while not opposed to reform, envisage a traditional
approach to regional affairs that prioritizes member-state security through commitments to sovereign equality and non-intervention. The ASEAN synthesis reconciles these two agendas by
legitimizing the discussion of human rights within the regional
framework while also reinforcing the principle of non-intervention, seriously curtailing the ability of regional institutions and
declarations to engage in proactive rights protection.

The argument unfolds in three parts. The discussion first
identifies the members and interests of the progressive and
traditionalist camps, placing them in the context of ASEAN's
evolution since 1967 and with particular attention to the 1997

Dr. Mathew Davies
is a Research Fellow
at the Department of
International Rela-
tions, School of Inter-
national, Political and
Strategic Studies, Col-
lege of Asia and the
Pacific, Australian
National University in
Canberra, Australia.

Financial Crisis as the trigger for their emergence. The second section examines the evolution of ASEAN from 1997-2012 and argues that this process can be understood as representing the synthesis of the progressive interest in human rights as aims and the traditionalist focus on orthodox practices. The final section examines the AHRD itself to reveal the influence of both interest groups.

Progressives, traditionalists and human rights in ASEAN. Indonesia, Malaysia, The Philippines, Singapore, and Thailand members (Brunei in 1984, Vietnam in 1995, Laos and Burma in 1997, and Cambodia in 1999), sought to join. The preoccupation with non-intervention rendered ASEAN hostile terrain for any concern with human rights.[4] Whilst ASEAN had engaged with gender issues through the ASEAN Women Leader Conference of 1975 and the subsequent ASEAN Sub-Committee on Women, these were always felt by regional elites to be non-political and so not threatening to elite understandings of the status quo.[5]

The Asian Financial Crisis of 1997 dis-

The preoccupation with non-intervention rendered ASEAN hostile terrain for any concern with human rights.

created ASEAN with the Bangkok Declaration of 1967.[2] Tensions between Southeast Asian states had seen the collapse of two previous efforts to create a regional arrangement, the ill-fated Association of Southeast Asia (1961) and Maphilindo (1963). ASEAN was designed to alleviate those tensions by promoting the "ASEAN Way," comprising both aims and a diplomatic culture. ASEAN members agreed to work towards greater cooperation in economic affairs and peaceful political relations between members. In order to realize these goals, members were bound together by a set of practices that cemented quiet diplomacy, consensus, cooperation, and a strong disinclination to comment on the domestic affairs of other members. This non-interventionist approach to regional governance was strengthened and refined with the Bali Accords of 1976.[3] So strong was this commitment that the ASEAN Way was one of the prime reasons new

solved the consensus that was previously sufficient to manage Southeast Asian affairs.[6] In particular, it divided ASEAN members along a progressive-traditionalist spectrum. There was a widely held belief that ASEAN members' failure to engage with the causes and consequences of the crisis was because of the refusal to comment on the internal affairs of others.[7] Progressives understood the crisis as revealing deep-seated limitations to ASEAN both in terms of its narrow aims and its non-interventionist diplomatic culture. Together these structures stopped ASEAN from effectively dealing with domestic issues such as good governance and the wellbeing of citizens that were now necessary to safeguard its legitimacy. This group was thus concerned with moving ASEAN towards an explicitly socially progressive agenda that would come to include human rights. It is unsurprising that the more progressive states were characterised by a greater embrace of liberalism and democracy domestically: the Philippines, Thailand, and Indonesia after its democratic transition.[8] Traditionalist members did not reject change completely but were strongly committed to ensuring that any changes worked to safeguard, not replace, the traditional pre-crisis ASEAN commitment to state sovereignty and security. Advocates of this position were diverse, the Indochinese states of Vietnam, Laos, and Cambodia along with Myanmar were in the vanguard, but states like Singapore and Brunei were concerned with avoiding overly strong commitments to liberal democracy.

The ASEAN Synthesis and regional reform. ASEAN's journey from 1997 with no commitment to human rights to 2012 and the Declaration only came about because of the emergence of the ASEAN synthesis between progressives and traditionalists. The synthesis consists of an agreement that human rights promotion should be an aim of regional cooperation, but that those aims should not trump the principles of non-intervention and sovereignty that traditionalists prioritize. New goals have been wedded to traditional practices.

This synthesis has been predicated on a gradualist approach to adopting rights within ASEAN. The ASEAN response to the financial crisis was to embark on an open-ended reform process aimed at strengthening ASEAN in light of the weaknesses the crisis had exposed. Ultimately this process would reshape the aims and institutions of regional cooperation. The key area of interest for discussion here was the growing commitment to demonstrate ASEAN's response to the social dislocation that its citizens had endured. From

1997 until 2003, the words "human rights" were almost never mentioned in ASEAN's community building efforts. Vision 2020 (1997) and more notably the Bali II Accords (2003) were limited to talking about a commitment to promote "caring communities" and good governance. The 2004 Vientiane Action Programme marked the first real commitment to rights and made the link between caring communities and human rights explicit. ASEAN states agreed to a stocktaking exercise of existing human rights mechanisms, establishing greater coordination between those mechanisms, developing a coherent and integrated work program towards human rights, building educative programs, and forming commissions for the rights of women and children.[9] Member states signified the importance of human rights by placing the above discussion within what was known as the Security Pillar. Since the Bali II Accords of 2003, ASEAN community building was, emulating in part the European experience, divided into three pillars: Security, Economic, and Socio-Cultural. Placing human rights efforts within the Security pillar, the pillar that primarily housed existing commitments to regional peace and security, the key traditional ASEAN goals, suggests that members were recognising the link between human rights for their citizens and the quality of regional security for states.[10]

Within the Security pillar human rights were successfully "sold" not as radically new, but as the logical continuation of ASEAN's traditional engagement with state security issues. Then Philippine Foreign Minister Alberto Romulo noted that ASEAN's continued ability to meet its commitment to interstate peace was "dependent on one crucial element – the commitment of each government to enact laws and policies that will promote this kind of environment. This must necessarily include the protection and promotion of human rights across the region." [11] This linkage was important in securing at least the acquiescence of more traditionalist states. The form that the commitment to rights would take was more far more important, however. It would be errone-

the sovereign independence of all members alongside an explicit commitment to "non-interference in the internal affairs of ASEAN Member States." [15] So central is non-intervention that the Terms of Reference for the 2010 AICHR itself commits the Commission to non-interference in article 2.1(b). [16]

One of the more progressive aspects
of the Declaration is that it provides detail to ASEAN's discussions about rights for the first time.

ous to view the emergence of rights as an unmitigated defeat of the traditionalist agenda. Traditionalist states agreed to the emergence of human rights norms within ASEAN as legitimate issues for discussion and even regional agreement, but they have ensured that the discussion of rights regionally be undertaken in a way that is compatible with their absolutist vision of non-intervention.

This synthesis has been prominent in all post 2004 community-building efforts. The ASEAN Charter of 2007 noted in Article 1/7 that one of the purposes of ASEAN was to strengthen human rights. [12] Article 14 of the Charter committed ASEAN to creating some sort of "ASEAN Human Rights Body," which was finally addressed with the creation in 2009 of the ASEAN Intergovernmental Commission on Human Rights (AICHR). [13] The AICHR is tasked with the promotion and protection of human rights and fundamental freedoms across ASEAN, although, until the release of the AHRD, it had no explicit rights to protect or promote. [14] In parallel, however, the Charter also re-affirmed

Progressive and traditionalist elements of the Declaration. The AICHR was tasked, as part of its Terms of Reference agreed in October 2009, with developing a human rights declaration "with a view to establishing a framework for human rights cooperation" within ASEAN. [17] The Declaration itself was released three years later in November 2012, adopted at the 21st ASEAN Summit in Phnom Penh, Cambodia. [18] The AHRD is the product of the progressive and traditionalist synthesis. One of the more progressive aspects of the Declaration is that it provides detail to ASEAN's discussions about rights for the first time. Every previous ASEAN agreement, including all of the ones mentioned above, had never moved beyond the words "human rights" to specify what those rights may actually be. The Declaration addresses civil, political, economic, cultural, and social rights, and gives details about how ASEAN members understand these rights. Particularly remarkable in this regard are sections 22-25 of the Declaration that outline fundamental political freedoms, including the freedom of thought, conscience and religion, opinion and expression, peaceful assembly and participation in "periodic and genuine" elections.[19]

These political freedoms, whilst not as detailed as those contained in the European and American regional systems, do describe a system of representative government that is far in advance of the situation prevalent in many ASEAN member states.[20] It is notable that Brunei, Malaysia, Myanmar, and Singapore are not signatories to the International Covenant on Civil and Political Rights, and, as such, the articles above are the strongest commitments these states have made to political rights given that the Declaration is more detailed than articles 18-21 of the Universal Declaration of Human Rights, which is widely considered to be of universal validity.[21] The situation in Myanmar is illustrative of this ongoing tension. Recent reforms and partial democratisation have not overturned the dominant role of the military in domestic affairs, given that the military retains a 25 percent block of seats in both houses of Myanmar's parliament. The tension between this situation and the AHRD's call for government to reflect the "free expression of the will of the electors" is clear, although whether the AICHR is ever allowed to examine that tension is considerably less assured.

One particularly worrying development, from the progressive end of the spectrum, is the continued relevance of cultural relativism. For example, Article 7 starts with the commitment that "[a]ll human rights are universal, indivisible, interdependent and interrelated. All human rights and fundamental freedoms in this Declaration must be treated in a fair and equal manner, on the same footing and with the same emphasis."[22] It then continues with "[a]t the same time, the realisation of human rights must be considered in the regional and national context bearing in mind different political, economic, legal, social, cultural, historical and religious backgrounds."[23] While innocuous on the surface, this reference to various contexts echoes the early 1990s debate about so-called "Asian Values," which saw Malaysia and Indonesia amongst others critique the global human rights regime as overly Western and, as such, damaging to the more communitarian minded societies of "the East."[24] The inclusion of such a clause immediately after the commitment to rights universality and indivisibility is notable and the future practice of the AICHR will need to be studied to see how states understand the relationship between universality and "regional and national context."

This echo of the past finds further resonance in Article 6 that notes "the enjoyment of human rights and fundamental freedoms must be balanced with the performance of corresponding duties as every person has responsibilities to all other individuals, the community and the society where one lives."[25] Article 8 extends this sentiment by indicating that rights can be limited "to meet the just requirements of national security, public order, public health, public safety, public morality, as well as the general welfare of the peoples in a democratic society."[26] It is not unusual for various rights declarations, charters, and conventions to contain within them a clause to suspend rights in "extreme circumstances," but were security, order, health, and safety not broad enough, the inclusion of "public morality" suggests a far more enduring curtailment of apparent "fundamental" freedoms. Such language caused the U.S. State Department to express serious worry about the Declaration.[27]

Finally, the Declaration is not legally binding on ASEAN members. Declarations are just that, declaratory. They may become binding over time, but that process is not inevitable and depends on the will, and perception, of states over time. The phenomenon of states with poor human rights records agreeing to human rights declarations and treaties, whether global or regional, is well documented.[28] Illiberal states tend to sign human rights treaties more to satisfy international pressure that they should sign than because of a true commitment to the moral weight of the documents themselves.

There is even ambiguity about the precise relationship between ASEAN and the

that body, and the closest that it comes to an endorsement of the AHRD is a commitment to promoting the implementation of ASEAN instruments, "related to human rights."[30] The Terms of Reference were written before the Declaration was finalized, but given the AICHR drafted the Declaration, and this fact was well known, the omission remains significant. Reading the five-year work plan established by the AICHR for the 2010-2015 period provides no greater clarity. Section 4.6, which talks of how the AICHR will facilitate the promotion and implementation of ASEAN instruments, talks only about compiling existing ASEAN instruments and ensuring translations are available.[31]

Illiberal states tend to sign human rights treaties more to satisfy international pressure that they should sign than because of a true commitment to the moral weight of the documents themselves.

Declaration. In Article 39 the Declaration, seemingly prosaically, suggests that rights and freedoms will be achieved through interstate cooperation as well as with "relevant national, regional and international institutions/organizations, in accordance with the ASEAN Charter."[29] The prime institution that we might expect to be referenced, the AICHR, is not explicitly mentioned. The AICHR was tasked with drafting the Declaration, but is not tasked explicitly with promoting and protecting the rights within the Declaration. The Terms of Reference for the AICHR in Article 4 identifies fourteen "mandates" for

Conclusion. The ASEAN Human Rights Declaration is not so much a compromise between progressives and traditionalists as representative of the synthesis of their positions. The document confirms the legitimacy of human rights as part of the framework of ASEAN cooperation, but it also confirms that the discussion of rights sits alongside traditional commitments to non-intervention and sovereign equality. Many have criticised the Declaration as being flawed. The AHRD is no great step towards increasing ASEAN's ability to proactively promote and protect human rights, but it does carefully allow agreement between ten highly diverse members. Given its genesis and the care that has gone into its crafting, the Declaration deserves some credit. In a very real sense, it was never designed to meet the expectations of external ASEAN critics.

The ASEAN synthesis exerts a powerful conditioning affect on the ability of the Declaration to live up to the expectations of human rights defenders within and beyond the region. In particular it develops little direct compliance pressure, especially when read alongside the AICHR and its weak enforcement mechanisms. There is nothing inherent about the Declaration that forbids further reform towards stronger regional oversight, but the histories of the progressives and traditionalists, together with the synthesis established between them, means that considerable, and radical, political will is needed if ASEAN is ever to live up to the expectations that some have of it.

NOTES

1 "Civil Society Denounced Adoption of Flawed ASEAN Human Rights Declaration," Internet, November 20, 2012, Internet, http://www.fidh.org/Civil-Society-Denounces-Adoption-12462.

2 ASEAN, *The Bangkok Declaration*, Bangkok, Thailand, August 8th 1967, Internet, http://www.asean.org/index.php?option=com_content&view=article&id=5.

3 ASEAN, *Treaty of Amity and Cooperation*, Jakarta, Indonesia, 24 February 1976, Internet, http://www.asean.org/news/item/treaty-of-amity-and-cooperation-in-southeast-asia-indonesia-24-february-1976-3.

4 Maznah Mohamad. "Towards a Human Rights Regime in Southeast Asia: Charting the Course of State Commitment." *Contemporary Southeast Asia* 24, no. 2 (2002): 223.

5 Li-ann Thio, "Implementing Human Rights in ASEAN Countries: Promises to Keep and Miles to go Before I Sleep," *Yale Human Rights and Development Law Journal*, 2, no. 1. (1999): 11.

6 Hadi Soesastro, "ASEAN During the Crisis," in *Southeast Asia's Economic Crisis*, ed. H.W. Arndt and Hal Hill (Singapore: Institute of Southeast Asian Studies, 1999). Zakaria Haji Ahmad and Baladas Ghoshal, "The Political Future of ASEAN After the Asian Crisis," *International Affairs* 75, no. 4 (1999).

7 Herman Kraft, "ASEAN and Intra-ASEAN Relations: Weathering the Storm?" *The Pacific Review*, 13, no. 3 (2000).

8 Alexander C. Chandra, "Indonesia's Non-State Actors in ASEAN: A New Regionalism Agenda for Southeast Asia," *Contemporary Southeast Asia* 26, no. 1 (2004).

9 ASEAN, *Vientiane Action Program*, Vientiane, Laos, 29 November 2004, Internet, http://cil.nus.edu.sg/2004/2004-vientiane-action-programme-2004-2010-signed-on-29-november-2004-in-vientiane-laos-by-the-heads-of-stategovernment-vap/.

10 Mathew Davies, "Explaining the Vientiane Action Programme: ASEAN and the Institutionalisation of Human Rights," *The Pacific Review*, (2013). DOI:10.1080/09512748.2013.788066

11 See Umar Hadi, "Human Rights Promotion in the ASEAN Security Community: An Overview" (paper presented at the AICOHR - ASEAN-ISIS Colloquium on Human Rights, Manila, 15-16 May 2006): 6.

12 ASEAN, The ASEAN Charter, November 20, 2007Article 1/7, Internet, http://www.asean.org/asean/asean-charter/asean-charter.

13 Ibid., Article 14.

14 ASEAN, *The ASEAN Intergovernmental Commission on Human Rights,* Terms of Reference, 2009, Internet, http://www1.umn.edu/humanrts/research/Philippines/Terms%20of%20Reference%20for%20the%20ASEAN%20Inter-Governmental%20CHR.pdf.

15 ASEAN, *The ASEAN Charter*, Article 2/E.

16 ASEAN, T*he ASEAN Intergovernmental Commission on Human Rights*, Terms of Reference, Article 2.1(e).

17 Ibid. Article 4.2.

18 ASEAN, *Phnom Penh Statement on the Adoption of the ASEAN Human Rights Declaration* (AHRD) 12 November 2012. http://aichr.org/?dl_name=Phnom-Penh-Statement-on-the-Adoption-of-the-ASEAN-human-Rights-Declaration.pdf

19 ASEAN, *ASEAN Human Rights Declaration*, November 12, 2012, Articles 22-25, Internet, http://www.asean.org/news/asean-statement-communiques/item/asean-human-rights-declaration.

20 See the European Convention on Human Rights at http://www.echr.coe.int/NR/rdonlyres/D5CC24A7-DC13-4318-B457-5C9014916D7A/0/Convention_ENG.pdf and the collected inter-American system, Internet, http://www.oas.org/en/iachr/mandate/basic_documents.asp.

21 *The Universal Declaration of Human Rights*, Internet, http://www.un.org/en/documents/udhr/.

22 ASEAN, *ASEAN Human Rights Declaration,* Article 7.

23 Ibid.

24 See Daniel A. Bell, *East Meets West: Human Rights and Democracy in East Asia* (Princeton NJ: Princeton University Press, 1998).

25 ASEAN, *ASEAN Human Rights Declaration*, Article 6. 26 Ibid., Article 8.

27 U.S. Department of State, "ASEAN Declaration on Human Rights, Press Statement," http://www.state.gov/r/pa/prs/ps/2012/11/200915.htm.

28 See Oona A. Hathaway, "Do Human Rights Treaties make a Difference?," *Yale Law Journal,* 111, 2002. See also Eric Neumayer, "Do International Human Rights Treaties Improve Respect for Human Rights?," *Journal of Conflict Resolution* 49, no. 6 (2005).

29 ASEAN, *ASEAN Human Rights Declaration*, Article 39.

30 ASEAN, *ASEAN Intergovernmental Commission on Human Rights*, Article 4.

31 ASEAN, *Sectoral Bodies*, Internet, http://www.asean.org/images/archive/21071.pdf.

Conflict&Security

Mali: This is Only the Beginning

Baz Lecocq

Finally, the situation in Mali was rotten enough for interna-
tional intervention. First because the mujahideen of Ansar
Dine, the Movement for Tawhid and Jihad in West Africa
(MUJWA), along with Al-Qaeda in the Islamic Maghreb
(AQIM), only had to exercise a little pressure at the front
in Konna, to let the last remnants of the Malian Army
fall apart.[1] Second because the Malian Interim President,
Dioncounda Traoré, installed after the coup d'état against
President Amadou Toumani Touré of 22 March 2012,
faced yet another coup d'état from this same decrepit army,
set heavily against foreign intervention as it might upset its
power within Mali, which led him to formally ask France
for military support, believing he had nothing to lose.[2]

Undoubtedly, the French Ministry of Defense and
French Military HQ *État-Major des Armées* had a plan
ready despite President Hollande's public assurances that
France would not pursue a neocolonial intervention in a
sovereign state. France has historically intervened militarily
in West Africa whenever the situation allowed.[3] In the past
decade, Mali had become more and more part of the U.S.
sphere of influence in Africa as U.S. armed forces trained
Malian troops in counter terrorism operations. This was

Dr. Baz Lecocq holds
a PhD in social sci-
ences from the Uni-
versity of Amsterdam.
Dr. Lecocq special-
izes in the history of
Africa and the Muslim
World. Dr. Lecocq is
senior lecturer in Afri-
can History at Ghent
University, Belgium.

without much success, as is now clear, but France must have looked with disquiet upon their loss of influence. Then there are the uranium mines at Imouraren in neighboring Niger, only a few hundred kilometers from the mujahideen controlled zone in Mali. A further degradation of the security situation in Mali would certainly pose a threat to these French strategic interests.

Now France is back in the game and with the support of the Malian population, at least for the moment. It has proven to be easy enough to free the cities of northern Mali from the mujahideen and their amputated interpretation of shari'a. The mujahideen hardly resisted as this is not their strength in war. Their strength lies in high-speed guerilla warfare in the desert, the whole desert. So what is next?

Both the intervention itself and the immediate post-conflict period will be determined by two main issues. The first is the state of Malian politics, its bureaucracy, and its army. At present, they are all in shambles and the subject of foreign interventions of various kinds, now and in the foreseeable future. The second is the geographic and socio-political position of the country. France and its allies are not fighting a containment operation in northern Mali, but a conflict on a Saharan scale.

Immediately after it became clear that Malian soldiers were preparing to stay in power after their coup d'état on 22 March 2012, the Economic Community of West African States (ECOWAS) reacted swiftly and efficiently with an economic boycott, forcing the putschists into negotiations and a partial restoration of constitutional civilian rule, as House Speaker Dioncounda Traoré was installed as Interim President.[4] ECOWAS has managed to keep the initiative in subsequent international efforts to end the crisis in Mali, to the detriment of traditional mediators such as France or Algeria, but with mixed results and uncertain prospects.

ECOWAS is an organization which partly serves as a platform for West African states, to play out their national and regional interests and influences. Mali's case is no different. ECOWAS' main negotiator, the President of Burkina Faso, Blaise Compaoré, managed to have Malian Speaker of Parliament Dioncounda Traoré appointed as Interim President, according to constitutional rule. However, the constitutional legitimacy of this move has by now expired.[5] The legitimacy of Malian state rule now fully depends on the credibility its leaders have in the eyes of ECOWAS and international leadership, possibly with destabilizing consequences. ECOWAS President Alassane Ouattara is the President of Ivory Coast, a position he won in elections intended to end a decade-long civil war splitting the country in half. Ouattara could only claim his presidency after foreign intervention by ECOWAS and France.[6] The presence of large numbers of Malian and Burkinabe immigrants played an important role in the Ivorian conflict, and their continued political presence influences Ouattara's take on the Malian conflict. ECOWAS' main negotiator in Mali, Burkina Faso's President Blaise Compaoré, is one of West Africa's longest-reigning dictators who has to deal with a small Tuareg minority in Burkina Faso's border area with Mali and Niger, a desert area easily accessible to the mujahideen perhaps still present in Mali, but soon on the move. These two factors undoubtedly leave Compaoré with security concerns of his own, which influence his take on negotiations. The approaches of these two West African leaders to the crisis in Mali, and their direct interests, are therefore not necessarily the same, which could affect events on the ground. Especially Compaoré managed to gain a strong position of influence when he managed to have his long time friend Cheick Modibo Diarra installed as Prime Minister in April 2012.[7]

Further complicating the mission, the military coordination of the African Support Mission in Mali (AFISMA) is in the hands of Nigeria, but the largest contingent is delivered by Chad, which is not an ECOWAS member and which so far has over 2000 troops on the ground.[8] Undoubtedly, Chad's president, Idriss Déby Itno, did not send such a strong contingent to Mali only for humanitarian commitments or his desire to see Malian democracy restored. There are strategic positions to be gained here in a future denouement of Saharan politics. This might lead to squabbles over leadership in the field, which the Chadians might win simply because they have far more experience in the kind of high-speed desert warfare required in the Sahara (a tactic they practically invented). Moreover, Chad is not an ECOWAS member, which will further complicate coordination, unless the AFISMA mission will be transformed into a

UN peace keeping mission, as is now projected.[9]

Under the leadership of ousted President Touré from 2002 to 2012, Mali developed externally as a success story for democracy and development. This could not hide what was evident for the Malian population: the creation of a patronage network through which the political elite enriched itself by, among other things, participating in the growing international drug trade passing through the country.[10]

Few would regret that Touré's second presidential mandate would end with the upcoming April 2012 elections, in which both Interim President Dioncounda Traoré and former Prime Minister Cheick Modibo Diarra ran.[12] However, when these elections were cancelled after the putsch, neither man put his political rivalry aside for the good of the country. Instead, they worked antagonistically as if they were still engaged in the struggle for votes in Mali's annulled elections.

To their credit, both Traoré and Diarra tried to curb the power of putsch leader Captain Amadou Sanogo behind the scenes, mainly by lobbying actively for international intervention. Sanogo feared international intervention as it might lead to a restoration of democratic civilian rule, to the detriment of his power, which he gained by violating Mali's constitution and military law. On 10 December 2012, Prime Minister Diarra was arrested on vague accusations by the military and forced to step down, mainly as he had pleaded openly at the United Nations for foreign intervention.[12] It is almost a miracle that Traoré found the courage to call for French help after the advance of the mujahideen in early January 2013 since he was clearly facing a coup d'état, a second in less than two years, at that same moment.

The political infighting has lowered Malian voters' already low confidence in their government and the country's democratic institutions, hampering the necessary confidence building in the new democracy that is so badly needed after the end of the conflict. Presidential elections are now projected for July 2013, but the question remains as to whether Mali's old political class will muster enough confidence from voters to stay in power, or whether the political landscape will be drastically altered, making way for a new but inexperienced generation of leaders. Neither option will provide the necessary stability needed for the country's post-conflict reconstruction efforts to achieve success.

As for the military, the putschists arrested the entire Malian General Staff during the coup.[13] A number of them have been released and subsequently co-opted by the putchists, who have taken control of operations. This means the logistic and strategic aspects of national defense are in the hands of men hardly trained for the job. The Malian armed forces had two well-trained and experienced elite combat units. The best known is the airborne regiment, nicknamed 'the Red Berets', which also forms the presidential guard. The Red Berets were especially loyal to ousted President Touré who commanded the regiment before entering politics in 2001. In late April 2012 members of this unit staged an aborted counter-coup, after which the regiment was officially disbanded, its members disarmed and integrated into regular army units under control of the putchists around Sanogo. Some were arrested and tortured. Following the Islamist offensive in early January 2013, the Red Berets pleaded long in vain to be reformed and sent to the front. Instead they were further engaged in violent conflict with troops loyal to the former junta in the streets of Bamako in March this year.[14] Only in April was the regiment reformed, but on less than its former strength and probably without sufficient equipment, which sheds doubt on their efficiency in securing Northern Mali.

The second elite combat unit is the Standing Battalion of the Gao Military Region, under command of Colonel Elhaj Gamou. Like their commanding officer, most men in this battalion are former Tuareg rebels who integrated the Malian Armed Forces after the rebellion of the 1990s. The battalion is complemented with an auxiliary force equipped from the Malian Armed Forces arsenals, called 'Delta Force' (in reference to US Special Forces), consisting entirely of men with Colonel Gamou's own tribal affiliation. These units are extremely loyal to the Malian state as they were backed by President Touré in recent years in their decades old local and very deadly struggle with the Tuareg Ifoghas tribe, which dominates the MNLA, Ansar Dine, and the recently created Islamic Movement of Azawad (IMA). Elhaj Gamou and Ansar Dine leader Iyad ag Ghali have been sworn enemies for over a decade. Gamou's battalion defended the city of Kidal against mujahideen forces in early 2012 but were outnumbered and outgunned. Gamou nevertheless managed to negotiate safe retreat in exchange for surrender.[15] This battalion has spent much of 2012 demobilized in Niger's capital Niamey, but have remained ready to engage the enemy. They are in fact the only military unit capable of engaging their former brothers in arms, whose tactics and terrain they share. Gamou's reinstated and rearmed battalion entered Gao alongside French troops in early February, and its men served as guides to French and Chadian forces for operations in the Tigharghar Mountains, but they are eyed with great suspicion by their Malian brothers in arms for two reasons. The first is that they are Tuareg fighters, former rebels at that.[16] The second, and more importantly for the future political field, is that

operational level means starting from the ground up, restoring a well-trained officer corps, restoring trust between units, restoring the army's loyalty to the Malian democratic state, and restoring trust between the army and the nation it is supposed to defend.

The mujahideen retreat from the cities and villages of the north has already led to small-scale acts of vengeance by civilians and army elements alike against people suspected of supporting them. It is feared by local civic leaders and analysts alike that such acts of vengeance will develop into large scale ethnic violence between the various peoples of the north: the Arabs, the Tuareg and the Songhay.[17] The region witnessed similar such violence in the mid-1990s. Then too, the Malian army

Rebuilding the Malian military to an operational level means starting from the ground up.

Colonel Elhaj Gamou is among the few superior officers of the Malian armed forces who has not been under arrest or under control of the putschists. Additionally, he is very popular and respected by Malians despite being a Tuareg. This status would perhaps allow him to mobilize forces against Captain Sanogo and his henchmen, and even have them arrested and court martialed for insubordination, mutiny and high treason.

Whatever else was left of the Malian armed forces after the coup was scattered by the first advances of the mujahideen in early January 2013. Rebuilding the Malian military to an

did nothing to protect its citizens from bloodshed. To the contrary, soldiers of Songhay origins effectively helped to organize and carry out pogroms, while soldiers of Tuareg and Arab origins - rebels integrated in the armed forces - made counter strikes against Songhay villages.[18] It is clear by now that Malian soldiers have again committed acts of vengeance and atrocities against civilian populations in the current conflict, leading to further fears for ethnic conflicts. It is unlikely that Chadian or Nigerian soldiers will be able to halt such violence once it starts. The deployment of Nigerian soldiers in ECOWAS forces in Liberia and Sierra

Leone in the 1990s has shown that they are more likely to become part of the problem than help solving it.

What many observers do not appreciate is that northern Mali forms part of the Sahara, an internally coherent socio-political and cultural space with a long history of internal political struggles and alliances. National borders within the region are politically disputed and create opportunities for smuggling, but do not in any way restrict the movement of goods or people. Indeed fighters are able to easily move from country to country, with or without the tacit support of state organizations.

The Tuareg have been fighting for autonomy or independence of their homeland of Azawad since before Malian independence in the 1960s. The current conflict is the fourth episode in this ongoing struggle. They are not the only ones disputing existing political borders. The most important disputed border is that between Morocco on the one side, and Algeria and the Western Sahara on the other. Morocco and Algeria fought the undecided 'War of the Sands' over their border in 1963. Since then, relations between these countries have been extremely tense. Morocco annexed the former Spanish West Sahara in stages in the 1970s.

The annexation was directly opposed by the Western Saharan POLISARIO movement, which has been fighting for national independence ever since, operating from Algerian soil with Algerian support. POLISARIO has been kept alive by Algeria and the international community. A UN-organized referendum should decide on the political future of the Western Sahara, but this is eternally postponed on ever-more obscure grounds, much to the despair and disillusionment of the Sahraoui youth. Living in permanent refugee camps without hopes for a political solution or improvement in their living conditions, these youths have turned abroad for salvation. While the vast majority turn to Western Europe, especially Spain, a small minority living in the El Aayoun camp have turned to jihadi-salafism and to trans-Saharan smuggling.[19] An unknown number of Sahraoui's have integrated into AQIM and have been active recently in northern Mali, along with tribal kin from Mauritania. It is generally estimated that Mauritanian Arabs provide the vast majority of mujahideen fighters active in AQIM's Saharan battalions or its offshoot MUJWA, although part of its leadership is believed to be of local origins, especially from the Arab Lamhar tribe.[20]

Some analysts, and some jihadists, believe that MUJWA is supported by Moroccan Secret Services as part of its campaigns against POLISARIO.[21] Similar theories on the creation and/or support of AQIM's predecessor (the GSPC) and of AQIM itself by Algeria's intelligence service have been in circulation for about a decade.[22] Support of either secret service for either movement has never been definitively proven or refuted.

These various political struggles make the political and economic problems of the vast Saharan borderland between Algeria, Mali, Mauritania, and Morocco key to understanding the current conflict in Mali: this region may be the next to explode once France and its allies have managed to chase the mujahideen from Mali to their respective homelands.

The borders and border conflicts between Saharan states and peoples have never disrupted Saharan tribal political and commercial relations. The trans-Saharan and intra-Saharan trade has been strongly revived in the past decades. Efficient trucks and fast four-wheel-drives ship food, migrants, cigarettes, arms, and drugs.[23] Mounted with extra gas tanks, 4x4's can cross the vastness of the Sahara in only a few days, which makes the interception of smugglers a near-impossible task, which is unlikely to be carried out at all. Customs officers, soldiers, bureau-

rupting food supplies to northern Mali, exacerbating an already dire food situation.

In addition to this commerce, the political world of tribal feuds and alliances has remained alive and well and plays an important part in the current conflict. The tribes have modernized over the past decades. They form political structures with effective political representation and power in the cities, as well as in the Saharan plains. In Libya, tribes formed the backbone of Khadafi's internal politics. At present many militias still operating in the country are based on tribal affiliation.[25] In Mauritania, Mali and Niger, Tuareg and Arab tribes constitute formal units

These various political struggles make the political and economic problems of the vast Saharan borderland...key to understanding the current conflict in Mali.

crats, and politicians of the various Saharan states are actively involved in the trans-Saharan trade, or look the other way in exchange for a share in the profits.[24]

The various trade and smuggling networks in the Sahara are not necessarily as strongly connected to the different Saharan political and military opposition movements as is generally thought, but they are at least facilitating the logistics of these movements at present. At the same time, they have provided the populations of northern Mali with a minimum of affordable bare necessities over the past months. Disrupting the smuggling means dis-

of administration and local democracy.[26]

The living areas and political domains of these tribes often stretch over national borders. The Arab Lamhar tribe, believed to be leading in MUJWA, for example, is transnational in nature with many connections and actual tribe members living in southern Algeria. The same holds for those so-called 'Mauritanian Arabs' in MUJWA and AQIM, or those in Ansar Dine: many belong to tribes such as the Berabish, Rgeybat, Kunta or Tajakant, which have always lived dispersed between West Sahara, Mauritania, Algeria, and Mali. They are not so much foreign as they are simply choosing between nationalities, while sometimes holding multiple ones. The mayor of Timbuktu in the late 1990s, for example, was a member of the Tikna tribe, living between Morocco, Mauritania, and Mali, and he was locally known to hold both Moroccan and Malian citizenship.

Trade, tribal loyalty and jihad are closely intertwined. These political alliances now gain shape in the form of the MNLA, Ansar Dine, the MUJWA, and AQIM, but the differences between these movements remain subtle and dependent on tribal alliances. This helps to explain the dynamics of the factional splitting and regrouping witnessed over the past year, with first one group rapidly gaining dominance and then another, depending on where the commercial and political interests of the Saharan communities lie. At present, the Ifoghas tribe of Kidal and its allied Tuareg and Arab tribes from Mali, Algeria and elsewhere seem to have the upper hand again after some skillful political maneuvering by its ruling family.

But the MNLA, Ansar Dine, the MUJWA and even AQIM are not the only movements of significance in the Sahara. Next to tribal militias, the ongoing power struggle in Libya involves a number of jihadi-salafi movements, the most notorious of which is the Libyan Islamic Fighting Group (LIFG). One of the spearheads of the 2011 revolution, the LIFG was also implicated in the attack on the U.S. consulate in Benghazi on 11 September 2012.[27] The date of the attack is symbolic for the LIFG's declared alliance with Al-Qaeda. Although very little is known about

the movement and its further alliances, it is not unlikely that the LIFG will try to gain control over the unruly Libyan south in a coalition with local tribal militias, in which Tuareg from the Ajjer Mountains, Berbers from the Jebel Nafusa and Tubu from the Kufrah oases (get used to these names, you'll read them more often in the coming years) play alongside Fezzani Arab tribes who were loyal to Khadafi and who have no choice for their political survival but to form a block against those who want to undo every Khadafi legacy in politics, including those who were loyal to him. Khadafi's death has not dissolved all Khadafi powerbases.[28]

The southern Libyan Fezzan and Kufrah regions have been the turning points in trans-Saharan movements for centuries. Controlling the Fezzan means controlling a large part of the Sahara, something that local players have known for long, but which France, ECOWAS and other interested parties might realize too late. It is by now clear that a large part of the logistics of the movements in northern Mali ran via jihadi-salafi and tribal networks between Mali, Tunisia and Libya, via the Fezzan and the Tamesna Plain - a borderland between Libya, Algeria, Niger, and Mali entirely controlled by Tuareg tribesmen and international smuggler networks. Tuareg and AQIM fighters who left Libya in late 2011 to return heavily armed to Mali took this road. They were not the first, nor will they be the last to do so.

However impressive the advance of Operation Serval might have looked, the French and African troops moved at a turtle's pace in comparison with the high-speed guerrilla tactics of their adversaries. Moreover, where the forces of Operation Serval and its successors MINUSMA and AFISMA are bound by national borders, their mujahideen opponents feel no such restriction. By the time the French arrived in Timbuktu, the various movements in northern Mali had had ample time to reorganize themselves, withdraw men and materiel into the desert, and move across borders. The attack of casualties, strengthening support for the mujahideen as it does in Afghanistan and Pakistan.

France and its allies should realize that they are not fighting a limited containment operation in northern Mali against 'foreign fighters' that can be clearly differentiated from local Tuareg. They will be fighting a war in the Sahara against coalitions of various Saharan political factions

France and its allies should realize that they are not fighting a limited containment operation in northern Mali against 'foreign fighters' that can be clearly differentiated from local Tuareg.

Mokhtar Belmokhtar's new jihadi Brigade 'Those Who Sign in Blood' at the gas fields of In Amenas is proof of that speed and tactical efficiency over a vast terrain.

Unless the Chadian and Nigerien forces within Serval teach their comrades how to drive a 'technical' combat vehicle at close to 200 km/h over rocks and through mull sand, the ECOWAS allies have no chance of effectively beating the mujahideen. They might, however, have managed to disperse them over the various Saharan states until the situation is ripe for them to return to northern Mali, or until the situation in southern Libya is rotten enough to take over local power in ways not unlike we have seen in Mali in the last year. Permanent drone and air warfare, as waged in the Afghanistan-Pakistan border area, will undoubtedly lead to many civilian and economic networks of national, tribal, economic and jihadi-ideological nature. Unless this viewpoint is taken and unless all the various alliances, conflicts, and political contestations in the Sahara are taken into account, any solution to the current crisis in Mali will be ephemeral.

Building stable - let alone good - governance in Mali, to say nothing of building a viable democracy, or establishing peace and prosperity in northern Mali, will be a task of many years comparable to that in Afghanistan. The difference is that while the international community at least pretends to be interested in making an effort in Afghanistan, it has yet to realize this effort needs to be made in Mali on a similar scale.

In recent months there has been much talk of the "Afghanistanisation" of West Africa or "Africanistan".[29]

Until the start of Operation Serval these comparisons were out of place. With every step the international community takes in Mali, "Africanistan" could become more of a reality. Politics is largely a self-fulfilling prophecy.

Notes

1 Adam Thiam, "Affrontement armée-jihadistes," *Le Républicain*, 11 January 2013.

2 "Le président malien Traoré mercredi à Paris pour rencontrer Hollande", *AFP*, 11 January 2013.

3 According to one study, France has intervened militarily forty-six times in Africa between 1960 and 2005. Christopher Griffin, "French Military Interventions in Africa: French Grand Strategy and Defense Policy since Decolonization," a paper prepared for the International Studies Association 2007 Annual Convention, Internet, http://research.allacademic. com/meta/p_mla_apa_research_citation/1/7/8/6/2/ p178629_index.html, internet (date accessed: 01 April 13).

4 Lydia Polgreen, "Mali Coup Leaders Suffer Sanctions and Loss of Timbuktu," *New York Times*, 2 April 12.

5 Lydia Polgreen, "Junta in Mali to Step Down", *New York Times*, 07 April 2012.

6 UNOCI: United Nations Operation in Côte d'Ivoire, "Post Election Crisis", Internet, http://www. un.org/en/peacekeeping/missions/unoci/elections. shtml (date accessed: 04 March 2013).

7 "Mali: nomination du Premier ministre de transition, Cheick Modibo Diarra", *RFI*, 17 April 2012, Internet, http://www.rfi.fr/print/812685? (date accessed: 17 April 2013).

8 "Mali: 1.800 soldats tchadiens sont entrés dans Kidal pour sécuriser la ville", *AFP*, 5 February 2013.

9 UN News Centre , "UN peacekeeping mission in Mali increasingly possible, says top official", 6 February 2013, Internet, http://www.un.org/apps/news/ story.asp?NewsID=44087#.UTRzPo6tzx0, internet (date accessed: 4 March 2013).

10 Bruce Whitehouse, "The problem with the political class", *Bridges from Bamako* (blog), 16 May 2012, Internet, http://bridgesfrombamako.com/2012 May 16/political-class/ (date accessed: 04 March 2013).

11 Diara was installed after negotiations between ECOWAS and the Junta in March 2012. "Mali: nomination du Premier ministre de transition, Cheick Modibo Diarra", *RFI*, 17 February 2012, Internet, http://www.rfi.fr/print/812685 (date accessed: 04 March 2013).

12 "Mali: le Premier Ministre Cheick Modibo Diarra arrêté par des militaires (entourage)", *Mali Actualités*, 11 December 2012, Internet, http://mali-actu.net/mali-le-premier-ministre-cheick-modibo-diarra-arrete-par-des-militaires-entourage-2/, (date accessed:11 December 2012).

13 "Mali: nomination du Premier ministre de transition, Cheick Modibo Diarra", *RFI*, 17 February 2012, Internet, http://www.rfi.fr/print/812685, (date accessed: 04 March 2013).

14 "Nouvel affrontements entre bérets rouges et bérets verts: L'irréparable honte", *Le 26 Mars*, 12 February 2013, Internet, http://www.maliweb.net/ news/armee/2013 February 12/article,126942.html, (date accessed: 04 March 2013).

15 "Mali: Les raisons d'un désertion", *Afrique en ligne*, 2 April 2012, Internet, http://www. afriquejet.com/mali-les-raisons-dune-deser-tion-2012040236126.html (date accessed: 2 April 2012).

16 "Mali des soldats touareg malien de retour à Gao, où certains les ont 'à l'oeuil,'" *AFP*, 4 February 2013, Internet, http://www.malijet.com/en-direct-du-front/63744-des-soldats-touareg-maliens-de-retour-a-gao-ou-certains-les-ont-.html (date accessed: 4 February 2013).

17 Nouhoum Dicko, "El Hadj Baba Haïdara dit Sandy, député élu de Tombouctou à propos de la crise du nord: 'Après la libération de nord nous craignons la guerre civile et il faut dès à présent y faire face'", *Le Prétoire*, 21 January 2013, Internet, http:// www.nord-mali.com/index.php/home/3363-el-hadj-baba-haid...faut-des-a-present-y-faire-facer (date accessed: 21 January 2013).

18 Baz Lecocq, *Disputed Desert: Decolonisation, Competing Nationalisms and Tuareg Rebellions in Northern Mali* (Leiden: Brill, 2010).

19 François Soudan, Mali: Polisario Connection", *Jeune Afrique,* 1 November 2012 and "Qui se cache derrière Mujao?", *Temoust.org*, Internet, http://www. nord-mali.com/index.php/home/952-qui-se-cache-derriere-le-mujao-?, Internet (date accessed: 04 July 2012).

20 "Morocco Terror Risk Spikes", Magharebia, 18 January 2013, Internet, http://magharebia.com/ cocoon/awi/xhtml1/en_GB/features/awi/report-age/2013 January 18/reportage-01 (date accessed: 18 January 2013).

21 Kal, "Early Perspectives on the Mali Crisis from a Jihadist Forum (I)", *The Moor Next Door* (Blog), Internet, http://themoornextdoor.wordpress. com/2012December 22/early-perspectives-on-the-mali-crisis-from-a-jihadi-forum-i/#more-8721 (date accessed: 06 March 2013).

22 The most notable theorist of Algerian intelligence involvement in Saharan Jihadi movements is Jeremy Keenan. See Jeremy Keenan, *The Dark Sahara: America's War on Terror in Africa* (London: Pluto Press, 2009).

23 Julien Brachet, Migrations Transsahariennes: *Vers un désert cosmopolite et morcelé, Niger* (Belle-

combe-en-Bauges: Croquant, 2009); Georg Klute, "Die Rebellionen der Tuareg in Mali und Niger" (Habilitationsschrift, Universität Siegen, 2001).

24 Lacher, Wolfram. "Organized Crime and Conflict in the Sahel -Sahara Region," in *The Carnegie Papers,* Washington: Carnegie Endowment for International Peace, 2012.

25 Moisseron, Jean-Yves and Nadia Belalimat, "L'après-Kadhafi : nouveaux défis en Libye et au Sahel", in Mansouria Mokhefi and Alain Antil (eds.), *Le Maghreb et son sud : vers des liens renouvelés* (Paris: CNRS, 2012), 73-90.

26 Lecocq, Baz. "This Country Is Your Country: Territory, Borders and Decentralisation in Tuareg Politics." *Itinerario: European Journal of Overseas History* 27, no. 1 (2003): 58-78.

27 "Pro-al Qaeda group seen behind deadly Benghazi attack", *CNN,*13 November 2012, Internet, http://edition.cnn.com/2012 September 12/world/ africa/libya-attack-jihadists (date accessed: 06 March 2013).

28 Dida Badi, "Les rélations des Touaregs aux Etats: le cas de l'Algérie et de la Libye", *Note de l'IFRI Le Maghreb dans son environnement régional et international* (Paris, 2010); Moisseron and Belalimat, *op. cit.*

29 *Time Magazine*, 4 February 2013. The *Economist* of that same week dubbed 'Afrighanistan', while in Germany 'Maliban' has become the common denominator.

Since its founding in 1919, Georgetown University's Edmund A. Walsh School of Foreign Service in Washington, D.C. has devoted itself to educating the next generation of global leaders.

The Master of Science in Foreign Service (MSFS)

is the longest-standing graduate program in the School. With an emphasis on creative leadership, ethics and service in the international arena, it prepares women and men from around the world for careers with impact in the public, private and non-profit sectors of international affairs.

The MSFS Advantage

- Distinguished faculty of leading scholars and practitioners
- Diverse and dynamic community of students
- Small class sizes and personalized attention
- Unparalleled internship and career opportunities in Washington, D.C.
- Network of more than 3,000 alumni around the world

Concentrations

- International Relations and Security
- International Development
- International Commerce and Business
- Self Designed/Regional Studies

New Focus Areas

- Environment and Energy
- Global Institutions and Partnerships
- Social Entrepreneurship and Enterprise

Certificate Programs

- Asian Studies
- Arab Studies
- Russian, Eurasian & East European Studies
- International Business Diplomacy
- Refugee and Humanitarian Emergencies

"With fantastic faculty, students, curriculum and location, MSFS was the ideal graduate program for me. It prepared me for my subsequent government, international organization and NGO positions, and fostered friendships that will last a lifetime."

Rob Boone, MSFS '95
Director, American Bar Association Rule of Law Initiative, Washington, DC

GEORGETOWN UNIVERSITY
School *of* Foreign Service
Master of Science in Foreign Service

17 89

msfs.georgetown.edu
msfsinfo@georgetown.edu
202/687-5763

The Kurdistan Region of Iraq: Stabilizer or Spoiler?

Denise Natali

Despite the contentious Iraqi political arena, the Kurdistan Region of Iraq is pressing ahead with its ambitious agenda for economic development and greater autonomy. The Kurdistan Regional Government (KRG) continues to negotiate large-scale energy deals with foreign governments and international oil companies (IOCs), expand its commercial and investment interests, and assure internal stability by controlling the use of force within its borders. Economic opportunities have encouraged political cooperation with regional states, especially Turkey, while reaffirming shared border security commitments. The KRG not only has become Ankara's key—if not only—regional ally, but its partner in checking the Kurdistan Worker's Party (Partiye Karkaren Kurdistane-PKK) and its expanding trans-border affiliates.

Yet, the Kurdistan Region's particular condition as a quasi-state also makes it a political spoiler, or a potential one. In the absence of external sovereignty, the region thrives on international recognition, external patronage, and a weak central Iraqi government to advance its nationalist ambitions.[1] While these features of quasi-statehood help affirm the KRG's autonomy, they challenge the Iraqi government's

Denise Natali holds the Minerva Chair at the Institute for National Strategic Studies (INSS) of the National Defense University, and is an adjunct associate professor at the Georgetown University Center for Security Studies. She has authored numerous publications on Kurdish identity, economic and regional politics, including *The Kurds and the State: Evolving National Identity in Iraq, Turkey and Iran and The Kurdish Quasi-State*.

The views expressed are the author's own and do not reflect the official policy or position of the National Defense University, the U.S. Department of Defense, or the U.S. government.

own state-rebuilding efforts that seek to consolidate its authority and territorial integrity. Additionally, the region's landlocked position and absence of an independent revenue source leave it highly dependent upon Baghdad and regional states for its economic and political survival.[2] These geopolitical and financial realities may encourage deal-making to secure Kurdish interests or the status quo in Iraq; however, they can also source conflict within and across Kurdish nationalist communities beyond Iraq's borders.

Underdeveloped and Unstable. If economic and political opportunities have encouraged relative stability in the Kurdistan Region, their absence has helped foster volatility. Since the state formation period in the early twentieth century, successive Iraqi elites officially recognized the ethnicity of the Kurds and referred to their territory as "the Autonomous Region." However, they left the Kurdish north underdeveloped and isolated from official international alliances and regional markets and their integrative functions. Clandestine external aid was sporadically offered to Kurdish leaders but it targeted particular tribal elites and elevated the Kurds' role as proxies for foreign powers seeking to undermine Iraqi Arab Ba'athist governments. These constraints, as well as Baghdad's ethnically exclusionary and violent policies toward the Kurds after 1968, helped create a climate of volatility and resistance in the region. This resistance was symbolized by the Kurdish peshmerga (militia), whose *raison d'être* was to revolt against the

state and "face death" on behalf of Kurdish nationalism.

Indeed, the relationship between the Kurds and Baghdad was not always hostile and even involved politically expedient negotiations and distinct alliances. In 1970 then Iraqi vice president Saddam Hussein negotiated the March Autonomy Agreement with Kurdish leader Mullah Mustafa Barzani. In 1991, three years after Baghdad's chemical gassing of the Kurds as part of the al-Anfal campaign, Kurdish leaders met with Saddam for nine months to negotiate Kurdish autonomy. Certain Kurdish tribal elites and communities also allied with the Iraqi state against other Kurdish nationalist and tribal leaders.

Still, these negotiations generally broke down over Kirkuk and did not lower the costs of sustained conflict for the Kurds. Even after the 1990 Gulf War, when the region was administratively separated from the rest of Iraq and received large international aid in the form of a safe haven and no fly zone, it was still subject to a double embargo and political marginalization. Moreover, tribal, local, and religious identities remained highly salient, which allowed power struggles to continue between the two main Kurdish leaders and their parties, Ma'sud Barzani's Kurdistan Democratic Party (KDP) and Jelal Talabani's Patriotic Union of Kurdistan (PUK). The four-year civil war that ensued (1994-1998) further destabilized the region and left it politically and administratively fragmented.[3]

The Benefits of Political Stalemate. Whereas Iraqi Kurds had little to lose by engaging in armed resistance against the Ba'athist state and each other, after 2003, their calculus for conflict changed in important ways. The overthrow of Saddam and creation of a weak federal state not only reconfigured the balance of power between Sunni and Shi'a Arabs, but it legitimized and elevated the KRG as a political entity in Iraq. In fact, the 2005 Constitution was a political and financial windfall for the KRG. It disfranchised the central government in the central government. Kurdish President Ma'sud Barzani also brokered various "Erbil Agreements" to assure the Constitution's power sharing agreements and check Iraqi Prime Minister Nuri al-Maliki's consolidation of power after 2010.

Assuring Kurdish interests also meant expanding external patronage networks and international recognition. With its large revenue base from Baghdad, business-friendly regional investment and oil laws, and internal security, the KRG attracted some of the world's largest IOCS, service

---

Turkey has become one of the KRG's most important external patrons, with large-scale investments in infrastructure, construction, and the energy sector.

---

and its Sunni Arab foundation and gave the Kurds recognition, rights, and revenues as a distinct ethnic group and region. Part of these benefits assured the Kurdistan Region 17 percent of the Iraqi budget, which increased exponentially from 2005 to 2013 from about $2.5 billion to $13 billion.

As the KRG integrated into legitimate political structures, its *modus vivendi* altered as well. The region's survival was no longer tied to sustained warfare against Baghdad, but on supporting a federal Iraq and benefiting from the large opportunities it accorded to the region. To this end, Kurdish leaders worked to keep Iraq together, or prevent warfare. Iraqi President Jelal Talabani became an invaluable mediator between the fractious groups industries, and foreign consulates to the region. According to the KRG Investment Board, from 2006 to 2011, the region attracted over $16 billion in foreign investment, 60 percent of which has targeted the capital city of Erbil.

Turkey has become one of the KRG's most important external patrons, with large-scale investments in infrastructure, construction, and the energy sector. Approximately 70 percent of Ankara's $12 billion trade with Iraq in 2011-2012 was with the Kurdistan Region, making it the KRG's largest external trading partner, or more precisely import market.[4] And even though the KRG has no effective export market (excluding trucking Kurdish crude and other "bartered" items across Turkey's border), it aims to export its hydrocarbons through pipelines to Turkey, which needs them to help source its own domestic energy demand and become a regional energy hub.

The Erbil-Ankara alliance has

with an estimated value of over $4 billion in exports to the region expected in 2013, or over 65 percent of Iran's total trade with Iraq ($6 billion).[6] These exchanges are particularly important to the PUK-Goran (Change Movement) influenced Suleymaniya prov-

By moving Kurdish *peshmerga* forces into the territories and 'Kurdifying' the populations, the KRG has unilaterally reconfigured the internal coundaries of what it perceives as Iraq and the Kurdistan Region.

helped stabilize the shared border region, particularly as PKK influence extends beyond Turkey and into Iraqi Kurdistan (Qandil Mountains), Iran, and Syria. In fact, as the Syrian civil war continues to destabilize Turkey's border and the PKK-influenced Democratic Union Party (PYD) assumes control over most Syrian Kurdish territories, Ankara has turned to the KRG for political and security assistance. Barzani has become Erdogan's unofficial envoy in attempting to check the PKK and moderate Syrian Kurdish demands.[5]

The KRG also assures relative security on its eastern border, having developed important commercial/security pacts with Tehran. In exchange for an open border and special trade agreements—including trucking Kurdish crude oil to Iran—the KRG checks Iranian Kurdish dissidents, in much the same way it attempts to control Syrian and PKK nationalist groups on Turkey's border. Iran has become the region's second largest trading partner,

ince, which shares a 150-kilometer border with Iran and largely depends upon Iranian goods to source its local economy.

The Snake Bites the Snake-Charmer. Internal sovereignty in particular has helped advance Kurdish economic and political interests and has encouraged regional cooperation. Yet, by taking advantage of the weak Iraqi state and ambiguous constitution, perhaps more than its framers had expected, the KRG has challenged Baghdad's own state-rebuilding efforts and the country's territorial integrity. Arab and non-Kurdish populations have become critical of what they perceive as Kurdish political overstep and increasingly maximalist demands. Consequently, despite shared anti-Maliki sentiments with other Iraqi Arab groups, the Kurdistan Region has no significant support from Iraqi populations for its key nationalist issues (disputed territories, *peshmerga* budget, and oil law). The 2013 budget was recently passed regardless of the KRG boycott.

Some of the most provocative measures involve KRG penetrations into Iraq's disputed areas. By moving Kurdish *peshmerga* forces into the territories and "Kurdifying" their populations, the KRG has unilaterally reconfigured the internal boundaries of what it perceives as Iraq and the Kurdistan Region.[7] This strategy may have given the KRG de facto control over parts of the territories and its resources—namely oil—but it has undermined regional stability and negotiations with

to Ninewa and its resources, despite the private energy deals negotiated between Mosul governor Atheel al-Nujaifi and Ma'sud Barzani, and commercial exchanges between Mosul and Dohuk. Even though Sunni Arabs have recently protested en masse against Maliki, particularly after the Hawija riots in April 2013, and seek an alliance with the Kurds against Baghdad, they remain committed to their view of Iraqi sovereignty and land. The KRG's movement of *peshmerga* further into Kirkuk after the riots has increased

Despite the appearance of increased economic autonomy, the KRG has become more dependent upon Baghdad than ever before.

Baghdad. Signing contracts with IOCs in the territories has merged oil and land disputes, further complicating ratification of a National Hydrocarbons Law (NHL), while placing local populations in the territories on the front line and at increasing risk of conflict and instability.

The KRG's claims to Ninewa have been particularly unsettling. Arab Iraqis regard the province as the heartland of Sunni Arab and Iraqi nationalism that has no history of administrative ties to the region.[8] They consider it as a fundamental part of Iraq and not the Kurdistan Region—in much the same way they regard Kirkuk as Iraqi territory. Counterclaims to Ninewa have led to increasing brinkmanship and threats of violence. Local Sunni Arab groups, including the Sons of Ninewa, have affirmed their willingness to pursue armed resistance to Kurdish claims

potential for future land disputes.

Indeed, one can argue that the KRG is simply reacting to Baghdad's failure—or refusal—to negotiate the territories, revenue sharing, and a NHL through constitutional means. The Iraqi government indefinitely postponed the planned December 2007 referendum to determine the status of the territories. Draft oil laws debated in the Iraqi parliament also failed to reach consensus and ratification. The Iraqi central government also has refused to fully pay the KRG for its limited oil exports through the official Iraqi pipeline, despite the KRG's affirmation that its hydrocarbons would benefit all of Iraq and publishing partial contracts to assure greater transparency. From a KRG perspective the only option left is to circumvent Baghdad and attempt to export Kurdish crude oil through an independent pipeline to Turkey.

Still, these measures have occurred unilaterally and are perceived by Arab Iraqis as threatening the territorial integrity of the country. For instance, instead of making maximalist claims to the territories, including redefining them as "Kurdish regions outside Kurdistan" the KRG could have opted for a more moderated approach that gave Kirkuk "special status" as proposed by local populations and the UN plan.[9] Rather than signing oil contracts in the disputed areas the KRG could have avoided these sensitive regions altogether. In fact, some local Kurdish populations have become increasingly concerned about what they perceive as Barzani's overreach and the implications for the region's stability.[10] The KRG's threats to independently export crude oil to Turkey while Kurds in Syria are trying to carve their own autonomous region amidst an active PKK also has heightened concerns about Kurdish political ambitions by Iraqi Arab populations and regional states, including Turkey and Iran, despite Turkey's recent attempts to negotiate with the PKK and the ongoing ceasefire.

Even then, the prospect of a sustained civil war between the KRG and Baghdad is unlikely because the costs of conflict for the region remain high. Kurdish leaders and their parties are significantly vested in the Region's multi-billion dollar economy and need to assure internal stability, the KRG's international recognition, and external patronage networks. Additionally, despite the appearance of increased economic autonomy, the KRG has become more dependent upon Baghdad than ever before. About 95 per-

cent of its annual budget is sourced from the central government, three quarters of which is allocated to public sector salaries. The majority of KRG social welfare services—essentially the functioning of the region—is dependent upon Baghdad funding. This dependency further checks the KRG's potential to act independently, including its ongoing threat to secede from Iraq. Further, given the KRG's landlocked condition, relying on Turkey as a sole energy transit route would only increase its vulnerability, threaten its revenues from Baghdad, and undermine its foreign policy autonomy and internal sovereignty.[11]

Backlash of the Ankara-Erbil Alliance. The Ankara-Erbil alliance also is having unintended consequences on Kurdish-state relations and intra-Kurdish dynamics. Ankara's ties to Erbil have developed while its relationship with Baghdad has deteriorated, reinforcing the growing sectarian policies of Turkish Prime Minister Recep Tayyip Erdoğan and the "Sunnification" of Turkish foreign policy.[12] As a proxy for Turkey, the KRG has become implicated in Ankara's domestic and foreign policy decisions, which has brought Iraqi Kurds into Turkey's regional power struggles and exacerbated Erbil's tensions with Baghdad and some cross-border Kurdish groups.

In particular, the KRG has become part of Erdoğan's attempts to weaken Baghdad by creating a Sunni-Arab and Kurdish alliance against Maliki. Similarly, Erdoğan's backing of the SNC and its Salafist affiliates have further compromised Barzani's potential to influence Syrian Kurds, the vast majority of whom are tied to the secular PYD or acting independents. Barzani's message of political moderation may appease Ankara and regional governments, but it has antagonized Syrian Kurds who seek no less politically than what Iraqi Kurds have realized. Power struggles have emerged between Barzani-influenced Syrian Kurds in the KNC and PKK/PYD groups, reflecting the larger tensions between Turkey and Iran, Islamist and secular influences, and their local proxies. Intertwined in these tensions is a power struggle between Barzani and the PKK over leadership of the Kurds.

The Erbil-Ankara alliance also has reinforced political divisions in the Kurdistan Region. It has developed as the KDP-Barzani has consolidated power in Erbil and PUK influence has declined, aggravating concerns about the aggrandizement of Barzani family power. Some PUK and Goran circles have renewed efforts to check what they perceive as Barzani's unilateral decisions that are gambling with the security of the Kurdistan Region.[13] These internal divisions have been manifested in distinct approaches to the KRG relationship with Baghdad, Syria, and Kurdish hydrocarbons policy. While most KDP circles see the region's future tied to Turkey and apart from Baghdad, others within the PUK and Goran regard the Erbil-Ankara connection as limited and affirm the region's future is part of Iraq, despite a shared anti-Maliki sentiment. This is why, when Barzani attempted to secure a vote of no-confidence against Maliki in 2012, the PUK and Goran did not offer their support. It also explains the emergent divisions within the KNC between PUK and KDP-backed factions that are further fragmenting Syrian Kurdish groups.

Finally, while the KRG's internal security measures have helped establish a positive investment climate they have further checked political openings in the region. Increasing authoritarianism and the evident gap in wealth caused by uneven, rapid economic development has led to rising criticisms of the KRG by local populations. Despite urbanization and education trends, the region remains deeply embedded in traditional patronage networks. The KDP and PUK still control virtually all aspects of society, political life and the economy, and have deepened their patronage networks with the rising oil wealth. While the Kurdish uprisings in spring 2011 may have remained limited to Suleymaniya province and were eventually quelled by KRG-KDP security forces, they mark a growing challenge to regime legitimacy that could undermine the region's development potential and stability.

Looking Forward. The Kurdistan Region has benefitted significantly from the federal Iraqi system and has used these opportunities to enhance its international status, internal autonomy, relative stability, and economic development. No other region in Iraq has realized these accomplishments in the post-Saddam era. The Region has the potential to further develop and encourage regional cooperation on energy, commerce, and other sectors such as tourism. In this sense, the KRG can play a positive role in stabilizing the region and should be supported internationally to do so.

The problem, and where the Kurdistan Region can be a political spoiler, is where Kurdish nationalist ambitions undermine—or are perceived to undermine—Iraq's territorial integrity. In this sense, the KRG's actions have not only antagonized Baghdad, but also Iraqi Arab groups and other non-Kurdish communities in the disputed areas. While neither Baghdad nor Erbil has an interest or capability in engaging in a sustained civil war, the zero-sum mentality and increasing centralization of power on both sides will likely result in ongoing brinkmanship, a continuation of the status quo, destabilized border areas, and constraints on economic development, especially energy sector potential.

Additionally, given the increasing complexities of trans-border Kurdish nationalism, the deal-making required to sustain the region politically and financially is highly susceptible to power struggles between regional states and non-state actors. In particular, as the KRG becomes engulfed in the geopolitical tensions between Turkey and Iran, and as different Kurdish groups seek to benefit from the political vacuum in Syria, the region may become vulnerable to Syrian spillover and intra-Kurdish divisions. Similarly, rising fragmentation between Iraqi Kurdish parties will continue to play out in Syria, reinforcing competitions between Kurdish groups.

The real concern is the future of KRG relations with the Iraqi state. Maliki's consolidation of power and his sectarian policies certainly have heightened tensions with the Kurdistan Region and Sunni Arab groups. However, the Iraqi government, whether under Maliki or another leader, will have the same need and interest in consolidating power and reaffirming authority as any other state seeking to secure its borders, including the Kurdistan Region. The degree to which the KRG can balance the realities and external support of Iraqi sovereignty, the benefits of political stalemate and its own nationalist ambitions will shape the prospects for its future development and stability.

NOTES

1 Kolsto, Pål. 2006, "The Sustainability and Future of Unrecognized Quasi-States," *Journal of Peace Research* 32, no. 6: 723-740: 724.

2 Natali, Denise, *The Kurdish Quasi-State: Development and Dependency in Post-Saddam Iraq*, 2010, (Syracuse: Syracuse University Press): xxii-xxiv.

3 The Kurdish civil war was official terminated by the 1998 Washington Agreement; however, two KRG administrations continued to operate in Erbil and Suleymaniya under the KDP and PUK influence respectively. The administrations reunified into one regional government again in 2006, based on a strategic power-sharing agreement between the two parties.

4 Mohammed, Fryad. "Most of Turkey-Iraq US$12 billion trade exchange in Kurdistan: minister", 19 January 2012, Internet, http://www.aknews.com/en/aknews/2/2r85281/.

5 Specifically, Ankara's expectation is that Barzani will nudge the Kurdish National Council (KNC), a disparate group of moderate Syrian Kurdish parties, to join the Syrian National Council, to which Ankara, Qatar, and Saudi Arabia are key sponsors.

6 "Iran, Iraqi Kurdistan to further expand trade cooperation," Kurdnet, 26 March 2013, Internet, http://www.ekurd.net/mismas/articles/misc2013/3/irankurd926.htm.

7 Kane, Sean, "Iraq's Disputed Territories: A View of the Political Horizons and Implications for U.S. Policy," The United States Institute of Peace (2011); 19-21.

8 Kean: 19-21.

9 This statement was in response to Maliki's referral of the territories as "mixed territories" and not disputed. "Roundup: Disputed, Mixed or Kurdistan Territories?" *Insight Kurdistan*, 16 December 2012, Internet, http://insightkurdistan.om/disputed-mixed-or-kurdistan-territories/1050/.

10 Author interviews and discussions with Kurdish groups in Erbil and Suleymaniya, in the Kurdistan Region. 26-28 April 2013.

11 Avinoam Idan and Brenda Shaffer, "The Foreign Policies of Landlocked Energy States," *Post-Soviet Affairs*, 27 no. 3, 2011: 241-268. The Kurdistan Region faces similar constraints as landlocked Caspian states.

12 Idiz, Semeh, "The Sunnification of Turkish Foreign Policy", *al-Monitor*, 1 March 2013, Internet, http://www.al-monitor.com/pulse/originals/2013/03/akp-sunni-foreign-policy-turkey-sectarianism.html.

13 "Yekiti oo Goran hawran ley ser Gerandenewehey destur bo perleman," *Awene*, 24 September 2012. In an effort to check Barzani's centralization of power Talabani and Nowsherwan Mustafa Amin, head of Goran (Change Movement), issued a joint declaration to rewrite the existing draft KRG constitution. The statement was to assure that the Region follows a parliamentary system like Baghdad and not a presidential system emergent in the KRG, Internet, http://awene.com/article/ http://awene.com/article/%DB%8C%D9%-87%E2%80%8C%D9%83%DB%8E%D8%AA%D-B%8C%E2%80%8C%E2%80%8C%D9%88-%DA%AF%DB%86%DA%95%D8%A7%D9%86-%D9%87%D8%A7%D9%88%DA%95%D8%A7%D9%86--%D9%84%D9%87%E2%80%8C%D8%B3%D9%87%E2%80%8C%D8%B1-%DA%AF%D9%87%E2%80%8C%DA%95%D8%A7%D9%86%D8%AF%D9%86%D9%87%E2%80%8C%D9%88%D9%87%E2%80%8C%DB%8C%E2%80%8C-%D8%AF%D9%87%E2%80%8C%D8%B3%D8%AA%D9%88%D8%B1-%D8%A8%DB%86-%D9%BE%D9%87%E2%80%8C%D8%B1%D9%84%D9%87%E2%80%8C%D9%85%D8%A7%D9%86

Georgetown Journal

of International Affairs

religion& power *to...*

Espionage Exposed

- - - *tackling the issues that shape our world* - -

CALL FOR PAPERS

The *Georgetown Journal of International Affairs* is accepting submissions for the Winter/Spring 2014 issue. The submission deadline is 15 August 2013. Articles must be about 3,000 words in length. They should have the intellectual vigor to meet the highest scholarly standard, but should be written with the clarity to attract a broad audience. For submission details please refer to our website: http://journal.georgetown.edu/submissions/

Building Community Resilience to Violent Extremism

Stevan Weine

The Obama administration's landmark new approach to countering violent extremism through engaging community partners calls for no less than a paradigm shift in how we understand the causes of terrorism. The shift is away from a pathways approach focused on how push and pull factors influenced one person's trajectory toward or away from violent extremism, and towards an ecological view that looks at how characteristics of the social environment can either lead to or diminish involvement in violent extremism for the persons living there.

The core idea of this new paradigm, conveyed in the White House's December 2011 *Strategic Implementation Plan for Empowering Local Partners to Prevent Violent Extremism in the United States* (SIP), is that of countering violent extremism through building resilience.[1] Denis McDonough, former Deputy National Security Advisor to President Obama, expressed this at an Islamic center in Virginia, stating, "we know, as the President said, that the best defense against terrorist ideologies is strong and resilient individuals and communities."[2] Subsequent White House documents have further unpacked this, for example, in stating: "[n]ational security draws on the strength and resilience of our citizens, communities, and economy."[3]

Resilience usually refers to persons' capacities to with-

Stevan Weine is Professor of Psychiatry and Director of the International Center on Responses to Catastrophes at the University of Illinois at Chicago. He leads a federally supported program of research on refugees and migrants, and has received two NIH career scientist awards. Weine is author of *When History is a Nightmare: Lives and Memories of Ethnic Cleansing in Bosnia-Herzegovina* (Rutgers, 1999) and *Testimony and Catastrophe: Narrating the Traumas of Political Violence* (Northwestern, 2006).

stand or bounce back from adversity.[4] It is a concept derived from engineering perspectives upon the durability of materials to bend and not break. In recent years, resilience has come to the forefront in the fields of public health, child development, and disaster relief.[5] To scientists and policymakers, resilience is not just a property of individuals, but of families, communities, organizations, networks, and societies.[6] Resilience-focused policies and interventions that support or enhance its components have yielded significant and cost effective gains in preventing HIV/AIDS transmission, and helping high-risk children and disaster-impacted populations. Though the present use of resilience sounds more like resistance, today's hope is that such approaches could also keep young Americans away from violent extremism.

A resilience approach offers no quick fix, not in any of the aforementioned fields or in countering violent extremism. It depends upon adequately understanding what resilience means for a particular group of persons and how it has been shaped by history, politics, social context, and culture. It also depends upon government establishing and sustaining partnerships with the impacted families, communities, networks, and organizations. Additionally, it depends on government working in partnership to design, implement, and evaluate what interventions can really make a difference in building resilience, a process certain to involve trial and error.

Responding to the Threat of Homegrown Terrorism. The current shift in counter-terrorism policy to-wards building resilience was driven in part by the surge in al-Qaeda inspired "homegrown terrorism" in the U.S. that peaked in 2008.[7] Government officials and terrorism experts came to believe that the United States shared similar vulnerabilities as European countries for terrorist recruitment and needed to develop appropriate responses. Especially of concern for U.S. government officials were Somali-Americans, given that between late 2007 and fall of 2008, at least seventeen adolescent boys and young men left the Minneapolis-St. Paul area without telling their parents and went to Somalia to join al-Shabaab militant training camps.[8] All indicators were that this effort was well-organized, involving both transnational and local associates who had conspired to obtain passports and to purchase airline tickets. What was so striking about this effort, though, was that it was possible to get some of the best and brightest young people in that community to return to the war-torn country from which their parents had fled less than twenty years before.

Consider Burhan Hassan, a seventeen year-old Somali-American high school senior and student at Roosevelt Senior High. Osman Ahmed, Hassan's uncle, described Burhan as, "a brilliant student with straight A's and on top of his class. He was taking college courses, calculus, advanced chemistry, as he was about to graduate from high school... He was an ambitious kid with the hope to go to Harvard University to study medicine or law and become a medical doctor or a lawyer ... Like his peers, Burhan was never interested in Somali politics or understood Somali clan issues... He used to go to school, home and the mosque ... and there's no way you could get that ideology from the school or home."[9]

If recruiters could influence Burhan, a smart, well-liked teenager with apparently strong connections to his family and community, then they could likely influence anyone. The power of recruiters over young men as seemingly solid as Burhan has been of grave concern

Tamerlan Tsarnaev, provided another example of sudden lapse to violent extremism in young adults who came to the United States as refugees from a war-torn country. This attack reminded Americans of the need to act to prevent terrorist attacks at home in part through the new policies that emphasize community engagement and partnering so as to build resilience.

The power of recruiters over young men...has been of grave concern to family members, community advocates, and law enforcement.

to family members, community advocates, and law enforcement. The recruiters not only had the logistical networks that could secretly move young people out of the country, but they also had ways of reaching young people's hearts and minds. For a time, U.S. government concerns about al-Shabaab's capacities to speak to youth were focused on Omar Hammami, a young man who left Alabama and joined al-Shabaab in Somalia, where he became known as Al-Amriki.[10] In March 2009 Hammami made a recruitment video which has been widely watched on the Internet. Hammami had a clever way of speaking to the yearnings and grievances of diaspora youth, and it appeared that neither the U.S. government nor local communities found responses that could effectively counter such recruitment messages.

The April 2013 Boston Marathon bombing committed by two Chechen-American brothers, Dzhokhar and

Studying Somali-Americans in Little Mogadishu. On one of my first visits to Minneapolis in February 2009, I met with Osman Ahmed, Burhan's uncle, who had recently testified to the U.S. Senate's Committee on Homeland Security and Governmental Affairs. There, he said, "[f]amily members whose children went to Somalia to join al-Shabaab were scared to even talk to the law enforcement. We have been painted as bad people within the Somali community by the mosque management. We have been threatened for just speaking out." Ahmed was taking considerable risks in speaking openly in resistance to al-Shabaab. On behalf of the families of the missing or youth he asked for the federal government to, "create special task force to combat the al-Shabaab recruitment," and to, "educate members of the Somali community on the importance of cooperation between law enforcement and the community."[11]

When Ahmed and I met at a local community center, I told him that I agreed with his goals and supported his advocacy. He and I agreed that research was one activity that could help to advocate for and inform policy changes. We proposed a study of family and community protective resources among Somali-Americans in Minneapolis-St. Paul, which in 2010 was funded by the U.S. Department of Homeland Security through its University of Maryland START Center of Excellence. This was an ethnographic study that looked at the everyday lives of Somali-American adolescent boys and young men in the context of their families and communities in Minneapolis-St. Paul. Now that the results of that study are public, demonstrating what building resilience to violent extremism means in one U.S. community under the threat of al-Qaeda inspired terrorism. Based on em-

pirical data and informed by relevant theory, it identified themes and built a model, Diminishing Opportunities for Violent Extremism (DOVE), which can help to inform prevention strategies for building community resilience to violent extremism in the Somali-American community in Minneapolis-St. Paul.

The research results help in understanding how to implement the White House Strategy on Empowering Local Partners to Prevent Violent Extremism. The overall finding is that building community resilience to violent extremism depends on sustaining and strengthening (or in some cases initiating) protective resources through collaborations between family and youth, community, and government. According to the DOVE model, these protective resources should focus on three risk opportunity levels:

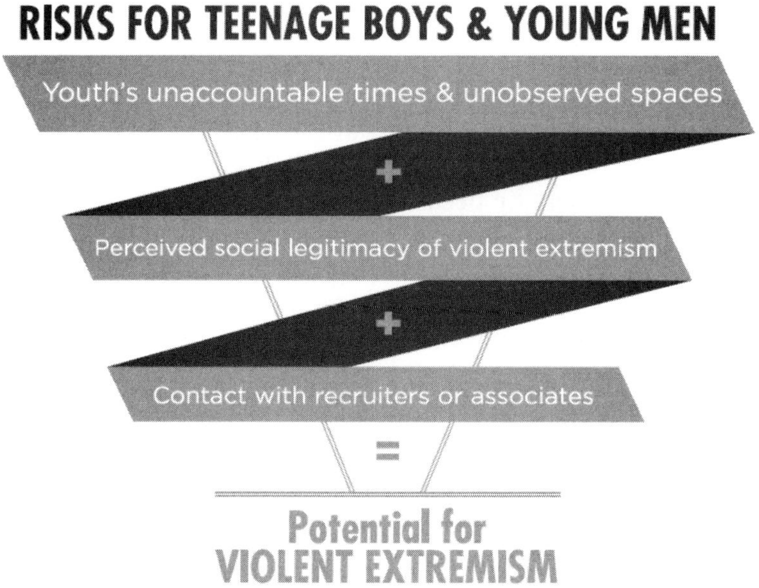

Figure 1: DOVE model.

1. Diminishing youth's unaccountable times and unobserved spaces (the times when adolescent boys are not answerable to parents or other adults and are in spaces where they are out of their sight);
2. Diminishing the perceived social legitimacy of violent extremism (perceptions of the appropriateness and necessity of violent extremist ideology and actions); and
3. Diminishing contact with recruiters or associates (adolescent boys and young men interacting directly with either recruiters or companions who facilitate their increased involvement in violent extremism).

These were the three levels of opportunity in the model that were supported by empirical evidence from the research. These three levels represent the interaction of multiple risk factors at the peer, family, community, global, state, and societal levels; in total, we identified thirty-six such factors. Further, we found that no one risk factor explained involvement in violent extremism. Parents, community leaders, and the government should be concerned that many youth are exposed to level one, and decreasing but still substantial proportions of youth are exposed to levels two and three. In other words, the risks for their involvement in violent extremism are characteristic of the environment in which they grow up.

From talking with parents and community service providers, we found evidence not only of risks but also of protective resources among Somali-Americans. For example, we learned about parents who are their children's confidants and who make an effort to monitor and supervise their youth's activities. We also learned about elders who advise parents and youth about the dangers posed by violent extremism, even though they have never had formal support for those efforts. We learned about community-based service providers, including teachers, imams, coaches, and police officers, who tried to help youth to avoid violent extremism both directly and through their parents, but who hadn't yet been trained in how to do so.

Overall, this study demonstrated not only the centrality of resilience to countering violent extremism, but also that resilience is complex and not limited to individual resilience. Our findings indicate that through additional changes in their social environment, we may be able to diminish the likelihood of their involvement in violent extremism. Family resilience happens to be an important, but often overlooked, component of community resilience. One very important meaning of resilience is parents talking to their children about these matters and supervising and monitoring their activities. But in order for many parents to do so, they need additional support from communities, which in turn need help from the government. For example, a Somali elder said, "[e]lders should organize meetings in the community and explain the consequences if we don't build communication with our kids and explain our culture and true religion. Nobody can take our kids advantage if all community are well alerted about the radicalization." Helping to support an elders' network is one promising path to achieving the White House's call for "well-equipped families" to stand up to recruiters.

Of course this model does not explain all kinds of terrorism. For example, it does not explain the so-called lone wolf terrorists, like Major Nidal Hassan, who have acted in a variety of contexts and could also emerge in communities threatened by al-Qaeda inspired terrorism.[12] However, the attention currently given to lone wolf terrorists in the public discourse should not detract from the need for developing the social environmental paradigm which underlines the SIP and its resilience approach to countering violent extremism.

Building Resilience to Violent Extremism. Everything known about resilience tells us that it cannot simply be dialed up by turning a single knob. As a policy undertaking, building resilience to violent extremism will be at least as complicated as was building resilience to gang violence, HIV/AIDS risks, and domestic violence. It is achievable but

eda inspired terrorism.

How can public policy use our study's findings on resilience to advance the paradigm shift that underlines the SIP's resilience approach?

One specific way to use the results of this study would be for the government to collaborate with the community to develop, pilot, and evaluate a multilevel community resilience-based prevention strategy based on the DOVE model in Minneapolis-St. Paul, or perhaps adapted for other communities under threat. The findings indicate that this should include these three components: 1) building a web-based resource on risks and safeguards to assist parents and community providers; 2) providing logistical support and training to elders and other critical community voices; 3) creating alternative opportunities for community or humanitarian service for young Somalis.

A second way is to take the DOVE model that was developed and to use

One very important meaning of resilience is parents talking to their children about these matters and supervising and monitoring their activities.

not straightforward or easy and will depend in part upon increasing scientific knowledge. Our research is just one study of one Muslim-American community in one U.S. city with limited generalizability to other communities. Nonetheless it is the first study focused on building resilience to violent extremism and may have important implications for public policy in other communities under the threat of al-Qa-

it to study other communities under threat of al-Qaeda inspired violent extremism. This could include other Somali-American communities in the U.S. as well as other Muslim-American refugee and immigrant communities that share the common elements of failed state politics, terrorist organization actively recruiting in the area, and challenges in the diaspora. The goal would be to see whether the model holds up or needs to be modified in order to become generalizable and useful in informing the prevention of terrorist recruitment.

A third way that the results of this study could be used is to inform the development and implementation of the Obama administration's new policies for building resilience to counter violent extremism. The DOVE model's three opportunity levels should be considered as possible priorities for which new tasks, indicators, and measures could be developed. The DOVE model also strongly supports the SIP's claim that this work should involve cooperation between federal, state, and municipal governments and collaboration with communities. Of course, precisely how to implement these priorities and claims regarding "building resilience" in a manner powerful enough to reshape government, community, and family capacities will be a major challenge.

To accomplish these policy changes concerning resilience and countering violent extremism, there are some additional steps that the federal government could take to address the challenges to developing the SIP resilience approach. The first is to convene meetings that bring together multidisciplinary researchers, policymakers, practitioners, and advocates from different agencies, service fields, disciplines, and communities, to come up with integrated models for preventing violent extremism. For example, the federal government can arrange for interchanges that otherwise wouldn't happen, such as bringing together resilience from child development with those trying to develop ways to counter violent extremism.

Second is to bring together different federal funding agencies to create innovative funding mechanisms to support the kind of multidisciplinary, collaborative research that is needed to create a sound scientific basis for a resilience approach to countering violent extremism. It is especially important to include long-term efforts at implementation, monitoring, and evaluation, as well as community collaborative approaches. Research on building resilience to violent extremism isn't only a matter of homeland security but also necessarily involves social services, mental health resources, education, and more, and we need funding mechanisms that are prepared to fully embrace this complexity.

Third is to conduct a thorough review of refugee resettlement and immigration policy in the U.S. with a view towards making policy changes that would reduce the inequities, vulnerabilities, or grievances that recruiters can exploit. It is no accident that recruitment was successful among Somali-Americans in Minnesota, who are surely one of the most vulnerable refugee groups in the history of U.S. refugee resettlement. For example, a large epidemiological survey conducted in Minneapolis-St. Paul in 2004 found that 37 percent of Somali women and 25 percent of Somali men had been tortured. In 2008, among Somali-Americans in Minneapolis-St. Paul, the unemployment rate was 17 percent, the median income $14,367, and the poverty level 42 percent.[13]

Guiding Principles and Conclusions. Finally, in light of our study findings and these public policy challenges, we have identified seven guiding principles for building resilience to counter violent extremism.

1. Ensure that resilience approaches are well supported by theory, empirical evidence, and community collaboration.

2. Shift from individual level to multilevel analyses of risk factors and protective resources in communities under threat.

3. Intervene on all multiple opportunity levels, not just one, and sustain interventions over time.

4. Involve government, community, and families working collaboratively to improve each other's capacities to address each level.

5. Utilize a comprehensive approach to countering violent extremism with key contributions from law enforcement, immigration, public health, labor, housing, education, and media.

6. Adopt balanced, fair and transparent approaches to partnerships not limited by the biases of particular gatekeepers.

7. Conduct research in communities under threat to examine which acts of building community resilience work with whom under what circumstances and why.

In conclusion, a resilience building approach has substantial potential to help with countering violent extremism. It is supported by theory, research findings, practical knowledge, and policy successes. However, paradigm shifts as ambitious and complex as this do not happen accidentally or overnight, which is why we hear policymakers refer to building resilience to violent extremism as truly a generational undertaking. To best realize its potential for Somali-Americans and other U.S. communities under threat, building resilience to violent extremism will require a longstanding, well-informed, and collaborative commitment by federal, state, and local government.

Notes

1 The White House, *Strategic Implementation Plan for Empowering Local Partners to Prevent Violent Extremism in the United States* (Washington DC, December 2011).

2 Denis McDonough, "Remarks at the Adams Center," Sterling, Virginia, 8 March 2011.

3 The White House, National Security Strategy (Washington DC, May 2010).

4 Per Bodin and Bo L.B. Wiman, "Resilience and Other Stability Concepts in Ecology: Notes on Their Origin, Validity, and Usefulness," *ESS Bulletin* 2, no 2 (October 2004): 33-43; Fran H. Norris, Susan P. Stevens, Betty Pfefferbaum, Karen F. Wyche, and Rose L. Pfefferbaum, "Community Resilience as a Metaphor, Theory, Set of Capacities, and Strategy for Disaster Readiness," *American Journal of Community Psychology* 41, no 1-2 (2008): 127-150; Froma Walsh, "Family Resilience: A Framework for Clinical Practice," *Family Process* 42, no. 1 (2003): 1-18.

5 Mary Ellen O'Connell, Thomas Boat, and Kenneth E. Warner (eds.), *Preventing Mental, Emotional, and Behavioral Disorders Among Young People: Progress and Possibilities* (Washington, D.C.: National Academies Press, 2009); Partick H. Tolan, Laura D. Hanish, Mary M.McKay, and Mitchell H. Dickey, "Evaluation Process in Child and Family Interventions: Aggression Prevention as an Example," *Journal of Family Psychology* 16. no. 2 (June 2002): 220-236; Froma Walsh, "Traumatic Loss and Major Disasters: Strengthening Family and Community Resilience," *Family Process* 46, no. 2 (2007): 207-227.

6 Norris, "Community Resilience as a Metaphor."

7 Stevan M. Weine, Yael Hoffman, Norma Ware, Toni Tugenberg, Leonce Hakizimana, Gonwo Dahnweigh, Madeleine Currie, and Maureen Wagner, "Secondary Migration and Relocation Among African refugee families in the United States," *Family Process* 50, no. 1 (2011): 27-46.

8 Brian Michael Jenkins, *Would-be Warriors: Incidents of Jihadist Terrorist Radicalization in the United States Since September 11, 2001* (Santa Monica: The Rand Corporation, 2010); Charles Kurzman, "Muslim American Terrorism in the Decade Since 9/11," A Report by Triangle Center on Terrorism

and Homeland Security (Chapel Hill: University of North Carolina, 2012).

9 Andrea Elliot, "A Call to Jihad, Answered in America," *The New York Times*, 11 July 2009; Stevan M. Weine, John Horgan, Cheryl Robertson, Sana Loue, Amin Mohamed, and Sahra Noor, "Community and Family Approaches to Combating the Radicalization and Recruitment of Somali-American Youth and Young Adults: A Psychosocial Perspective," *Dynamics of Asymmetric Conflict: Pathways Toward Terrorism and Genocide* 2, no. 3 (2009): 181-200.

10 Osman Ahmed, "Violent Islamist Extremists: Al Shabaab Recruitment in America," (Congressional Hearing Before the United States Senate Committee on Homeland Security and Governmental Affairs, Minneapolis, MN, 8 March 2009).

11 Andrea Elliot, "The Jihadist Next Door," *The New York Times,* 27 January 2011.

12 Ahmed, "Violent Islamist Extremists," 2009.

13 Stevan Weine and Osman Ahmed, "Building Resilience to Violent Extremism Among Somali-Americans in Minneapolis-St. Paul," *A Report by START support by the U.S. Department of Homeland Security* (College Park: START, 2012), Internet, http://www.start.umd.edu/start/publications/Weine_BuildingResiliencetoViolentExtremism_SomaliAmericans.pdf.

14 Sophia Moskalenko and Clark McCauley, "The Psychology of Lone-Wolf Terrorism," *Counselling Psychology Quarterly* 24, no. 2 (2011): 115-126.

15 James M. Jaranson, James Butcher, Linda Halcón, David Robert Johnson, Cheryl Robertson, Kay Savik, Marline Spring, and Joseph Westermeyer, "Somali and Oromo Refugees: Correlates of Torture and Trauma History," *American Journal of Public Health* 94, no. 4 (2004): 591-598.

16 Eric Kasper, Peter Fleck, and Leah Gardner, "Engaging Somali Young Adults in Cedar-Riverside: Opportunities for Programming and Collaboration," *CHANCE Capstone* (Humphrey Institute of Public Affairs, 2009); City of Minneapolis, *Cedar-Riverside Population - Minneapolis Neighborhood Profile*, (Minneapolis, 2009).

Georgetown Journal

of International Affairs

religion&power *to...*

Espionage Exposed

- - tackling the issues that shape our world - -

CALL FOR PAPERS

The *Georgetown Journal of International Affairs* is accepting submissions for the Winter/Spring 2014 issue. The submission deadline is 15 August 2013. Articles must be about 3,000 words in length. They should have the intellectual vigor to meet the highest scholarly standard, but should be written with the clarity to attract a broad audience. For submission details please refer to our website: http://journal.georgetown.edu/submissions/

Politics&Diplomacy

The Most Dangerous Country on Earth

Joseph Cirincione

In any given week, there is significant competition for the title of "most dangerous country in the world." Some may believe it is Syria or Mali, Iran or North Korea, China or Russia, or dozens of others. As tragic as conditions may be in these countries, as potentially harmful as their policies may seem, no state truly comes close to the multiple dangers inherent in Pakistan today. Trends in this nation may converge to form one or more nuclear nightmares that could spread well beyond the region to threaten international security and the lives of millions.

Experts estimate that Pakistan has between 90-110 nuclear weapons and enough fissile material to produce 100 more.[1] It has an unstable government, a fragile economy, strong extremist influences in its military and intelligence structures, and Al Qaeda, as well as half a dozen similar terrorist groups operating inside the country. The confluence of these factors not only increases the potential for a nuclear escalation between Pakistan and its regional rival, India, but perhaps the even more terrifying scenario that a terrorist group will acquire fissile material, or an intact weapon, from Pakistan's burgeoning stockpiles. Both of these risks are unacceptable. The United States can and

Joseph Cirincione is president of Ploughshares Fund, a global security foundation. This article is adapted from his forthcoming book, *Nuclear Nightmares* (Columbia University Press, 2013). The author gratefully acknowledges the substantial research work by Alyssa Demus and Leah Fae Cochran for this article and the earlier research of Rizwan Ladha, all of whom worked as research assistants at Ploughshares Fund.

must take concrete steps to reduce the risks posed by Pakistan's unique combination of instability, extremism, and nuclear weapons.

A Nuclear War on the Subcontinent? Nuclear terrorism is just one of the scenarios that should frighten policymakers. South Asia is often overlooked in discussions of the gravest nuclear threats. And yet, South Asia remains the area of the world most likely to see nuclear weapons used in combat. Pakistan's decades-long conflict with its nuclear-armed neighbor, India (with which it has fought three wars since independence), combined with the general instability of the region, contribute to this grim assessment. Relations between Pakistan and India are fragile and tenuous, with tensions dating back to the birth of the two countries. Armed conflict between the two states broke out in in 1999 in the disputed Kashmir region, marking the first Indo-Pakistani conflict after both states developed nuclear arms, and the only direct, conventional conflict between two nuclear-armed states to date. If these South Asian neighbors do clash again, it is very likely to escalate to a nuclear exchange.

A South Asian nuclear war would not just destroy the subcontinent, the most densely populated region on Earth, but this unprecedented catastrophe would likely also have global consequences, though it is important to note that the exact environmental impact is debated among experts in the field. Scientists calculate that the mega-fires started by the use of just 100 nuclear weapons could pour so much smoke and particulates into the atmosphere that the planet would be blanketed by clouds, blocking sunlight, dropping global temperatures two to three degrees.[2] The resulting massive crop failures would trigger worldwide famine, leaving up to one billion people dead. The use of a nuclear weapon in South Asia would also set a dangerous precedent, undermining the decades-old nuclear taboo and have catastrophic consequences for the global economy.

Could that many weapons possibly be used? Yes. While Pakistan's capabilities and doctrines are not entirely clear, one former nuclear official, giving an example of the type of calculations that Pakistani planners might make, said that for a set of ten possible targets, a country might need sixty-eight to seventy warheads (without taking into account the risk of a pre-emptive strike).[3] India's calculations are likely similar.

Pakistan has the fastest growing nuclear arsenal in the world. Within this decade, experts estimate that Pakistani nuclear capability could include 150 to 200 warheads, new production facilities, and new nuclear-capable ballistic missiles.[4] Analysts Hans Kristensen and Robert Norris of the Federation of American Scientists provide the best independent estimates of national nuclear arsenals: "[w]ith four new delivery systems and two plutonium production reactors under development...the rate of Pakistan's stockpile growth may even increase over the next 10 years."[5]

The risks that this arsenal would actually be used are increased by Pakistan's aggressive nuclear doctrine. Owen Bennett Jones documents in his book, *Pakistan: Eye of the Storm*, several instances during the 1999 Kargil Crisis when Pakistani leaders considered the use of Pakistan's nuclear arsenal.[6] They did so again during another crisis in 2002, where both militaries were on high alert at the border after India mobilized in response to a terrorist attack on its New Delhi parliament building. According to Jones, General Musharraf said, "[i]f Indian troops moved a single step across the international border or the Line of Control, they should not expect a con-

nuclear weapons to offset India's superior conventional military forces just as the United States and its allies deployed hundreds of tactical nuclear weapons in Europe to defeat the more numerous Soviet forces. From Pakistan's point of view, given its significant conventional inferiority, it is a strategically sound move to escalate early on in a conflict. This makes peaceful and stable Indo-Pakistani relations all the more important and the prospect of conflict all the more dangerous.

Pakistan has the fastest growing nuclear arsenal in the world. Within this decade, experts estimate that Pakistani nuclear capability could include 150 to 200 warheads.

ventional war from Pakistan."[7]

Analyst Tom Hundley warns that Pakistan's new production of tactical nuclear weapons increases the risk that full-scale nuclear war could develop from "miscalculation, miscommunication or panic." Specifically, Hundley argues that, "as these ready-to-use weapons are maneuvered closer to enemy lines, the chain of command and control would be stretched and more authority necessarily delegated to field officers."[8] Hundley goes on to suggest that these less experienced Pakistani field commanders, who have been armed with tactical nuclear warheads to deter or defend against an overwhelming conventional attack, may actually use these weapons if provoked. In this sense, Pakistan's military leaders have taken a page from NATO's Cold War playbook, using

Security of Pakistan's Nuclear Weapons. Experts are divided on the security of this growing nuclear arsenal. Notably, specialists at the International Institute for Strategic Studies (IISS), the Atlantic Council, and the Carnegie Endowment for International Peace have believed for years that Pakistan's nuclear weapons are secure, and that the integrity of the military forces responsible for protecting those assets will not be compromised. Those who support this analysis believe that the main risks today are not that weapons will fall into the wrong hands or that Islamists will take over the country. Rather, the main risks concern the deliberate use by the military of nuclear weapons in wartime. They also worry about the potential for the loss of control of the weapons if they are moved into the battlefield and the low-level leaks of WMD expertise, or a radiological incident in peacetime.[9]

Other well-respected experts believe the military's control over these weapons is overestimated, and have grave concerns over the safety and security of the Pakistani nuclear complex. Their worries have deepened with increasingly frequent reports[10] corroborating long-standing suspicions that Pakistan's military and intelligence services have been compromised by extremist elements.[11] In May 2009, former U.S. intelligence official Rolf Mowatt-Larssen argued, "the insider threat combined with outsiders" could take over a nuclear facility.[12]

A subgroup of experts is more worried about the security of the fissile material manufactured and stored in the sprawling Pakistani nuclear complex. Shaun Gregory of the University of Bradford believes that "the safety and security of nuclear weapons materials in Pakistan may very well be compromised at some point in the future."[13]

It is not just a question of the security of the weapons or fissile material; it is a question of the security of the government. If the government falls, if the army splinters, who gets the weapons? Who gets the nuclear materials for building these weapons? Where do the scientists and technicians who know how to make the material and build the weapons go? Pakistan could transform from a major non-NATO ally to our worst nuclear nightmare overnight.

As former CIA case officer Valerie Plame Wilson said, "Here you have a nation state that is essentially imploding. You have a very unstable nation-state that is nuclear-armed. Their intelligence service is deeply infiltrated with those that are antithetical to U.S. national security interests."[14]

In his report "Pakistan's Nuclear and WMD Programmes: Status, Evolution, and Risks," Bruno Tertrais acknowledges, "[i]n the longer term, the legal and institutional barriers that have been put into place to protect the arsenal could erode." He says, "[a] weakening of the state and an increased sympathy for radical militants within the armed forces or the nuclear establishment would make for a dangerous combination."[15] In short, the security of the weapons is highly dependent on the security of the government.

Dangers Posed by Terrorism. Three scenarios in particular disquiet experts and policymakers. One concern is that terrorists could acquire an assembled nuclear warhead or enough fissile material to construct a bomb. A second is that terrorists operating from Pakistan could launch another attack on India, similar to the 2001 New Delhi attack and the 2008 coordinated attacks across Mumbai, which would force India to retaliate, thrusting both into a military conflict that could escalate to a nuclear exchange.

A third scenario combines these two concerns. Pakistan guards its nuclear weapons very tightly, but it also plans to move newly-developed, mobile tactical weapons into the field for possible use should a conflict with India develop. MIT Professor Vipin Narang explains the risks associated with such a maneuver:

Terrorist organizations in the region with nuclear ambitions, such as al-Qaida, may find no easier route to obtaining fissile material or a fully functional nuclear weapon than to attack India, thereby triggering a crisis between India and Pakistan and forcing Pakistan to ready and disperse nuclear assets—with few, if any, negative controls—and then attempting to steal the nuclear material when it is being moved or in the field, where it is less secure than in peacetime locations.[16]

These are not abstract concerns or implausible scenarios. There have been repeated instances in which extremist groups have staged major attacks on military bases, including ones suspected of housing nuclear weapons. These include a suicide bomber who killed eight Pakistani Air Force personnel and wounded forty others at a Punjab Air Force Base that housed the military headquarters for the control of Pakistan's nuclear arsenal; a suicide bomber attack on a bus at the Kamra Air Force Base in Peshawar province that includes facilities likely associated with the storage and maintenance of nuclear weapons; a major attack on the Karachi Naval Base that killed ten and wounded forty in a sixteen-hour gun battle; and an August 2012 attack on Pakistan's main air force base near Islamabad.

These examples demonstrate that the risks of terrorist acquisition, unintended or unauthorized use of the weapons, or deliberate escalation to nuclear war are too great to continue with the failed policies of the past. The United States should leverage its considerable diplomatic influence and technical expertise to help mitigate the threat posed by an unstable, nuclear-armed Pakistan. Concrete steps must be taken and greater commitments must be made if a nuclear catastrophe is to be avoided.

Reevaluating U.S.-Pakistani Dialogue. The U.S. government should reassess how it pursues its dialogue with Pakistan. There is little question that the United States should lend more support to the civilian leadership of the Pakistani government and be firmer when dealing with the military leadership so that recognition of, and long-term support for, the civilian government is not undermined. Although ostensibly a democracy, Pakistan has bounced back and forth between civilian and military leadership since its creation. The military often acts without the knowledge of elected officials and vice-versa.

The United States historically has close ties to the military because of close collaboration against the Soviets in the 1980s. However, Bruce Riedel and other experts agree that going straight to the military with American concerns - even if there is a more productive relationship there - damages civilian institutions and severely undermines the legitimacy of the elected government.[17] The International Crisis Group argues that, "the interests of the international community, the U.S. and EU in particular, are best served by a politically stable, democratically-governed state, and not a military-backed government with a civilian façade."[18] A Council on Foreign Relations task force suggests that,

The United States cannot rectify

the civil-military power imbalance that plagues the Pakistani state. It can, however, regularly reiterate its preference for democratic rule and take pains to involve Pakistan's civilian leaders in all major bilateral dialogues. Washington should target support to partners and institutions that share common goals.[19]

Dealing primarily, or even exclusively, with the Pakistani military leadership has had its tactical benefits, but at great strategic cost. The Soviets, and later the Taliban, were defeated in Afghanistan with Pakistani military aid. But, extremism in the region has grown and the Pakistani state has not

larly in the textile sectors, will help the relationship at no cost to the American economy.[21] This would both help strengthen Pakistan's private sector and help combat its chronically high unemployment rates.

Another productive step would be for the United States to quietly encourage expanded trade between Pakistan and India. In 2011, there was a mere $2.6 billion worth of trade between the two countries, compared with trade between India and China, which is approaching $100 billion.[22] Some suggest that the U.S. should offer to compensate Pakistan for any initial losses occurred from importing Indian goods.[23] Though the aid might be a

Dealing primarily, or even exclusively, with the Pakistani military leadership has had its tactical benefits, but at great strategic cost.

provided a stable, democratic, and economically vibrant alternative.

Promoting Economic Stabilization. In the end, the threat posed by an unstable, nuclear-armed Pakistan can only be addressed by strengthening the country's domestic economy. The United States is Pakistan's top export market, and a full one-third of Pakistani foreign direct investment comes from the United States.[20] This is advantageous for the United States, and experts almost unanimously agree that encouraging stronger trade ties by offering Pakistan preferential trade status and lowering tariffs, particu-

tough sell in today's fiscal climate, this trade could stimulate Pakistan's economy, employ millions of young and economically displaced Pakistanis who otherwise might be prime targets for recruitment by terrorist organizations, and put more money in the pockets of the Pakistani consumers–all without putting United States producers at risk. There is much opportunity for greater prosperity on both sides of the border, increased bi-lateral dialogue as well as enhanced regional stability. Lastly, a more productive Pakistani economy would have the added benefit of potentially weaning Pakistan off of American aid that is already being reduced due to U.S. domestic budgetary constraints, hostile public opinion, and the U.S. exit from Afghanistan. That said, even generous economic aid would not by itself solve Pakistan's problems, and the impact of aid would take decades to manifest. However, it is a vital component of a comprehensive strategy towards Pakistan.

Advocating for Improved Indo-Pakistani Relations. The United States is interested in "preventing a South Asian nuclear war, slowing the Pakistani nuclear weapons program, and avoiding a nuclear arms race with India," notes Moeed Yusuf of the U.S. Institute of Peace. He continues, "these goals will be served by reduced tensions and increased confidence between India and Pakistan, and the U.S. should clearly work to promote this movement."[24] Michael Krepon, co-founder of the Stimson Center, agrees. He finds that "the safest route to reduce nuclear dangers on the subcontinent is through concerted efforts to improve relations between Pakistan and India."[25] To this end, the United States should encourage India and Pakistan to pursue initiatives that will help to stabilize their bilateral political relations, thereby creating a more secure regional environment. Many of the experts mentioned above, along with others, have put forward a number of policy recommendations for the two nations to undertake mutually.

First, the United States should continue to encourage Pakistan and India to maintain their bilateral dialogue. Although there have been bilateral talks on trade, water security, and other issues, the major problem continues to be Kashmir. Tensions over Kashmir precipitated three of the four conflicts between the countries and have inspired the Pakistani government to support a low-level insurgency that has had disastrous consequences for relations. However, there are fragile signs of progress, such as the 2012 talks between Pakistan and India on the subject of demilitarizing the Siachen glacier in Kashmir. Though without resolution, the discussion at least temporarily defused a tense standoff.

The two neighbors could also benefit from increasing and strengthening their economic ties. Krepon argues, the "surest way" to improve relations between Pakistan and India and reduce nuclear dangers in the region is through "greatly increasing cross-border trade."[26]

A nuclear arsenal built on very weak economic foundations is inherently unstable, which is reason enough for India to pursue sustained and accelerated trade and investment opportunities with Pakistan. These methods, which have dampened tensions between China and Taiwan, could also serve a similar purpose on the subcontinent.[27]

India and Pakistan could reduce some of the impetus behind their nuclear arms race by becoming more transparent on their fissile material stocks. Moeed Yusuf suggested in January 2011 that, "both sides need to discuss the logic of their fissile material stockpile trajectories."[28] They could start by exchanging information on un-reprocessed spent fuel. This is fuel that has been removed from reactors after use, but not yet chemically treated to extract plutonium created in the reactor and any unused uranium. This would allow each country to extrapolate from the gathered data the other's potential for plutonium stockpiling, which would increase transparency in the near term and build confidence in the long term, creating space for India and Pakistan to discuss additional nuclear-related confidence building measures.

The United States could also encourage the two neighboring states to establish a direct executive hotline. Similar to the Moscow-Washington hotline that was born of the lessons learned from the 1962 Cuban Missile Crisis, India and Pakistan could create a similar direct connection that links together the prime ministers of both countries for immediate and direct communications during periods of crisis escalation. A similar hotline was set up in March 2011 between the Pakistani Interior Ministry and the Indian Home Ministry to share terrorist-related information in real time,[29] and, before that, a hotline was agreed upon between the Foreign Ministries.[30]

Similarly, India and Pakistan could further enhance their regional stability by establishing nuclear risk reduction centers. Such centers could follow the U.S.-Russia model, which facilitate data and information sharing, and lower the potential for escalation during a crisis. Mohammed Badrul Alam of the Institute of Peace and Conflict Studies (IPCS) in New Delhi notes, "The idea of having a nuclear risk reduction center in each country has received favorable reactions both within and outside of South Asia, including from skeptics who had felt such a proposal to be too

unrealistic."[31]

Lastly, India and Pakistan should engage in exchanges between the authorities in both countries who are responsible for managing the civilian uses of nuclear energy to share best practices. The July 2011 Track II Ottawa Dialogue that took place between current and retired Indian and Pakistani government officials yielded some concrete recommendations, including an endorsement of nuclear risk reduction centers.[32] The Ottawa Dialogue participants recommended that officials and scientists from the Indian and Pakistani civilian nuclear programs convene to share their regulatory experiences and discuss nuclear safety.

Looking Ahead. The United States must stay engaged with Pakistan, despite the difficulties of the relationship. As Daniel Painter at the American Security Project wrote, "in the frustrating, complex process of working with Pakistan, it is tempting to simply walk away, writing Pakistan off as [a] rogue state. This would be a mistake. National security demands the United States continue to engage Pakistan to address these nuclear threats."[33] Pakistan is too dangerous to ignore and too complex to resolve with a single sweeping policy. There is no magic bullet. There is no one diplomatic or economic fix that will repair the damage done by decades of mistakes (both Pakistani and American), nor can the U.S. military possibly seize or secure Pakistan's nuclear weapons in a crisis.

Pursued individually, the policy prescriptions laid out above cannot solve the Pakistani problem. But taken together, these actions can begin a more hopeful trajectory for the subcontinent by reorienting U.S. policy, strengthening Pakistan's economy, improving Indo-Pakistani relations, reducing incentives for violent upheaval, and decreasing grave misunderstandings during crisis. While Pakistan will likely remain the most dangerous country on earth for many years, these are actionable steps the United States and others can pursue to steadily reduce the risks of a nuclear catastrophe and allow Pakistan to one day realize its enormous potential.

The author is honored to serve on the International Security Advisory Board to the Secretary of State, however, the views expressed in this article and elsewhere are his alone and do not necessarily represent those of the U.S. Department of State or of the U.S. Government.

Notes

1 Hans M. Kristensen and Robert S. Norris, "Pakistan's Nuclear Forces, 2011," *Bulletin of the Atomic Scientists* 67, no. 4 (July 2011): 91-99, Internet, http://bos.sagepub.com/content/67/4/91.full.

2 O. B. Toon, A. Robock, R. P. Turco, C. Bardeen, L. Oman, and G. L. Stenchikov, "Consequences of Regional-Scale Nuclear Conflicts," *Science* 315, no. 5816 (March 2007): 1224–25; A. Robock, L. Oman, G. L. Stenchikov, O. B Toon, C. Bardeen, and R. P. Turco, "Climatic Consequences of Regional Nuclear Conflicts," *Atmospheric Chemistry and Physics* 7, (April 2007): 2003-2012.

3 Bruno Tertrais, *Pakistan's Nuclear and WMD Programmes: Status, Evolution and Risks,* (London: International Institute for Strategic Studies, July 2012), 3, quoted in Naeem Salik, *Minimum Deterrence and India-Pakistan Nuclear Dialogue: Case Study on Pakistan* (Como, Italy: Landau Network-Centro Volta Publications, 2006) 14.

4 Kristensen and Norris, "Pakistan's Nuclear Forces, 2011," 94.

5 Ibid.

6 Owen Bennett Jones, Pakistan: Eye of the Storm (New Haven: Yale University Press, 2003), 207.

7 Ibid.

8 Tom Hundley, "Race to the End," *Foreign Policy*, 5 September 2012, Internet, http://www.foreignpolicy.com/articles/2012/09/05/race_to_the_end?print=yes&hidecomments=yes&page=full.

9 Tertrais (2012), 1.

10 Fareed Zakaria, "The radicalization of Pakistan's military," *The Washington Post*, 22 June 2011, Internet, http://www.washingtonpost.com/opinions/the-radicalization-of-pakistans-military/2011/06/22/AGbCBSgH_story.html.

11 Pervez Hoodbhoy, "A state of denial," *The New York Times*, 6 January 2008, Internet, http://www.nytimes.com/2008/01/16/opinion/16iht-edhood.1.9260885.html.

12 Ben Arnoldy, "Could Taliban get keys to Pakistan's A-bomb?" *The Christian Science Monitor*, 15 May 2009, Internet, http://www.csmonitor.com/World/Asia-South-Central/2009/0515/p06s11-wosc.html.

13 Shaun Gregory, "Terrorist Tactics in Pakistan Threaten Nuclear Weapons Safety," *CTC Sentinel* 4, Issue 6, (June 2011): 1-28.

14 Interview with Valerie Plame, *The Daily Beast TV*, 21 June 2012, Internet, http://www.thedailybeast.com/videos/2012/06/21/valerie-plame-on-pakistans-nuclear-program.html.

15 Tertrais (2012), 15.

16 Vipin Narang, *Pakistan's Nuclear Posture: Implications for South Asian Stability*, (Cambridge, MA: Belfer Center, 2010), 2; For a more detailed argument, see Vipin Narang, "Posturing for Peace? Pakistan's Nuclear Postures and South Asian Stability," *International Security* 34, no. 3 (Winter 2009/10): 38-78.

17 Bruce Riedel, *Deadly Embrace: Pakistan, America and the Future of Global Jihad* (Washington, DC: The Brookings Institution, 2011), 128-9.

18 International Crisis Group, *Reforming Pakistan's Electoral System: Asia Report No. 203* (Brussels, Belgium: International Crisis Group, 2011), 25-6.

19 Richard L. Armitage and Samuel R. Berger, *U.S. Strategy for Pakistan and Afghanistan*, Independent Task Force Report No. 65 (New York, NY: Council on Foreign Relations, 2010), 53.

20 Ibid.

21 Ibid, 7.

22 "Clever Steps at the Border," *The Economist*, 12 May 2012, Internet, http://www.economist.com/node/21554526.

23 Moeed Yusuf, *The Silver Bullet: India-Pakistan Normalization*, U.S. Institute of Peace, 23 May 2011, Internet, http://www.usip.org/publications/the-silver-bullet-india-pakistan-normalization.

24 Ibid

25 Michael Krepon, "Nuclear Race on the Subcontinent," *The New York Times*, 4 April 2013.

26 Ibid.

27 Ibid.

28 Moeed Yusuf, Stability in the Nuclear Context: Making South Asians Safe (Karachi, Pakistan: Jinnah Institute, 2010), 6.

29 "India, Pakistan agree to 'terror hotline,'" *International Herald Tribune*, 29 March 2011, Internet, http://tribune.com.pk/story/139313/india-pakistan-agree-to-terror-hotline/.

30 Justin Huggler, "India and Pakistan to have nuclear hotline," *The Independent*, 21 June 2004, Internet, http://www.independent.co.uk/news/world/asia/india-and-pakistan-to-have-nuclear-hotline-732980.html (accessed August 17, 2011).

31 Mohammed Badrul Alam, "CBMs in South and Northeast Asia: The Sum of Two Parts," Institute of Peace & Conflict Studies, 16 July 2004, Internet, http://www.ipcs.org/article/south-asia/cbms-in-south-asia-and-northeast-asia-the-sum-of-1436.html (accessed August 17, 2011).

32 "Ottawa Dialogue recommends nuclear agreements for India and Pakistan," University of Ottawa, 13 July 2011, Internet, http://www.uottawa.ca/media/media-release-2370.html, (accessed August 17, 2011).

33 Daniel Painter, *Why the U.S. Cannot Ignore Pakistan*, (Washington DC: The American Security Project, 2012), 7.

From Tehran to Khartoum: Thirty-Five Years as An American Diplomat

Ambassador Joseph D. Stafford III

GJIA: What has been your favorite part about being a career Foreign Service Officer, and why?

Stafford: I think my favorite part has been having the opportunity to live and work overseas, in other cultures, and to work on issues of importance to the United States and our international relations. The assignments in Washington have also been interesting but, in my mind, the most stimulating and enjoyable part of my Foreign Service career has been the chance to work overseas and meet ordinary citizens and members of civil society across the world, and to represent the US government.

GJIA: During your first tour, you were forced to flee the embassy in Tehran while it was under siege. How did that experience influence your career in the State Department?

Stafford: That was certainly a stimulating first tour. In a number of ways it reinforced my interest in the Foreign Service. I realize my wife and I were very lucky to be able to seek refuge with the Canadians, and then leave surreptitiously and avoid being taken hostage. I would say on

Joseph D. Stafford III is a career Foreign Service Officer with the U.S. Department of State, holding the rank of Ambassador. He joined the Foreign Service in 1978, serving his first assignment in Tehran, Iran. Ambassador Stafford and his wife, Kathleen, were among the six diplomats who evaded capture during the Iranian Hostage Crisis, eventually being smuggled out of Iran by the CIA. In June 2012, he was assigned to Khartoum, Sudan as Chargé d'affaires of U.S. Embassy, Khartoum.

balance, recognizing that it was not a typical first tour in the Foreign Service, that nonetheless, in a way, it only heightened my interest in continuing that type of career. We also had the opportunity a couple months before the assault on the embassy to travel around Iran a little bit, and we interacted with Iranians on a daily basis on the visa line. Those experiences were formative for me, and they only furthered my desire to be a Foreign Service Officer.

GJIA: What was your first reaction when you found out that Ben Affleck was making *Argo*, a film about your experience during the hostage crisis? How did you feel about having such a deeply personal and terrifying experience relived in the public spotlight?

Stafford: I have to tell you, I was sort of bemused. It was not the first film that had been made. A Canadian outfit had done some sort of film a year or two after the event, and there had been a couple of books. I guess I was sort of bemused. I viewed it that way. For me it was an experience that happened a long time ago. Memories of it for me—to tell you the truth—have faded. I do appreciate the fact that the film has served to highlight, in a positive way, the role of the U.S. Foreign Service, the CIA and, of course, the important, vital role of the Canadian government, to whom we are eternally grateful. That is my take on it. I hope to see the film myself someday. My wife has seen it and she says my character comes off well.

GJIA: What are your impressions of Iran today, and what do you think the future holds for U.S. engagement with the Iranian government?

Stafford: I have not, to tell you the truth, followed events in Iran very closely in recent years. I recognize what an important country it is, and I certainly hope that there will be a change in the Iranian government's behavior and that we can find a modus vivendi in the form of normalized relations someday. Iran is a large, strategically located country. It has a rich culture, rich history—a mosaic of cultures, peoples, and languages, really. I know it is an important challenge for U.S. foreign policy, and I'd say for the international community generally,

> # I know it is an important challenge for U.S. foreign policy...to press the Iranian government for responsible behavior on issues.

to press the Iranian government for responsible behavior on issues ranging from developing nuclear capabilities, to combatting terrorism, to promoting peace, stability, and democracy in the Middle East. It is obviously quite a tough endeavor, but I recognize that we have to keep at it, in the hopes that someday Iran can regain a respectable place in the international community.

GJIA: As an expert on the Middle East, and as an Arabic speaker, what do you envision for the future of U.S. diplomacy in the Middle East and North Africa? Who will be our key allies? And what will be the key challenges for policymakers?

Stafford: I have spent some time in the Middle East, and I have been in North Africa in recent years. I would say, of course, the fundamental issues of Arab-Israeli peace, in particularly Israeli-Palestinian peace are extremely pressing. We must do everything we can to encourage the parties to move forward constructively. The establishment of a viable Palestinian state is part of that process, but also the normalization of the Arab-Israeli relationship needs to be considered, more generally. In the aftermath of the Arab Spring, there is a need to be as supportive as we can be in every way of the processes of reform and development underway in the Middle East. It is important to bolster the forces of moderation, and those forces, in general, seeking peace, modernization, and development. It is also important that we work to isolate extremist forces in cooperation with our moderate Arab friends in the region, within the greater context of combatting global terrorism.

We also have an ongoing challenge of impressing upon Muslims—and people in the Middle East are obviously a key element of the Muslim world—that the United States has a deep respect for Islam, and that we as a nation do not equate Islam with terrorism, death, or destruction. On the contrary, Islam has noble teachings and those that resort to violence under the guise of Islam are distorting it.

In any case, I'm confident that we will remain deeply engaged in the Middle East. We have compelling reasons for doing so.

GJIA: In the wake of the Arab Spring and continued violence in Syria and Egypt, what role should the international community play (if any) in helping to shape new democracies?

Stafford: I think that it's important, in engagements with leaders of the Arab Spring states, to make clear that we support the development of democratic institutions. It's also important to conduct vigorous outreach efforts with civil society, and with forces for reform, democratization, and political openness. We must also make clear our opposition to violent extremism.

In Syria, of course, the ongoing horrific violence is a reminder that regimes that steadfastly reject the forces of change and reform and resort to such brutal repression cause tremendous damage to their countries. The ongoing death and destruction we are witnessing in Syria is so regrettable.

We have to continue our efforts on different fronts and respond to the situation in Syria as we have been doing. Doing our best to mobilize the international community, working with key friends and allies, and helping to shape an international consensus to pressure the Bashar al-Assad regime to make way for the forces of democracy, reform, and change in Syria.

GJIA: September 2012 saw increased protests at Western embassies across the Middle East and North Africa, and the U.S. Embassy in Khartoum was certainly not immune to this trend. What challenges do you envision the United States having to contend with as a result of the Arab Spring movement?

Stafford: I think it is important in Sudan, as elsewhere in the region, to impress upon the government and public that we are aligned with the forces of reform, but that we recognize the process of democratic transitions can be a difficult one. When one considers the experience of the United States, with the decades and decades, or really centuries, that it took for our democratic experiment, including a bloody civil war, it puts things in perspective. So our effort needs to be one of patient work with the governments in question, while also making full use of the diplomatic and public outreach tools at our disposal, such as official dialogue, economic cooperation, and

with and outreach to pro-democracy activists, our civic education work with political parties, our efforts to strengthen election commissions and to enable them to conduct free, fair, and transparent elections, are all key ways that American engagement can help during this critical transition period.

Additionally, beyond official economic assistance, I believe that private commercial cooperation with these countries is very important, not just for the trade, investment, and economic benefits, but also in the sense that people in these countries gain exposure to U.S. companies that operate and respect the democratic values and the rule of law. This is also good experience for U.S. companies. Unfortunately, in the case of Sudan, this type of interaction does not really occur due to the array of sanctions over the years that the U.S. government has imposed upon Sudan, for various rea-

I think it is important in Sudan, as elsewhere in the region, to impress upon the government and public that we are aligned with the forces of reform, but that we recognize the process of democratic transitions can be a difficult one.

humanitarian assistance. In the case of Sudan, for example, we are providing a considerable amount of humanitarian assistance in the conflict areas—first and foremost to Darfur, but also in the southern part of Sudan, where conflict continues to rage. Beyond those more critical, lifesaving efforts, our dialogue

sons, including the issue of genocide in Darfur and the ongoing violence there going back years, previous associations with terrorist elements, and the latest violence that erupted over a year ago in the southern part of Sudan following the secession of South Sudan. So we have some special challenges in the case of Sudan, but I would still say that it is important to draw upon the wide array of tools in promoting peaceful change and reform, as well as development.

GJIA: You arrived in Sudan under difficult political conditions: Sudan is fighting rebel movements and political unrest in the West, South, and East, including a deadly campaign against both rebels and civilians in the Southern Kordofan and Blue Nile; Sudan and South Sudan still have not fully implemented aspects of the Comprehensive Peace Agreement that ended decades of bloody civil war; the oil lifeline that both countries depend upon was shut off due to disputes and both countries now face grave economic crises; and for a moment, the armed forces of both countries looked to be on the path back to full-scale war, with northern warplanes bombing southern territory and southern troops seizing the northern oil field of Heglig. As a career diplomat who certainly has not shied away from countries with seemingly intractable political rows, what hope do you see on the horizon for the two Sudans, and for the U.S. relationship with the Khartoum government?

Stafford: In terms of the relationship between Sudan and South Sudan, I think that we need to continue our robust support of the African Union mediators' efforts to get the two countries to move forward on the cooperation agreements that they've signed in September 2012. The process has already been delayed far too long in the actual implementation, so that has

to be a key focus with the ultimate aim of securing a renewed sense of goodwill and commitment on both sides in implementing those agreements. Now, I think that both sides recognize that a return to war has to be avoided at all costs, that the vital interests of the two peoples are at stake and so it's vital that they implement the security arrangements they agreed upon last September, and, particularly the agreements to resume oil flow and to open up the border for badly needed trade between the two countries. These things are essential for the two countries' development, and for the hopes of improved standards of living for the people. Those considerations must be paramount in the minds of the two leaders and their two governments. So I am cautiously optimistic that we will see progress, simply because the two parties will realize that there is no alternative or that the alternatives are unacceptable; war, a status quo of tension, of a frozen relationship in a certain sense, and closed borders are not viable for either country in terms of coming to grips with the challenges each faces. So, the bottom line is that both sides recognize that a return to war must be avoided, and that we will see progress in implementation, delayed as it has been, of the cooperation agreements.

On the U.S. relationship with Khartoum, I think the key there is to look for opportunities—and encourage the government of Sudan to look as well—for the expansion of our dialogue and our search for ways to deal with these fundamental issues of peace and stability, democracy, good governance, and development for Sudan. Our fundamental objective remains to promote the emergence of a Sudan that is at peace internally and with its neighbors, particularly with South Sudan. So we need to continue finding ways to expand that dialogue and develop that dialogue with the Government of Sudan and encourage responsiveness on the questions of peace that are fundamental in moving forward in the relationship. In that respect, there are many salient issues we hope to address, including: progress in removing sanc-

it is vital to expand our public outreach and demonstrate to the people of Sudan that we are not hostile toward them, that we are committed to providing close to $300 million a year in humanitarian assistance, as well as some development assistance. So that's quite an investment we're making. Our work with members of Sudanese civil society, with political parties, and with the national election commission that we've been involved with in the past, will hopefully present

Our fundamental objective remains to promote the emergence of a Sudan that is at peace internally and with its neighbors.

tions, a process for removing Sudan from the list of State Sponsors of Terrorism, moving forward on the peace process in Darfur, resuming political talks with the Sudan People's Liberation Movement-North and reaching an agreement on the cessation of hostilities, permitting humanitarian access that has been delayed far too long to displaced persons in the Two Areas, and of course, moving forward with implementation of the cooperation agreements with South Sudan. So that's quite an agenda, as you can imagine—and governance and respect for human rights will always be a central theme permeating that agenda—but we hope for an expanded, productive dialogue with the Government of Sudan to deal with these challenges, and remove some of the obstacles on the path to normalization and improvement of ties.

Beyond our engagement with the Sudanese government, I also think

a multitude of opportunities for us to engage with the Sudanese during the run-up to national elections in 2015. So we have quite the agenda here in Sudan, an important country and an important relationship for us, as strained as it has been in recent years.

GJIA: You have experience serving in countries that have been sanctioned by the U.S. government and the international community, such as Iran and Sudan (granted, in the case of Iran, sanctions were imposed after you left). Do you think that sanctions are effective instruments in getting a regime to change its behavior?

Stafford: Well, the sanctions need to be, in my view, accompanied by a robust diplomatic process with the international community to ensure that there is, beyond the pressure resulting from sanctions, the diplomatic pressure from the international community in general. It is not a quick or easy process, that of applying pressure on regimes to get them to change policies that the international community finds objectionable, but it is, again, going back to the idea of tools, a tool of diplomacy—the tool of economic pressure embodied in sanctions—while I think that another important part has to be the provision of humanitarian assistance and making every effort to mitigate the impact of sanctions on ordinary citizens because after all, the target is the governments whose behavior we are trying to change through sanctions, through diplomatic pressure. Again, I return to the idea of the patient, hard-slogging efforts of using every available channel to apply pressure on these governments, and sanctions is part of the package, but it's not the only part. Diplomatic pressure and humanitarian assistance also have to be essential parts of the overall strategy.

Joseph D. Stafford was interviewed by Warren Ryan via telephone on 19 February 2013.

Science&Technology Politics&Diplomacy Culture&Society Business&Economics Law&Ethics Conflict&Security Books Science&Technology Politics&Diplomacy Culture&Society Business&Economics Law&Ethics Conflict&Security Books Science&Technology Politics&Diplomacy Culture&Society Business&Economics Law&Ethics Conflict&Security Science&Technology Politics&Diplomacy Culture&Society Business&Economics Law&Ethics Conflict&Security Books Business&Economics Politics&Diplomacy Culture&Society Business&Econ

Georgetown Journal

of International Affairs

Each Section. Every Issue. One Journal.

for more information or to subscribe

visit http://journal.georgetown.edu or email gjia@georgetown.edu

now featuring bi-weekly short essays, commentaries and analyses online

On Leadership and American Power

A Discussion about the Role of Leadership in U.S. Foreign Policy

Joseph S. Nye Jr.

On 26 March 2013, former Dean of the Harvard Kennedy School Joseph S. Nye led a seminar on presidents and the creation of the American era at Georgetown University's Mortara Center for International Studies. Professor Nye discussed about to what extent leadership mattered in establishing the United States as the dominant country in the twentieth century, and what lessons can be drawn for leadership and U.S. foreign policy in the twenty-first century. The *Journal* sat down with Professor Nye after the event to hear more about his views on the role of leadership in shaping and promoting U.S. foreign policy.

GJIA: You have argued that providing American education to more international students enhances U.S. soft power by helping them better understand American culture and political ideals. Today we have a record-high number of international students studying in the United States – what can U.S. colleges do to not waste this opportunity and positively influence the thoughts of future global leaders?

Joseph S. Nye Jr. is University Distinguished Service Professor at Harvard Kennedy School. He previously served as Dean of the Kennedy School, Assistant Secretary of Defense for International Security Affairs, Chair of the National Intelligence Council, and Deputy Under Secretary of State for Security Assistance, Science and Technology. In 2004, he published *Soft Power: The Means to Success in World Politics* and has just published *Presidential Leadership and the Creation of the American Era*.

Nye: The most important thing is to not try to shape minds of students in a propagandistic way, but to let students see the United States with all its virtues and all its flaws, and let them be able to make up their own minds. That is a lot more convincing than trying to have special programs to make foreign students love the United States, which will probably backfire. If we treat the foreign students well, integrate them into classes and courses with other ing horizontal education. It is not just foreign students, but also American students who can benefit from such experience.

GJIA: With the tenth anniversary of the Iraq war just passed, this period has been a time of reflection for many who have traced how American power has been transformed over the last decade. Looking towards the future, what do you think the role of the

> **By having ways in which** foreign students and American students interact informally as well as formally, you are creating horizontal education.

students so that they can make friends while others help them as they try to cope with the new environment, that is more likely to produce beneficial outcomes than by deliberately trying to shape their minds.

When I was Dean of the Harvard Kennedy School, I doubled its proportion of foreign students among the entire student body from 22 percent to 44 percent. People would say to me, "Why are you giving away these very rare, scarce resources to foreign students?" I replied, "Well, for one thing, we are in the business of educating bright people, but the other point is that every foreign student here at the Kennedy School is basically a teacher to an American who wishes to learn more about the rest of the world." By having ways in which foreign students and American students interact informally as well as formally, you are creat-

United States will be and should be in the world? What role will leaders have in making this shift?

Nye: The United States is likely to remain the most powerful country in the world for next several decades. I doubt that China will be able to pass the United States in military power, and I think their economy would probably become larger in terms of total GNP and the size of the United States simply due to their large population, but their per capita income will not be equal to that of the United States for several decades, if ever. On soft power, Chinese have a long way to go to equal the United States. The reason I mention China is that I think they are closer than any other country to the United States; they are the second largest economy, after all. That said, I do not see the Chinese passing the

United States in overall power. On the other hand, with the rise of China, the rise of India, and the rise of Brazil—and the rise of the rest—the United States does not have the same degree of dominance that it had in the late twentieth century after the decline of the Soviet Union. That means we have to have a smarter approach to foreign policy, which is to realize that the largest country is crucial in provision of global public goods. If we do not provide them, it is not clear whether or not any other nation can. If we do and do it well, it is beneficial to us, but it is also good for other countries. That, in the end, is our power and our attractiveness: both hard and soft power.

The right strategy for an American leader in the twenty-first century is to understand this context of American power. It is not declining, but it is coping with the rise of the rest. We have advantages in the way we are positioned, such as our existing alliances with Europe, Japan and others, and we have capacity to organize networks, which is very important in organizing collective action on problems that no one country can do by itself. These are problems like financial instability, pandemics, terrorism, and so forth. These are the things that we ought to be focusing on when we plan for a strategy for the twenty-first century.

For some of the transnational changes like climate change, financial stability, pandemics, or international cyber security, developing new sets of norms and institutions—ways through which you can organize cooperation to deal with these issues—is crucial. At the same time, it is important to maintain America's position as military power—not for intervention to try to reorganize the internal lives of the countries as we tried to do in Iraq and Iran, but rather to hold a balance of power in the world. For example, the American role in the Pacific that President Barak Obama has placed at the center of his foreign policy is important not as means of containing China, but rather as a means of making sure that we shape the environment so that China has incentives not to be a bully towards its neighbors. That itself is a type of public good—that sense of broader framework of security, so that countries can essentially enjoy the prosperity of rising economic interdependence without feeling threats to their security when one country grows stronger than its neighbors.

The United States will have to deal with traditional issues such as security issues, but we will have to deal with these new transnational issues at the same time. Security issues are sometimes described as zero-sum or power over others, and transnational issues are sometimes described as positive-sum or power with others, in which you need others to be able to get the outcomes you want. I think we are going to have to focus on both of these issues.

GJIA: Speaking of Asia, to what extent do you think the recent leadership transitions—Xi Jinping in China, Shinzo Abe in Japan, and Park Geun-hye in South Korea—will affect the region's geopolitical dynamics and its relations with the United States?

Nye: It is early; all these leaders are new to their job. However, I remain relatively optimistic from what we have seen of Xi Jinping. He does seem to want to cure some problems that China faces—from corruption to climate change and growing income inequality—as well as to have reasonable relationship with the United States. With Japan and South Korea, new leaders are from conservative sides, and there are some reactions against the rise of China, but both have thus far been reasonable in ways they have responded. I think the prospects there are encouraging rather than discouraging.

Yet, we should never forget that problems in international relations often rise with surprises and miscalculations. If in the bluffing and the tactical maneuvering over the Senkaku/Diaoyu Islands somebody makes

those events would be.

GJIA: The question of a defined role of the international community or individual foreign actors in cases of mass atrocity is one that has continued to elude global policy makers to a certain extent. Is there further legislation that should be crafted to make the obligations of international parties more clear, or is intervention destined to be dealt with on an ad hoc basis going forward and norms exist in a state of 'organized hypocrisy?' What role does the United States play in this process?

Nye: There are norms related to intervention now, but the problem is that they are not always clear-cut and sometimes have contradictory

There are norms related to intervention now, but the problem is that they are not always clear-cut and sometimes have contradictory effects.

a mistake, we might see things quickly getting out of control. Or, if North Korea tries to do something that takes high risk such as the sinking of the Cheonan in 2010, and since President Park has said that she is not going to tolerate such provocations—which I think is also a broad opinion held by the South Korean people—that could also lead to disruptive surprise. Overall, I tend to be relatively optimistic, but with a realization that—as Harold McMillan has said—a lot of the problems in history are caused by surprising events and you don't know what

effects. The UN Charter was an effort toward a framework that was largely not interventionist unless action was agreed upon by the permanent members of the Security Council under Chapter Seven, but we also have more recent norms like the "Responsibility to Protect," which was voted by the General Assembly in 2005. R2P states that if a government is not exercising its responsibility to protect its own people, then the outside world and international community can play a role in resolving conflict. What type of intervention is justifiable is not entirely clear and what we have seen is that sometimes these different approaches conflict with each other.

When the United States and the Europeans tried to persuade China and Russia to support a resolution under Chapter Seven authorizing use of force under the justification of the responsibility to protect Libya and the people of Benghazi from Muammar Gaddafi's attacks in 2011, the outcome in the eyes of Chinese and Russians led to regime change, which they argued they had not voted for. Partially because of this perception, we now cannot get the resolution in the Security Council, with the support of Chinese and Russians, in Syria. You might ask how R2P could exist and not be applied to intervention Syria, and part of the reason is that the Russians say that the norm they are observing is the norm of the UN Charter and they think that it was abused in the case of Libya. Even within Western governments it is not hundred-percent clear whether people understand what the full implications of use of force in Syria would look like so it is not just the absence of Security Council action.

You have to remember the Hippocratic Oath—above all do no harm—so you have to ask, "Do we know how to intervene in given situations without making things worse rather than better?" You will get differences in opinion about that. It is not just the problem of norms; it is also problem of how do you make sure as you try to take an action that you are getting intended outcomes, not unintended worse outcomes. Partly it is problem of norms, partly it is problem of institutions, and it is also problem of enormous uncertainty of intervention. On that, it is worth going back to the book written by Princeton Professor Gary Bass. In American foreign policy, we have been going through arguments about intervention as long ago as the 1820s. This is not a new issue.

Joseph S. Nye was interviewed by William Handel and Daye Shim Lee on 26 March 2013.

Georgetown University
Institute for Law, Science, and Global Security

International Engagement on Cyber

20

Developing International Norms for a Safe, Stable & Predictable Cyber Environmer

Georgetown Journal
of International Affairs

The Role of Syria in Israeli-Turkish Relations

Moran Stern and Dennis Ross

This article argues that, since the end of the Cold War, developments in or associated with Syria have proved instrumental in determining Israeli-Turkish relations, for better and worse.[1]

Syria borders both Israel and Turkey. Not surprisingly, its geographic location, regional strategic conduct, relations with Israel's and Turkey's regional rivals, military capabilities and, more recently, the implications of its civil war have affected both Israel and Turkey, and their relationship with each other. While strategic cooperation between Turkey and Israel reached a high point in the 1990s, and then soured and largely dissipated over the last several years, Syria's civil war has posed a new set of challenges and opportunities for renewed Israeli-Turkish ties. Indeed, shared interests on Syria may propel new possibilities for cooperation between Turkey and Israel on security, economic and humanitarian issues.

Through the historical analysis presented in this article, the authors attempt to explain the evolution of Israeli-Turkish relations through the prism of Syria. Understanding the historical background provided herein is relevant for contemporary analyses aimed at finding new ways to

Moran Stern is an Adjunct Lecturer at the Program for Jewish Civilization in Georgetown University's Edmund A. Walsh School of Foreign Service and at American University's Center for Israel Studies.

Dennis Ross is a Counselor at the Washington Institute for Near East Policy and Professor of the Practice of Diplomacy at Georgetown University. He served in several Administrations in senior positions at the NSC, the State Department and the Defense Department.

renew Israeli-Turkish strategic cooperation and assist in securing a stable post-war Syria.

Israel, Turkey, and Syria after the Cold War.

Since the end of the Cold War, Syria has played a pivotal role in affecting the nature of Israeli-Turkish relations, for better and worse, due to Syria's location, its regional ambitions and relations with Iran and terrorist organizations, its chemical and conventional weapons arsenal and, more recently, the implications of its civil war.

Syria is situated between Israel and Turkey, and shares borders with both.[2] Throughout the years, both countries have experienced tensions and border disputes with Syria: Israel fought three wars against Syria in 1948, 1967, and 1973. As Turkish-Syrian tensions heightened during the 1990s, Turkey's security establishment classified Syria, together with Greece, as its primary source of external threat.[3]

Over the past five decades, Syria has attempted to use its unique strategic location to advance its national interests and geopolitical status, often at the expense of Israel and Turkey. One way of achieving these ends was by sheltering different terror organizations and providing them a base for operations.

In the mid-1960s, Syria provided refuge and logistical support to the Palestinian group, the Palestinian National Liberation Movement (Fatah), then a terrorist outfit. Headed by Yasser Arafat, Fatah's militants often used Syrian soil to raid Israeli villages and to execute terrorist attacks against Israeli civilians and soldiers. These attacks stopped after Israel's victory in the Six Days War in June 1967 and its occupation of the Golan Heights, which forced Fatah to relocate to Jordan.[4]

After the collapse of its Soviet patron, Syria further tightened its relations with Iran. Since the 1980s, Syria has been an important supporter of Iranian protégé, the Shia-Lebanese terrorist organization Hezbollah ("The Party of God"), supplying it with arms, money and training. In 1993 and 1996, Hezbollah triggered conflicts with Israel that escalated and required American mediation with Syria to restore peace. Syrian president Hafez al-Assad saw Hezbollah's attacks as a point of leverage against Israel, and would only act to curb them when it served Syrian interests to do so. In late 1999, after Jordan expelled the Islamic Resistance Movement (Hamas) from its territory, the movement's political leadership under Khaled Mashal relocated to Damascus, where it remained until 2011.[5]

As for Turkey, water disputes with Syria have almost evolved into a direct conflict. In 1992, after Turkey completed the Atatürk Dam on the Euphrates River, Syria protested that the project disrupted its water supply.[6] To exert pressure on Turkey, Syria harbored combatants of the separatist Kurdish terror organization, the Kurdistan Workers' Party's (PKK).[7] The PKK used Syria and the presence of a large Kurdish minority there to train and execute attacks against Turkey.[8,9] Furthermore, in 1995, reports surfaced regarding a developing military pact between Syria and Greece, which would have forced Turkey to mobilize forces on two fronts simultaneously in the event of conflict.[10]

Consequently, deterring Syria became a mutual interest for Israel and Turkey. In 1996 the two countries signed the most comprehensive strategic agreement in the history of the modern Middle East to this day: the Military Cooperation and Training Agreement. Coerced by the politically influential Turkish Armed Forces (TAF), the Islamist Prime Minister, Necmettin Erbakan, signed the agreement against his will.[11] Shortly after, Süleyman Demirel became the first Turkish president to visit Israel.[12]

At the core of the agreement were strategic and security cooperation. The 1996 visit by TAF Deputy Chief of Staff General Çevik Bir to Israel concluded with a series of military agreements covering intelligence sharing, electronic surveillance, joint training, naval strategy, weapons sales, and the upgrade of Turkey's Phantom F-4 jets by Israel, totaling $630 million.[13] The strategic agreement was later expanded to a Free Trade Pact that included commerce, technology, science, and the lifting of barriers on investment in certain sectors. Between 1987 and 1999, bilateral trade grew from $54 million to almost $1 billion.[14]

According to General Bir, the Turkish alliance with Israel had "the objective of keeping theocratic extremism and martial despotism at check."[15] The alignment of two regional powerhouses who had both suffered from Syria's strategic conduct was with a clear aim: to restrain the Syrian regime from hostile actions against Israel and Turkey. Syria was deterred by the possibility of the two countries coordinating a "strategic pincer," pressing it when necessary from the southwest and the north.

The military agreements between Israel and Turkey did not include the premise of mutual defense. Nonetheless, these agreements appeared to increase Turkey's assertiveness towards Syria. In March 1996, Turkey's Prime Minister Mesut Yilmaz threatened Syria, "Some of our neighbors shelter those who seek to destroy the unity of our land…Either this neighbor puts an end to this situation or it will sooner or later surely be punished for its enmity…when our patience runs out our reaction will be violent."[16]

In 1998, as PKK attacks continued, Turkey explicitly threatened Syria with an invasion. Succumbing under Turkish pressure, the countries signed the Adana Agreement whereby Syria agreed to classify the PKK as a terrorist organization and pledged to cease all aid to it. As testimony to Turkey's augmented leverage over Syria, the latter deported the now-jailed PKK leader Abdullah Öcalan even before the agreement was signed.[17]

Israeli-Syrian peace negations during the mid-1990s helped to promote Israeli-Turkish strategic cooperation. If Israel and Syria were to have finalized a peace agreement, Israel would no longer function as a deterring power, reducing Turkey's deterrence as well. Thus, the prospects for an Israeli-Syrian settlement magnified the urgency for strategic cooperation with Israel for Turkey.[18]

For Israel, any peace agreement with Syria would have required withdrawal from the Golan Heights, which would curtail its strategic depth, surveillance capability, and military training zones. Cementing ties with Turkey—negotiated in the early 1990s before and in parallel to the Syrian track—could compensate for what Israel would cede as a result of an agreement with Syria. Turkey's terrain would allow the Israeli air force (IAF) to diversify its training zones while providing a landscape resembling Syria.[19] Both militaries used Turkey's border with Syria to gather and share intelligence.[20]

Shifting Perceptions. By the beginning of the twenty-first century, Israeli-Syrian peace negotiations had decelerated. There were also far-reaching political changes taking place in Turkey: the Justice and Development Party (AKP), led by Prime Minister Recep Tayyip Erdogan, came to power in 2002. Domestically, the AKP's ascendance signaled the transition of power from the urban, elitist and secular Kemalist establishment (supported by the TAF) to the peripheral, conservative lower and middle classes represented by the AKP.

This political shift had direct ramifications on Israeli-Turkish relations as the old guard Kemalists and the TAF, who were the major promoters of the strategic alignment with Israel, gradually lost their political power. As part of its political reform the new leadership removed military men from positions of political power, enabling the government to drastically change its regional threat perception.

Seeking to promote its regional status, stability, and economic opportunities, the AKP government formulated a "zero problems with neighbors" regional policy. According to this policy, suspicious and defensive attitudes towards neighboring states would be assuaged through dynamic diplomacy and economic engagement.[21]

Consequently, Turkey began to perceive Syria as a business partner. In 2004, Syria's new president and Hafez's son, Bashar al-Assad, visited Ankara on the first presidential trip to Turkey since Syrian independence in 1946. Al-Assad said that Syria and Turkey "have together shifted from an atmosphere of distrust to trust."[22] In 2006, he added that both countries share "common views on regional issues."[23] In 2009, ten Turkish ministers met with their Syrian counterparts and declared the lifting of visa restrictions on their shared border.[24,25]

Erdogan began to travel to Syria frequently and the countries inaugurated the Turkey-Syria High Level Strategic Cooperation Council in 2009 to cover issues ranging from trade to security. A year later at the Fifth Turkish-Arab Economic Forum in Istanbul, Turkey and other Arab states, including Syria, signed a free trade agreement.[26] Evidently, Turkey and Syria have benefited from their mutual economic opening. Between 2009 and 2010, Turkish exports to Syria increased by nearly 30 percent and imports boomed by 104 percent, totaling almost $4 billion in bilateral trade.[27]

The change in Turkey's threat perception and regional priorities—as well as its increasing ties with Syria—began to reduce the Turkish leadership's view of the strategic values of its relationship with Israel.

That did not mean that Erdogan was prepared to undo the strategic ties with Israel. During the early 2000s Erdogan stressed several times that no change would occur in relations with Israel as they served Turkish national interest.[28] Further, it was during Erdogan's premiership that most trade deals with Israel were signed.[29] In 2004, bilateral trade hit a record at $2 billion—and in 2012 has grown to over $4 billion.[30,31,32] Military cooperation further developed as the Israeli, Turkish, and American navies conducted a joint marine exercise, Reliant Mermaid. Turkey also continued to purchase Israeli arms, implemented a contract with Israel to upgrade its tanks, and in 2005 bought Israeli UAVs worth $200 million.[33,34] In December 2005,

es in Syria to reinitiate the Israeli-Syrian peace process. According to Turkey, its mediation efforts were on the verge of delivering a peace agreement in the winter of 2008 when the talks were abruptly terminated because Israel had launched Operation Cast Lead against Hamas in Gaza that December.[37]

Turkey's disappointment and fury at the collapse of the negotiations, at least in part because of Turkish anger over Operation Cast Lead, has been evident in Erdogan and Foreign Minister Ahmet Davutoglu's intensi-

The deep political, economic, social, and regional policy changes that Israel and...Turkey have undergone in the last decade have adversely affected their relations.

Israel's Chief of Staff, Dan Halutz, traveled to Ankara and met with his Turkish counterpart, General Hilmi Özkök. The two officers agreed to continue the joint military exercises and to sell Israeli surveillance equipment to Turkey.[35] Moreover, Turkey did not cease to perceive Syria's secret military programs as dangerous for its own security.[36]

Nevertheless, the deep political, economic, social, and regional policy changes that Israel and, far more significantly, Turkey have undergone in the last decade have adversely affected their relations. Interestingly, the negative watershed moment in Israeli-Turkish relations is directly associated with Syria.

As part of its regional ambitions, Turkey attempted to use its good offic-

fied anti-Israeli statements and policies since then. From the perspective of the Israeli public, Turkey's anti-Israel rhetoric took on an entirely new character at the World Economic Forum in Davos, Switzerland in January 2009 when Erdogan verbally attacked Israeli President Shimon Peres.[38] In Israel, criticism focused on Turkish mediation with Syria: Given the delicacy and importance of its relationship with Turkey for Israel, the latter should never have involved the former in a complex process whose prospects for success were uncertain.[39]

Israeli-Turkish relations continued to deteriorate. In 2010, Turkey's National Security Council released its annual "Red Book," which lists Turkey's security threats. Turkey had omitted Syria from its list of threatening states and classified Israel's policies as a threat to regional stability.[40]

Following the flotilla incident of May 2010 in which nine Turkish citizens were killed onboard the *Mavi Marmara* vessel, both countries suspended defense contracts. Turkey recalled its ambassador from Tel Aviv, blocked Israel initiatives in NATO, supported legal procedures against Israeli decision-makers and soldiers who were involved in the incident, and cancelled joint military exercises.[41] Turkey conditioned the renormalization of relations on Israeli apology for the killing of Turkish citizens, monetary compensations to the victims' families and the removal of the blockade off the Gaza Strip.

A Resurgent Alliance? The outbreak of the Arab turmoil—and especially the developments in Syria—has gradually brought the two sides, with American assistance, to reassess their relations. Both Israel and Turkey are deeply concerned about al-Assad's chemical and conventional weapons falling into the hands of Hezbollah or jihadist groups fighting in Syria, not to mention Iran's involvement in Syria and the conflict's spillover to Lebanon and Jordan.

For Israel, the Syrian border that has remained stable since 1974 has turned into a source of major concern. To fight the rebels on other fronts, al-Assad redeployed most of his forces from the Syrian Golan Heights to the vicinities of Damascus and other strategic locations, enabling the rebels—some of whom are Jihadists with links to al-Qaeda—to gain control.[42]

Security deterioration immediately followed. Between March and May 2013, more than 20 monitors from the UN Disengagement Observer Force (UNDOF) were abducted and later released by Jihadist rebels. In response, some of the UNDOF contributing countries decided to withdraw their troops from the mission, widening the security vacuum on the countries' border and the mobilization of Jihadist rebels.[43]

Probably the most prominent Jihadist group is *Jabhat a-Nusra* ("the Support Front"), recently classified by the United States as a terror organization. Some of its forces are located in southern Syria, near the borders with Israel and Jordan. In April 2013, one of its leaders, Abu Muhammad al-Julani, announced the group's merger with the Iraqi branch of al-Qaeda with the intent to establish an Islamist state in Syria and Iraq under the guidance of al-Qaeda leader Ayman al-Zawahiri.[44,45]

As long as the Jihadists remain occupied with securing their strongholds in the Golan Heights, they are likely to refrain from provoking Israel. Nevertheless, since November 2012, the IDF has been involved in several exchanges of fire with Syrian forces shooting and rocket shelling from the Syrian part of the Golan Heights near Israeli villages and IDF patrols. While it remains unclear whether the fire was intentional or inadvertent and the identity of the forces remains unidentified, Israeli concerns about potential spillover of the conflict and terrorists infiltrations led the IDF to replace its reserve forces near the border with more qualified regular forces and construct a new border fence with sophisticated anti-infiltration devices.[46,47,48]

Among Israel's critical concerns are Syria's attempts to traffic conventional weapons to Hezbollah, thus jeopardizing Israel's air and sea forces.[49] Israel considers the trafficking of such weapons a "redline" that necessitates a pre-emptive response. Between January and May 2013, it was reported that the IAF had destroyed a convoy of trucks on the Syrian-Lebanese border and weapons' warehouses in Syria that carried and stored missiles destined for Hezbollah.[50]

Turkish pressure on al-Assad to stop violence against his countrymen has been futile. The Syrian president rebuffed efforts by Davutoglu and Turkish officials to end the civil war and implement democratic reforms.[51] Syria's interception of a Turkish F-4 jet in the summer of 2012 was followed by intensified condemnations by Erdogan calling for al-Assad to resign, imposing sanctions, and threatening military invasion to create safe zones on Syrian soil; none of which convinced the regime to cease its repression.[52,53]

The humanitarian and economic tolls of the war in Syria have directly affected Turkey too. Currently, there are approximately 500,000 Syrian refugees in Turkey living in refugee camps and costing the Turkish authorities over $600 million.[54] Due to the war, bilateral trade has plummeted by 75 percent to $568 million in 2012 compared to $2.3 billion in 2010 and previous forecasts to record $5 billion in bilateral trade in 2013 are no longer feasible.[55,56]

Syria's disintegration may also result in a nightmare for Turkey with nascent Syrian Kurdish self-rule adjacent to the countries' border that is already administrated by the Kurdish Democratic Union party (PYD), the Syrian franchise of the PKK, and guarded by its militia, the Popular Protection Units (YPG).[57]

Both Israel and Turkey share concerns regarding Iran's deepening involvement in Syria. Through its *al-Quds* force and Hezbollah, Iran is offering massive support in arms, training, combat support and money to the Assad regime.[58]

Despite their economic and diplomatic relations, Iran remains Turkey's main geopolitical rival. For its part, Israel sees Iran's support for terror and its pursuit of a nuclear capability as posing an existential threat. An established Iranian presence near Israeli and Turkish borders during and after the war in Syria severely endangers both countries' security.

Where It Stands. The radical changes in the region compelled Turkey and Israel to initiate discreet talks. During Operation Pillar of Cloud against Hamas and the Islamic Jihad in November 2012, reports leaked about a meeting between the director of the Israeli Mossad, Tamir Pardo, and the Undersecretary of Turkey's National Intelligence Organization, Hakan Fidan, in Cairo.[59] The same month, back-channel talks to break the diplomatic impasse were held in Geneva between Joseph Ciechanover, former Foreign Ministry director general, and Turkish Foreign Ministry Director Feridun Sinirlioglu.[60] These discussions continued in February 2013 in Rome between Prime Minister Binyamin Netanyahu's national security adviser, Yaakov Amidror, accompanied by Joseph Ciechanover, and Feridun Sinirlioglu.[61]

Other developments suggest that relations are taking a more positive turn. In February, Israel completed the delivery of an airborne reconnaissance system to Turkey, a deal previously suspended by both the Turkish authorities and the Israeli Ministry of Defense following the flotilla incident.[62] In addition, a delegation of Israeli and foreign energy companies and one of Netanyahu's senior aides traveled to Turkey to promote the joint construction of an underwater gas pipe from the Israeli Leviathan reservoir to

Obama, Netanyahu expressed Israel's apology for any operational mistakes that might have led to the loss of life or injury on the *Mavi Marvara*, agreed to compensate the victims' families, and to continue to work on improving the lives of Palestinians in the West Bank and Gaza Strip as long as quiet prevails. Both prime ministers agreed to restore diplomatic relations and re-dispatch their ambassadors. Erdogan, accepting Netanyahu's apology, promised to repeal all current and future legal proceedings against IDF soldiers who were involved in the flotilla raid.[64]

Talk of Israeli-Turkish strategic cooperation on Syria or a full rap-

Talk of Israeli-Turkish strategic cooperation on Syria or a full rapprochement between the two state is premature.

Turkey and from there to Europe.[63]

American efforts to end the crisis, facilitated by President Barack Obama and Secretary of State John Kerry, were instrumental in the process. Restoring normal relations between its two main allies in the region is a clear American interest, for it helps Washington to approach the diverse challenges in the region and those in Syria in particular. As a probable gesture to the United States and Obama's second administration, both Netanyahu and Erdogan exhibited readiness to restore Israeli-Turkish relations.

Concomitant with Obama's departure from his March visit to Israel, Netanyahu called Erdogan for the first time since 2009. During the conversation, joined at one point by President

prochement between the two states is premature. Referring to the Military Cooperation and Training Agreement as a guide for the countries' relations in other areas would be unrealistic in light of the aforementioned changes in Turkey and Israel, their high mutual suspicion, and Turkey's regional policy. In Turkey, Israel is not merely a regional player and former ally, but also a convenient symbol in domestic politics.

Under the AKP, mention is usually made of Israel to harshly condemn its policies on the Palestinian issue, to silence the Kemalist establishment that advocated strategic cooperation with Israel and—by the same token—to promote the image and credibility of the AKP government, and to advance

Turkey's status in the Muslim world.

Turkey's ambitions for greater influence in the Middle East-often by playing-up its Muslim identity in an effort to have common denominator with the Muslim population in the region and cultivating relations with Israel's foes - not only limits overt cooperation with the Jewish State, but also raises questions about whether Turkey still considers Israel part of its strategic outlook. Conversely, Israel might not trust the new political establishment in Turkey to be a reliable partner. If nothing else, these questions suggest that while normalization is likely, a return to the kind of strategic cooperation that existed previously is less immediately probable.

Turkey's siding with Hamas at the expense of President Mahmoud Abbas' Palestinian Liberation Organization (PLO) in the West Bank furthers Hamas' legitimacy and feeds Israeli suspicions regarding Turkey.[65] Additionally, the stalemate in the Israeli-Palestinian peace process delegitimizes relations with Israel in eyes of consecutive Turkish leaderships and the current one in particular.[66] Within Turkey, senior generals who served as a powerful lobby for strong relations with Israel are now stripped of authority, imprisoned or otherwise restricted.[67]

As in the past, time and circumstances will be the best judges. Here, again, Syria is a platform for renewed cooperation.

Conclusion. Whatever Syria will become—a unified state, a collection of largely independent entities, or a system of cantons—it will maintain a pivotal role in affecting Israeli-Turkish relations. While Israel and Turkey are limited in their ability to influence the civil war in Syria, both would prefer to see a unified, stable, moderate, and—optimally—democratic Syria emerge. Given the current status of their relations, the question becomes whether Israel and Turkey can find ways to use these shared interests to restore cooperation between them, and what role can the United States play in facilitating such cooperation.

The United States is uniquely positioned to promote initiatives with Israel and Turkey in a number of areas that reflect shared concerns about trying to end–or at least contain–the conflict in Syria and its possible spillover effects in the region.

In the short and medium terms, security remains Israel, Turkey, and the United States' main preoccupation. The disintegration of Syria's conventional and nonconventional military and the risk that these weapons may fall to radical groups, Iranian protégés, and warlords can drag Syria and its neighbors into long years of low-intensity, yet highly lethal, warfare.[68]

Preventing the trafficking of weapons to radical groups is a mutual interest for both Israel and Turkey. If Israel were to execute preemptive attacks to curtail weapons' trafficking, Turkey should refrain from publically criticizing these operations, as it has done in the past.[69] Such operations clearly serve Turkish national security interests. Furthermore, continued Turkish anti-Israel rhetoric, especially in light of Israel's apology regarding the flotilla incident, will contribute to prolonging Israeli concerns about whether Turkey is genuinely prepared to cooperate with Israel—and also take American concerns and interests into account.

In addition, discreet contingency planning between the security establishments in Israel, Turkey, and the United States—including intelligence sharing and future resumption of joint military exercises specifically related to Syria—will benefit coordination efforts in order to reduce unfavorable threats and outcomes from the war in Syria. Economically, both Israel and Turkey are export-oriented countries and can expand their economic cooperation to enhance broader regional stability by including other regional players in general and to affect Syria's population in particular. At the moment, a unique precedent is being established in the region. Blocked roads in Syria helped to facilitate a historic cooperation between the Israeli, Turkish, Jordanian, and Iraqi, enabling the continuation of trade between the Middle East and Europe. Israel's roads and ports have become alternative trade routes for Syria to freight goods to Turkey and Europe, estimated at tens of millions of USD per month. Israel considers this economic interconnectedness a rare opportunity to demonstrate its good intentions to its Muslim neighbors.[70]

Similarly, even a smaller-scale Israeli-Turkish, and possibly Jordanian and Iraqi, initiative to export goods from Syria to the Western markets can somewhat ease the current economic suffering of the Syrian people and, more importantly, function as a platform for future confidence building measurement between Israel, Turkey, Syria's civil-population, and other Middle Eastern countries.

Moreover, when the war in Syria ends the country will begin its reconstruction process. Israeli pharmaceutical, agriculture and software companies, and "know-how" may play a vital role in rebuilding post-conflict Syria. Turkey's large construction and civil engineer companies, which already have a strong foothold in other Middle Eastern countries, as well as Turkish consumer goods, will find renewed markets in Syria. Joint economic ventures between the already interconnected Israeli and Turkish private sectors in fields such as telecommunications and infrastructure can benefit all sides.

Lastly, humanitarianism is a value shared by Israel, Turkey, and the U.S. While Israeli and Turkish approaches to the crisis in Syria diverge, both are highly concerned by the human tolls of the war there—and so is the United States. Israel is a leading country in emergency preparedness and medicine. In the past months, the IDF has built field hospitals near the border with Syria to treat injured Syrians, some of whom were also treated in Israeli hospitals, while Turkey has long sheltered Syrian refugees.[71] Working together with the United States and various international organizations to establish services for the welfare of the Syrian people now can serve near-term humanitarian needs, and be a long-term opportunity to initiate better working relations and trust between Israel, Syria, and Turkey.

The political, economic, social, and strategic changes that Israel and, more significantly, Turkey have undergone in the last decade have adversely affected their relations. Nevertheless, the unfortunate reality in Syria creates a window of opportunity to foster Israeli-Turkish ties. American involvement in promoting its allies' relations is instrumental in serving the strategic interests of all three states and in the region's future prosperity.

NOTES

1 Many thanks to Aurora Nou and Alexandra West for their invaluable contributions to the researching of this article.

2 Syria shares a 76 km (47 miles) border with Israel and an 822 km (511 miles) border with Turkey. Central Intelligence Agency, "The World Fact Book-Israel," Internet, https://www.cia.gov/library/publications/the-world-factbook/geos/is.html (date accessed 9 June 2013); Central Intelligence Agency, "The World Fact Book-Turkey," Internet, https://www.cia.gov/library/publications/the-world-factbook/geos/tu.html(date accessed 9 June 2013)

3 Malik Mufti, "Daring and Caution in Turkish Foreign Policy," *Middle East Journal* Vol. 52, No. 1 (Winter, 1998): p. 34

4 Fatah remained in Jordan until "Black September" in 1970, when King Hussein ousted Fatah's members from the kingdom to Lebanon.

5 Following the outbreak of the war in Syria, Hamas's political leadership left Damascus and its members are currently in Qatar and Egypt.

6 The Atatürk Dam is used for energy production and irrigation

7 Malik Mufti, "Daring and Caution in Turkish Foreign Policy," *Middle East Journal* Vol. 52, No. 1 (Winter, 1998): p. 35.

8 Syrian Kurds make up between 15 and 20 percent of the total Syrian population. Michael Weiss, "Why Syria's Kurds Will Determine the Fate of the Revolution," *New Republic*, 16 November 2011.

9 Lesser, Ian and Larrabee, Stephan, *Turkish Foreign Policy in an Age of Uncertainty*, (Santa Monica: RAND, 2003), p.145.

10 Malik Mufti, "Daring and Caution in Turkish Foreign Policy," *Middle East Journal* Vol. 52, No. 1 (Winter, 1998): 35.

11 Ofra Bengio, *The Turkish-Israeli Relationship: Changing Ties of Middle Eastern Outsiders*, (New York City: Palgrave Macmillan, 2004) 110.

12 The Washington Institute for Near East Policy, " Timeline of Turkish-Israeli Relations, 1949–2006," Internet, 2006.

13 "The Strategic Glue in the Israeli-Turkish Alignment," in *Turkey in World Politics: an Emerging Multiregional Power*, (Boulder: Lynne Rienner Publishers, Inc., 2001), pp.119-120.

14 "The Strategic Glue in the Israeli-Turkish Alignment," in *Turkey in World Politics: an Emerging Multiregional Power*, (Boulder: Lynne Rienner Publishers, Inc., 2001), p.115.

15 Bir Cevik and Sherman Daniel, " Formula for Stability: Turkey Plus Israel," *Middle East Quarterly* (Fall, 2002): 31

16 Malik Mufti, "Daring and Caution in Turkish Foreign Policy," *Middle East Journal*, Vol. 52, No. 1 (Winter, 1998): 35.

17 Ely Karmon, "A Solution to Syrian Terrorism," *The Middle East Quarterly*, Vol. 6, No. 2 (June, 1999): 23-32.

18 Nachmani Amikam, "The Remarkable Turkish-Israeli Tie," The Middle East Quarterly, Vol. 5, No. 2 (June, 1998): 19-29

19 Between 2001 and 2009, the Turkish, Israeli, and U.S. air forces held the "Anatolian Eagle,"joint exercises over Konya, Turkey.

20 Ofra Bengio, *The Turkish-Israeli Relationship: Changing Ties of Middle Eastern Outsiders*, (New York City: Palgrave Macmillan, 2004) 94-112

21 "Turkey's Stature as a Middle Eastern Power," in *Turkish-Israeli Relations in a Trans-Atlantic Context: Wider Europe and the Greater Middle East* (Tel Aviv: Tel Aviv University, 2005), 47

22 Bülent Aras , "Turkey between Syria and Israel: Turkey's Rising Soft Power," *SETA Policy Brief* (May 2008): 1.

23 Bülent Aras, Rabia Karakaya Polat, "From Conflict to Cooperation: Desecuritization of Turkey's Relations with Syria and Iran," *International Peace Research Institute, Oslo* (2008): 510.

24 The list of ministers included those from the foreign affairs, defense, interior, economy, energy and agriculture ministries

25 Republic of Turkey-Ministry of Foreign Affairs, "Relations between Turkey-Syria," Internet, http://www.mfa.gov.tr/relations-between-turkey%E2%80%93syria.en.mfa (date accessed 9 June 2013)

26 Joshua Walker and Naber Habibi, "What is Driving Turkey's Reengagement with the Arab World?" *Middle East Brief*, (2011): 5.

27 Turkish Statistical Institute, "Foreign Trade," Internet, http://www.turkstat.gov.tr/VeriBilgi.do?alt_id=12 (date accessed 9 June 2013)

28 Inbar Efraim, "The Resilience of Israeli-Turkish Relations," *Israel Affairs*, Vol. 11, No. 4 (October, 2005): 599.

29 The Begin-Sadat Center for Strategic Studies (BESA), "Is Turkey Lost to the West as a Strategic Ally?" *The Begin-Sadat Center for Strategic Studies (BESA) Bulletin*, No. 25 (February, 2010): 7.

30 Inbar Efraim, "The Resilience of Israeli-Turkish Relations," *Israel Affairs*, Vol. 11, No. 4 (October, 2005): 591.

31 According to the Turkish Statistical Institute bilateral trade with Israel in 2012 totaled $4.04 billion. Turkish Statistical Institute, "Foreign Trade," Internet, http://www.turkstat.gov.tr/VeriBilgi.do?alt_id=12(date accessed 9 June 2013).

32 Following the flotilla incident in 2010 and the suspension of government-to-government contracts, bilateral trade was between the countries' private sectors.

33 Unmanned Aerial Vehicles

34 Inbar Efraim, "The Resilience of Israeli-Turkish Relations," *Israel Affairs*, Vol. 11, No. 4 (October, 2005): 592-603.

35 The Washington Institute for Near East Policy, " Timeline of Turkish-Israeli Relations, 1949–2006,"

Internet, 2006.

36 According to foreign sources, in 2007, the IAF bombed and destroyed a nuclear reactor in northeast Syria that was meant to produce plutonium for a nuclear weapon. On their way back to Israel, a technical problem in one of the jets forced the pilot to detach a fuel tank. The tank, labeled with Hebrew characters, was discovered on Turkish soil and Syria demanded clarifications from Turkey. Israeli sources reported that the IAF had not violated Turkish sovereignty — an explanation that was accepted by the Turkish government and suggested Turkish satisfaction with the reactor's destruction. Yossi Melman and Dan Raviv, "The Destruction of the Syrian reactor: The Untold Story," *Haaretz*, 3 August 2012.

37 Moran Stern, interview with Turkish Government Official, May 11, 2011.

38 At the Forum's panel, when Mr. Peres tried to explain Israel's reasons for the Israel's Cast Lead Operation, Erdogan told him: "When it comes to killing, you know well how to kill." Katrin Bennhold, "Leaders of Turkey and Israel Clash at Davos Panel", *New York Times*, 29 January, 2009.

39 Ehud Toledano, "AKP's Turkey and its Relations with Israel," *INSS Insight*, no. 225 (November, 2010): 12

40 Gallia Lindenstrauss, "Changes in the Turkish Threat Perception: Strategic Significance for Israel," *INSS Insight*, no. 220, (November, 2010). http://www.inss.org.il/publications.php?cat=21&incat=&read=4565(Accessed April 2013)

41 Tavernise, Sabrina, "Raid Jeopardizes Turkey Relations," *The New York Times*, 31 May, 2010; Julian Borger, "Turkey confirms it barred Israel from military exercise because of Gaza war," *The Guardian*, 12 October 2012.

42 Martin Chulov and Harriet Sherwood, "Syrian troop redeployments raise concerns over Golan Heights security," *The Guardian*, 7 April 2013.

43 Manuel Mogato, "Manila seeks Golan Heights peacekeepers pullout after abductions," Reuters, 10 May 2013; John Reed, "Tensions build on Israel-Syria border," *The Washington Post*, 17 April 2013; Jerusalem Post and Reuters, "Austria to pull peacekeepers from Golan Heights," *The Jerusalem Post*, 6 June 2013

44 Abu Muhammad al-Julani's surname indicates that his origins are the Golan (in Arabic, *Julan*) area

45 Yaron Friedman, " Meet our new neighbors: al-Qaeda in the Golan Heights," *Ynet*, 15 April 2013

46 Isabel Kershner and Nick Cumming-Bruce, "Israel Says Its Tanks Responded to Shots Fired From Syrian Side," *The New York Times*, 2 April 2013

47 John Reed, "Tensions build on Israel-Syria border," The Washington Post, 17 April 2013

48 Aron Heller, "Israel wary quiet on Syrian front about to end," Internet, http://news.yahoo.com/israel-wary-quiet-syrian-front-end-191516406.

html (date accessed: 9 June 2013).

49 Among these weapons are the Russian-made SA-17 anti-aircraft missiles , P-800 (*Yakhont*) anti-ship cruise missiles, and Scud-D surface-to-surcease missiles which is capable to cover all Israel; as well as the Iranian surface-to-surcease Fateh 110

50 BBC News, "Israeli 'air strike on convoy on Syria-Lebanon border'," Internet, http://www.bbc.co.uk/news/world-middle-east-21264632(date accessed: 9 June 2013); Anne Barnard, Michael R. Gordon and Jodi Rudoren, "Israel Targeted Iranian Missiles in Syria Attack," *The New York Times*, 4 May 2013.

51 Nada Bakri, "Turkish Minister and Other Envoys Press Syrian Leader," *The New York Times*, 9 August 2011; Sunday's Zaman,"Davutoglu: Assad following path Gaddafi once walked," *Today's Zaman*, 26 October 2011.

52 Sebnem Arsu, "Turkish Premier Urges Assad to Quit in Syria," *The New York Times*, 22 November 2011

53 Dan Bilefsky and Anthony Shadid, "Turkey Moves to Intensify Sanctions Against Syria," *The New York Times*, 30 November 2011

54 Nick Cumming-Bruce, "Number of Syrian Refugees Hits 1 Million, U.N. Says," *The New York Times*, 6 March 2013; Kevin Sullivan, " Turkey's Erdogan to Air Policy Differences with Obama," *The Washington Post*, 13 May 2013

55 Turkish Statistical Institute, "Foreign Trade," Internet, http://www.turkstat.gov.tr/VeriBilgi.do?alt_id=12 (date accessed 9 June 2013).

56 Dan Bilefsky and Anthony Shadid, "Turkey Moves to Intensify Sanctions Against Syria," *The New York Times*, 30 November 2011

57 Jonathan Spyer, "The Kurds Are for the Kurds," *The Weekly Standard*, 18 March 2013; Najmeh Bozorgmehr, "Iran reiterates support of Syrian regime," *Financial Times*, 7 January 2013.

58 Jim Michaels, "Mattis interview: Syria would fall without Iran's help," *USA Today*, 12 April 2013.

59 Duygu Güvenç and Veli Sarıboga, "Israel Seeking to Repair Ties with Turkey," *Sabah*, 24 November 2012.

60 Ilan Ben-Zion, "Turkey confirms holding back-channel reconciliation talks with Israel," *The Times of Israel*, 25 November 2012.

61 *Times of Israel* staff, "Israel fails in new effort to mend ties with Turkey," *The Times of Israel*, 23 February 2013.

62 Press TV, "Israel delivers airborne reconnaissance systems to Turkey," Internet, http://www.presstv.ir/detail/2013/02/18/289525/israel-delivers-awacs-systems-to-turkey/ (date accessed 9 June 2013).

63 Golan Hazani, "Netanyahu's Next Goal: Gas Pipeline with Turkey," *Calcalist*, 13 February 2013.

64 Sara Sidner. Ivan Watson and Joe Sterling, "Israel to Turkey: We apologize for deadly raid on Gaza-bound flotilla," Internet, http://edition.cnn.

com/2013/03/22/world/meast/israel-turkey-apology (date accessed 9 June 2013); To be sure, this deal must be finalized with an agreement on the compensation Israel is to pay and the return of ambassadors to the two countries.

65 Hamas is classified as a terrorist organization in both Israel and the U.S. and one that openly calls for the destruction of Israel.

66 Karen Kaya and Moran Stern, "Turkey, the U.S. and the Middle East Peace Process," *Washington Jewish Week*, 18 May 2013.

67 Among the prominent jailed or restricted Turkish generals are: General Ismail Hakkı Karadayı, Commander of the Army from 1993 to 1994 and Chief of the General Staff from 1994 to1998 was detained in January 2013 (but later released due to his age) and was forbidden from traveling outside Turkey on the condition that he check in with legal authorities weekly; General Bir was arrested in April 2012; and General Ilhan Kılıç, Commander of the Turkish Air Force from 1997 to 1999, was arrested in May 2012, their exclusion from pro-Israel circles in Turkey attenuates the voices in support of a Turkish-Israeli strategic rapprochement; Moran Stern, interview with Turkey analyst, Washington D.C. 19 April 2013.

68 Ehud Eilam, "Israel's Approach to Syria," *The National Interest*, 26 April 2013.

69 *Sunday's Zaman*,"US says Turkish comments on Israel 'troubling'," *Today's Zaman*, 6 February 2013.

70 Gad Lior, "Iraqi goods travel to Turkey via Israel," *Ynet*, April 5, 2013.

71 Yoav Zitun, "Israel sets up 'field hospital' to treat injured Syrians," *Ynet*, 28 March 2013.

Culture&Society

The Future Role of the Chinese Middle Class

Cheng Li and Ryan McElveen

When the Rolex store in the swanky Sanlitun shopping district of Beijing shut its doors earlier this year, sunk by lackluster sales, it was a sign that the government frugality campaign launched in December by the new Chinese Communist Party (CCP) leader Xi Jinping had begun to take effect. Similarly, after Xi described the ideal banquet to consist of "four dishes and a soup," upscale Beijing restaurants in January saw their revenues decline by 35 percent from the previous year. Not only do these instantaneous changes in habit among Beijing's financially well-off upper class reflect the power behind Xi's bully pulpit, but they also point to the irony that has emerged at the highest levels of Chinese policymaking. As China's leaders advocate for increased domestic consumption to stimulate the economy, the luxury goods market has taken a hit as leaders are pushed to avoid ostentation.

These two policy shifts may, on the surface, seem contradictory, but they are part of a larger push to placate a middle class that has emerged as a core constituency with its own unique needs and desires. As China's growth model shifts from an export-based model to a domestic consumption-based model, the middle class, more than any other group, holds the keys to the governance and prosperity of the country. Just as other countries are watching to see how this tran-

Cheng Li is the director of research and senior fellow at the John L. Thornton China Center in the Foreign Policy program at The Brookings Institution. He is also a director of the National Committee on U.S.-China Relations. He is the author of numerous books, including China's Emerging Middle Class. He holds a Ph. D. from Princeton University.

Ryan McElveen is a researcher at The Brookings Institution Thornton China Center. He holds a Master of International Affairs degree from Columbia University.

sition unfolds for geopolitical reasons, companies and banks abroad are also closely observing the rise of the Chinese middle class, knowing that its purchasing power will reshape the global economy. Hampering the transition to consumption-based growth, however, are significant negative feelings among the middle class. The Chinese Ministry of Health revealed in 2011 that the majority of Chinese professionals—51 percent—showed signs of depression.[1] Such widespread depression likely stems from the extreme socioeconomic pressures in Chinese society, including skyrocketing housing prices, environmental degradation, health scares, and official corruption, all of which have tainted the public's confidence in the government and the country's future.

Middle class grievances over government policy have become increasingly evident, partly because the expansion of the middle class has slowed and economic disparity has increased. Disillusionment over the CCP leadership during the past decade is arguably most salient among the members of the middle class who often complain that they, rather than the upper class, have shouldered most of the burden of former President Hu Jintao's harmonious society policies targeting assistance for vulnerable socio-economic groups. The high unemployment rate among recent college graduates, who usually come from middle-class families and are potentially future members of the middle class, should alert the Chinese government.

To express their displeasure, the middle class often turns to organizing "mass incidents" (protests involving more than 100 participants), more than 100,000 of which occur each year according to official estimates.[2] Xi Jinping apparently understands the link between these manifestations of public pessimism and CCP authority, and has sought to make very public—albeit basic—improvements to please the country's middle class.

The current political discourse in China reveals that the government recognizes the importance of addressing the needs of the middle class. After all, the party must do so to survive. As the party turned to the simultaneous implementation of a frugality campaign and policies to increase domestic consumption, the implications were clear: the party has the political will to change and motivate the middle class to become the optimistic consumers they have the potential to become. Indeed, only when middle class consumption reaches its potential and when middle class interest in public health, rule of law, and freedom of speech is institutionally protected will Xi Jinping's "Chinese Dream" of national rejuvenation truly become a reality.

This article presents the distinctive characteristics of the middle class, its multifaceted interests, and its political demands, arguing that the new administration faces a critical balancing act as it seeks to implement a sustainable consumption-based growth model.

The Distinctive Characteristics of the Chinese Middle Class. After years of debate regarding its existence, the Chinese middle class has now emerged as the driving force behind Chinese policy development and is in the process of becoming the largest body of consumers that the world has ever seen. It was not until the late 1980s that the term "middle class" began to appear in academic writings examining the rise of rural industrialists and private urban entrepreneurs. At that time, scholars generally agreed that the "middle class" term was not particularly apt because these groups tended to come from underprivileged and uneducated backgrounds. Over the past decade, however, a notable increase in globalization and urbanization, together with the government's endeavors of enlarging the middle class and promoting China as the world's largest consumer market, has made the term "middle class" increasingly common.

Although the middle class is made up of a complex mosaic of groups and individuals, it can be divided into three major clusters:

(1) An economic cluster that includes private sector entrepreneurs, urban small businesspeople, foreign and domestic joint-venture employees, stock and real estate speculators, and rural industrialists and rich farmers;
(2) A political cluster that includes government officials, office clerks, state sector managers, and lawyers; and
(3) A cultural and educational cluster that includes academics and educators, media personalities, public intellectuals, and think tank scholars.

Based on a definition of the middle class that combines occupation, income, consumption, and innovation, distinguished Chinese sociologist Lu Xueyi noted that in 2009 the middle class constituted 23 percent (243 million) of China's total population, up from 15 percent in 2001.[3] Lu predicts that the Chinese middle class will grow at an annual rate of 1 percent over the next decade or so. In other words, 7.7 million people (of a labor force of 770 million) will join the ranks of the middle class each year.[4] As a result of this consistent growth, members of the middle class will be better able to organize socially and politically, leaving the government with no other choice but to proactively address issues concerning the middle class. Although the past century has seen the rise of middle classes in many countries such as the United States, Great Britain, Spain, and Japan, the meaning of "middle-class nation" tends to translate in demographic and economic terms across borders, while its political and cultural meaning tends to differ by context. Lu holds that the PRC will become a true "middle-class nation" in twenty years when the middle class constitutes 40 percent of the Chinese population, a figure approximately on par with Western countries.[5] According to a study by two analysts at the Brookings Institution, China accounted for only 4 percent of global middle-class spending in 2009 (enough to be the seventh-largest middle-class country in the world) but could become the "largest single middle-class market by 2020, surpassing the United States."[6] Of course, the middle class is not evenly distributed throughout China. By 2009, the middle class already constituted 40 percent of the population in major cities such as Shanghai and Beijing. The proportion of Chinese urban residents is expected to increase by 34.8 percent between 2000 and 2030, the fastest urbanization rate in history, according to economist Hu Angang. By 2030, 71 percent of the Chinese population will live in cities, making up 21 percent of the world's total urban population.[7] Never before has such a huge, concentrated population existed, giving China the opportunity to blaze the trail for sustainable urbanization on a massive scale. In doing so, the economic opportunities for the middle class will be great, as will the costs. While the ability to buy a house, a car, and luxury goods is representative of Western middle class ideals, the potential for such unabashed consumption in a country fac-

like the American Dream (a big car, a big house, and Big Macs for all) then we need another planet."[9] That kind of "Chinese dream," however, is probably not what Xi Jinping has in mind. Xi has defined the "Chinese Dream" primarily as the rejuvenation of the Chinese nation. In the nationalistic sense, this kind of "Chinese Dream" could be interpreted as the revival of a strong China from its noble past, before it was invaded by Western or Japanese outsiders. But

The Chinese government must find the social equilibrium between middle class consumption desires...and ecological security and public health.

ing grave environmental, health, and housing crises has created for China its greatest socio-economic dilemma of 21st century.

The Multi-dimensional Interests of the Chinese Middle Class. With the growth potential of the middle class, the Chinese government will need to balance the need for increased domestic consumption with the harmful effects of such consumption. Although China is a vast territory with many natural resources, those resources will not be plentiful enough to support the needs of the growing population. For example, with 20 percent of the world's population, China only has 7 percent of the world's arable land and 7 percent of the world's water resources, much of which are polluted.[8] As New York Times columnist Thomas Friedman quipped, "[i]f Xi Jinping's dream for China's emerging middle class is just

the "Chinese Dream" could also be interpreted in a more socially-conscious sense: all levels of society banding together to collectively ensure they can live together prosperously while preserving China's finite resources. That idea was first expressed by Hu Jintao, who envisioned an "ecological civilization" balancing the demands of man and earth to realize sustainable development - a critical balance that China has yet to discover. The disparate ways in which the Chinese Dream can be interpreted, however, illuminate the ways in which the middle class could become mobilized, taking either a nationalistic or socially-conscious path. As the Chinese government (much like the middle class) continues to search for sustainable economic growth, it must also find the social equilibrium between middle class consumption desires on the one hand, and ecological security and public health on the other.

Consumption Desires: Hope and Fear. Some trends show the potential for strong future middle class consumption, but many economic hurdles have yet to be surmounted by the middle class. The realm of e-commerce reveals positive trends in consumption. In 2013, for the first time, retail e-commerce sales in China ($286 billion) are predicted to outperform those in the United Sates ($230 billion).[10] Currently, only 40 percent of the population uses the internet, presenting a great opportunity for growth in the online market.[11] However, a major problem with the bottled up consumption desires of the middle class is that investment opportunities other than those in the real estate market are lacking. In terms of reflecting one's social status and wealth in Chinese society, nothing is more important than homeownership—just ask any young man trying to find a wife. Since the housing reform in the late 1990s, housing prices have increased dramatically, especially in urban centers on the eastern coast. According to a study by Joyce Yanyun Man, the Chinese middle class faces a home price-to-income ratio that exceeds international standards, ranging from 5.1 to 6.9, indicating that many urban Chinese face "severely unaffordable" housing. She claims that "without an effective and coherent policy promoting affordable housing and a strong commitment by various levels of government to promote and strengthen a middle class in China, the prospects of a vibrant, stable, and affluent middle class may be less than encouraging."[12] Given how difficult it is to get a small-business loan, the opaque and poorly-regulated nature of the Chinese stock market, and

the general lack of investment opportunities, middle-class savings have flowed heavily into real estate. The nightmare of a bursting property bubble is a real possibility; some regions are dotted with massive but tenantless areas of new construction known as "ghost cities." A study conducted by the Beijing Municipal Security Bureau revealed that there are 3.8 million vacant housing units in the capital alone.[13] As prices have continued to skyrocket, the world has become fearful of a Chinese housing bubble. Specifically, the National Bureau of Statistics pointed out that prices rose in sixty-two out of seventy cities tracked in February 2013 from a year earlier, with prices in Beijing and Guangzhou increasing 5.9 percent and 8.1 percent, respectively.[14] In the midst of rising housing prices, the middle class still maintains the desire, fed by the incursion of foreign retailers, for high-quality goods. In 2009, China surpassed the United States to become the world's leading automobile producer and consumer.[15] In 2012, 19.3 million cars were sold in China, compared to 14.5 million in the United States, and the first two months of 2013 saw a 19.5 percent increase in sales compared to 2012. As for overseas travel, China's middle class is expected to generate $160 billion in spending in 2013, an increase of 34 percent from last year.[17] According to the China Tourism Academy, 200 million Chinese will potentially travel abroad annually by 2020.[18] In addition, while those travelers are overseas, they are likely to purchase luxury goods. On overseas trips in 2012, 48 percent of spending occurred while shopping.[19] At home and abroad, the market for luxury goods will likely only continue to grow, especially if the middle class sees gains in purchasing power. Yet what use is purchasing power if one cannot live long enough to enjoy it? What use is prestigious real estate if one cannot admire the view outside the window? And what use are lavish buffets of food if one cannot trust them to be safe? Until these questions—and fears—about basic Chinese quality of life can be addressed, the middle class will be unable to truly enjoy the fruits of its consumption.

Environmental Protection and Public Health. The best illustration of Chinese middle class fears regarding their health and environment can be found in a March 2013 tweet on Weibo (the Chinese version of Twitter) by Kaifu Lee, a well-known Beijing entrepreneur: "Beijing people say they are the luckiest – they open the window and get a free cigarette. Shanghai people say, 'Oh that's nothing, we turn on the tap and get pork chop soup.'"[20] Of course, the free cigarette refers to Beijing's persistently poor air quality, and the tweet's language is not far from the truth. A study at Tsinghua University has shown that "if the air quality index in the form of PM 2.5 concentration hits three hundred, it would amount to smoking twenty cigarettes a day" - a fate endured by citizens of Beijing, where measurements exceeded three hundred on at least fifteen days in January 2013.[21] The pork chop soup, on the other hand, refers to the more than fifteen thousand dead pigs recovered from Shanghai's Huangpu River in March 2013. The pigs suffered from the porcine circovirus, supposedly causing local farmers in Jiaxing, Zhejiang province to dis-

pose of their bodies in the river. The pig scandal, unfortunately, is only one in a long line of food safety scandals that have ranged from the discovery of the chemical melamine in dairy products in 2008 to the formal acknowledgement by KFC that Chinese suppliers were using high levels of antibiotics in their chickens in late 2012. These scandals have caused the middle class to lose trust in governmental food safety regulation. However, when members of the middle class hear about environmental issues on which they can exert influence, they often react by organizing protests through Weibo. Yang Dongping of Beijing University of Science and Technology believes that China has entered an era during which protests against environmental degradation will become more frequent.[22] These public protests arise due to a number of factors, including social dislocation, political injustice, lack of work safety or job security, inadequacy of consumer rights, and problems of internal migration. On the part of the government, the financial cost of "maintaining social stability" (weiwen), primarily through the police force, has become astonishingly high. The Chinese government budget for national defense in 2012 was 670.3 billion yuan, while the budget for police and public security was 701.8 billion yuan. Like its counterparts elsewhere in the world, the middle class in China needs a clean, healthy environment that will yield healthy food. But as long as the government's desire for social stability outweighs its allowance for uninhibited speech on these and other important issues, the middle class will remain politically cynical.

Increased Political Demands from the Chinese Middle Class. The growth of the middle class has brought with it increasing political power, and CCP leaders have embraced the fact that they need to recognize the important role of the middle class in order to retain power. As economic reforms were implemented in the 1980s and 1990s, Party leadership avoided injecting any sort of class analysis into society. In 2000, a major ideological and policy shift began with CCP Secretary General Jiang Zemin's "theory of the three represents," which called on the CCP to broaden its power base to include entrepreneurs, technocrats, and cultural elites. This was a major break from the Marxist notion that the Communist Party should be the "vanguard of the working class." With the "three represents" serving as a guiding principle of the Sixteenth National Congress of the CCP in 2002, the leadership called for "enlarging the size of the middle-income group."[23] Since then, the middle class has been treated as an asset and political ally with some officials embracing it. However, to a great extent during the past two decades, the CCP has relied on economic development and material incentives to prevent grassroots demand for socio-political challenges. New socio-economic forces, especially entrepreneurs and the middle class, are widely perceived to be political allies of the CCP regime. But this assumption should be subject to greater scrutiny. Just as yesterday's political target could be today's political ally, so too could today's political ally become tomorrow's political rabble-rouser. Recent studies conducted in China have found that the Chinese middle class, more than

other social groups, tends to be cynical about the policy promises made by authorities, more demanding of policy implementation, and more sensitive when it comes to official corruption.[24] If the Chinese middle class begins to feel that the voices of its members are being suppressed, that their access to information is unjustly being blocked, or that their space for social action is being unduly confined, increased political dissent may begin to take shape. At the twelfth National People's Congress in 2013, the government displayed an understanding of the needs of the middle class, pointing to middle class-friendly policies that will be implemented down the road. At the superficial level, Xi Jinping has committed to plainer speech and reduced spending on ceremony, government offices, buildings, and travel. He has also begun to crack down on corruption, prominent examples of which stained Hu Jintao's final year in office. In reaction to the well-publicized scandals over the past few years, the Ministry of Railways will be split into two agencies, with administrative functions being overseen by the Ministry of Transportation and commercial operations being handled by a company. This could be a first step in a crackdown on ever-growing monopolized State Owned Enterprises (SOEs). In addition, in response to food safety concerns, the State Administration of Food and Drugs will be elevated to a general administration, and oversight functions will be centralized. Finally, in an effort to prevent the housing bubble from further expansion, the Chinese government requested that local governments explore limiting home purchases in high-demand areas and ordered the central bank to increase interest rates and down-payment requirements.[25] While such policies might be met with concern from a middle class seeking to invest in property, the policy will protect them in the long run from problematic investments. To promote consumption, the government has pointed to implementing tax cuts for the middle class and providing loans to small-medium-sized enterprises (SMEs) down the road. The government must follow its well-meaning bureaucratic adjustments with policies like these that are friendly to the middle class, addressing and balancing their need for a healthy environment and their desire to consume.

Conclusion. Over the past decade, Chinese leadership has slowly recognized the middle class and its positive influence on China. Recently installed leaders have sought to both co-opt

acknowledges middle-class needs and reminds the middle class that the government considers their needs even if it cannot always act in their best interest. By adopting this kind of communicative approach, China's leadership will remain on the right path to further engage the middle class in political discourse. More importantly, however, the government must commit to putting its words into political action. In creating policy, the government's major challenge will be balancing the increased consumption desires of the middle class with the potentially harmful effects of increased consumption. Finding the sustainable social equilibrium between consumption and a healthy environment will be the Party's ultimate task in the coming years. If the government is unable to balance those desires and needs, the middle class will become imperiled. And even if an increasingly cosmopolitan and informed

The government must commit to putting its words into political action.

the middle class within a "Chinese Dream" narrative and begin addressing concerns of government excess. As the middle class continues to grow, so should the government's political attention toward it. A good example of a government that focuses politically on the middle class is that of the United States. Although there is a much higher degree of middle class self-identification in the United States than in China, the middle class label is effectively inserted into almost every policy speech in a politically advantageous way that

middle class can afford all the air and water purifiers it needs, its members will hardly endure an increasingly polluted and politically unresponsive environment. The Chinese Communist Party would also hardly endure under such conditions. The current balance between frugality and consumption serves as a guiding light for future leadership efforts, revealing a masterful molding of the political environment to the middle-class mindset. Of course, if leaders are effective in employing crowd-pleasing gimmicks like frugality campaigns, they will be the victims of their own success, and the middle class will demand successively deeper institutional reforms. The political road ahead is muddy, and Chinese leaders need to be ready to get their boots dirty.

NOTES

1 Wei Gu, "An Unhappy Middle in the Middle Kingdom," *The Wall Street Journal*, Internet, http://online.wsj.com/article/SB10001424127887323362880 4578345342201524964.html (date accessed: March 2013).

2 2013 Social Development Blue Book, *Chinese Academy of Social Sciences*, 18 December 2012.

3 Lu Xueyi, *Social structure of contemporary China*, Beijing: 2010: 402-06.

4 *China Newsweek*, 11 February 2010.

5 *China Newsweek*, 22 January 2010. Euromonitor International, a London-based research and consulting firm, predicted that China's middle class would reach 700 million in 2020, about 48 percent of the country's total populations, Internet, http://www.euromonitor.com/Chinas_middle_class_reaches_80_million.

6 Homi Kharas and Geoffrey Gertz, "The New Global Middle Class: A Crossover from West to East," in *China's Emerging Middle Class: Beyond Economic Transformation*, Cheng Li, ed. (Washington, DC: Brookings, 2010), 38.

7 Hu Angang, *China in 2020: A New Type of Superpower* (Washington, DC: Brookings, 2011), 62.

8 "Arable land decreases to 102.4mln hectares," Internet, http://www.gov.cn/english/2005-10/24/content_82778.htm (accessed 9 April 2013); "Will China run out of water by 2030?", Internet, http://www.china.org.cn/opinion/2012-11/30/content_27272141.htm (date accessed: 9 April 2013).

9 Thomas Friedman, "China Needs its own Dream," *New York Times*, Internet, http://www.nytimes.com/2012/10/03/opinion/friedman-china-needs-its-own-dream.html (date accessed: 18 March 2013).

10 Alibaba, "China's Internet is a Giant Shopping Mall," Internet, http://www.alibaba.com/activities/ibdm/china_online_consumer_infographic.html (date accessed: 14 March 2013).

11 Ibid.

12 Joyce Yanyun Man, "China's Housing Reform and Emerging Middle Class," in *China's Emerging Middle Class: Beyond Economic Transformation*, Cheng Li, ed. (Washington, DC: Brookings, 2010), 189-191. Price-to-income ratio (PIR) is the method used to calculate the ratio of a house's value to household income, determining the affordability for housing in a given area. A PIR equal or greater than 5.1 indicates housing as "severely unaffordable." This data was compiled by the Global Urban Observatory of UN-HABITAT.

13 Jia Lynn Yang, "As China's Growth Lags, Fears of a Popping Sound," *Washington Post*, 3 October 2012.

14 Bonnie Cao, "China's Home Prices Up in Most Cities, Posing Policy Challenge," *Bloomberg News*, Internet, http://www.bloomberg.com/news/2013-03-18/china-home-prices-rise-in-most-cities-posing-policy-challenge.html (date accessed: 18 March 2013).

15 Zhang Xue, "Domestic Auto Sector Undergoes Structural Adjustments," *Economic Daily*, 9 February 2010.

16 "China's auto sales up 19.5 percent in Jan-Feb," *Associated Press*, 11 March 2013.

17 "Outbound travel flying high," *Financial Times: China Confidential*, Internet, http://www.ftchinaconfidential.com/outbound2013 (date accessed: 18 March 2013).

18 China Tourism Academy, "China Tourism Review 2012 Published," Internet, http://eng.ctaweb.org/html/2012-11/2012-11-7-17-40-50787.html (date accessed: 18 March 2013).

19 "Outbound travel flying high" *Financial Times: China Confidential*, Internet, http://www.ftchinaconfidential.com/outbound2013 (date accessed: 18 March 2013).

20 Lee, Kaifu (KaifuLee), 12 March 2013. Weibo Tweet.

21 Atsushi Okudera, "Survey: Breathing Bad Air in Beijing Like Smoking 21 Cigarettes," *Asahi Shimbun*, Internet, http://ajw.asahi.com/article/behind_news/social_affairs/AJ201302030021 (date accessed: 18 March 2013).

22 Yang Dongping, ed., *Zhongguo huanjing fazhan baogao 2010* [Report on China's environmental development 2010] (Beijing: Shehuikexue wenxian chubanshe, 2010).

23 *Nanfang ribao* [Southern daily], 26 February 2000, p. 1. For more discussion of the background of Jiang's ideological innovation, the "three represents," see Cheng Li, "China in 2000: A Year of Strategic Rethinking," in Asian Survey 41, no. 1 (2001): 71-90.

24 "China's new leadership confronts many challenges: Voices of the middle class," *Global Time*, 13 March 2013, Internet, http://news.qq.com/a/20130313/000254.htm (date accessed: 18 March 2013).

25 Bonnie Cao, "China's Home Prices Up in Most Cities, Posing Policy Challenge," *Bloomberg News*, Internet, http://www.bloomberg.com/news/2013-03-18/china-home-prices-rise-in-most-cities-posing-policy-challenge.html (date accessed: 18 March 2013).

Georgetown Journal

of International Affairs

religion & power to...

Espionage Exposed

- - - *tackling the issues that shape our world* - -

CALL FOR PAPERS

The *Georgetown Journal of International Affairs* is accepting submissions for the Winter/Spring 2014 issue. The submission deadline is 15 August 2013. Articles must be about 3,000 words in length. They should have the intellectual vigor to meet the highest scholarly standard, but should be written with the clarity to attract a broad audience. For submission details please refer to our website: http://journal.georgetown.edu/submissions/

Dis-United Kingdoms?
What Lies Behind Scotland's Referendum on Independence

Roger Mason

On 18 September 2014, the people of Scotland will decide whether to remain within the United Kingdom or to secede from a 400-year-long union with England and form an independent state. It is harder to predict the outcome of the referendum than it is to explain what lies behind it. Before examining its immediate context, therefore, this article surveys the history of Anglo-Scottish relations and reveals some of the historical tensions which have led to the most significant constitutional crisis that the UK has faced since the creation of the Republic of Ireland in 1922.

Borrowing from the Canadian Prime Minister Pierre Trudeau's memorable description of his country's relationship with the United States, Scots often describe their country's relations with England as like sleeping with an elephant.[1] For Scotland, as for Canada, occupying the same bed as a much larger partner is a challenging experience. The size of that challenge can be illustrated demographically: England has a population ten times larger than Scotland's. More precisely, of the total population of the United Kingdom, 83.9 percent (53 million) live in England and 8.4 percent (5.3 million) in Scotland, the rest living in Wales 4.8 percent (3 million) and Northern Ireland 2.9 percent (2 million). In terms of population, England dwarfs all three of its smaller partners put together.[2]

Roger Mason is Professor of Scottish History at the University of St Andrews and Director of the St Andrews Institute of Scottish Historical Research. Professor Mason is general editor of the New Edinburgh History of Scotland, published by Edinburgh University Press. His main publications include *Scots and Britons: Scottish Political Thought and the Union of 1603*; *Kingship and the Commonweal: Political Thought in Renaissance and Reformation Scotland*; and *George Buchanan: Political Thought in Early Modern Britain and Europe*.

To add to the discomfort, the bed these countries occupy is decidedly cramped. Britain and Ireland, Europe's off-shore islands, are relatively small, and since 1922 the United Kingdom has been comprised only of mainland Britain and the six counties of Northern Ireland. The troubled history of England's involvement in Ireland is significant here only in so far as it reflects the elephant's failure to impose its will on its surrounding territories. England's repeated attempts at conquest and colonization of Ireland began in the twelfth century and were renewed and given a vicious confessional twist following the protestant Reformation in the sixteenth century. Yet they were never wholly successful, and England's Irish 'problem,' and the bitter legacy it bequeathed, has never gone away.

Scotland's relations with England are similarly rooted in a long and troubled history, but critically the Scots never suffered conquest and colonization. On the contrary, it is precisely Scotland's past independence, and the negotiated nature of its union with England, that lie behind the referendum with which Scots will answer the simple question:

ment and ostensibly a new state called the United Kingdom of Great Britain. Put in contrasting nationalist terms, a yes vote will result in Scotland re-emerging as the fully-fledged nation-state it was before the union of 1603.

Before considering what has triggered the referendum, therefore, we need to set Anglo-Scottish relations, and the unions of 1603 and 1707, in longer historical perspective. This means beginning with what the Scots call their Wars of Independence, fought against an aggressive English monarchy from the 1290s until the 1320s, and vindicating the Scottish kingdom's right to the independent existence that contemporary nationalists are intent on reasserting. For all its historical inaccuracies, and they are legion and egregious, Mel Gibson's movie *Braveheart* (1995) captured for a modern audience the compelling romance of a small nation's struggle for freedom when confronted by the bullying imperialism of a larger one.[3] The reality was no doubt very different. Yet the central truth remains that the hegemony over the British Isles to which England aspired in the middle ages proved elusive.

Critically the Scots never suffered conquest and colonization.

Should Scotland be an independent country? If they vote yes, it will bring to an end a union that has lasted since 1603, when a Scottish king happened also to inherit the English throne, and which was made more complete a century later, when the 1707 Treaty of Union did away with a separate Scottish parliament and created a new parlia-

As a result, and crucially for current developments, Scotland emerged as an independent kingdom ruled over by its own royal dynasty and possessing its own political and legal system, its own religious and secular culture, and its own commercial and diplomatic relations with the outside world. In origin, the Scots were Gaels, but the late medieval kingdom was made up of a variety of ethnic and linguistic groups, and increasingly the dominant language was Scots, a variant of English that was maturing into a language in its own right. By the early 1500s, Scotland had developed the full range of markers of nationhood, and was recognized as a small but distinct state on the international stage, usually allied with France against its threatening English neighbor.

Small states were as vulnerable to super power rivalry in the past as they are in the present, and the most serious threat to Scotland's survival in the sixteenth century stemmed from England's hostile relations with France and Spain. Initially, the Scottish kingdom benefitted from this rivalry, and from the religious schism - the Protestant Reformation - that rapidly became inseparable from it. However, the reign of Mary Stuart proved a critical turning-point that witnessed the overturn of Scotland's traditional loyalty to France and the Papacy in favor of an enduring alliance with Protestant England. Mary's marital exploits (three weddings and a surfeit of funerals) are now the stuff of romance, but they triggered a series of religious and political revolutions that resulted not just in her captivity and execution in England, but more significantly in the birth of an heir to her Scottish kingdom James VI who by 1603 was also the only viable successor to Elizabeth Tudor's English throne.

This union of the Scottish and English crowns was hardly planned, but it had been anticipated. Indeed, the idea of a dynastic union was long-standing, promoted even by Scots, provided it was based on parity of status and es-

teem rather than assumptions of English superiority. Moreover, the potential benefits of union - the peace dividend for both countries - were now supplemented by a compelling religious imperative: the idea of creating a Protestant island, safe from the corrupting influence of continental Catholicism. After 1603, James VI of Scotland and I of England exploited this Protestant British rhetoric to promote a much closer Anglo-Scottish union, a union not just of language and culture, but of laws, religious practices, and governments. But his arguments fell on deaf ears. In England, his accession to the throne was accepted grudgingly as the only alternative to civil war and served to strengthen the traditional hostility that the English felt towards the Scots. In Scotland, closer union was seen as tantamount to absorption into a greater England, a loss of the country's historic identity that has proved a sticking point from that day to this.

In fact, what resulted from 1603 was a multiple British monarchy that bears comparison to the modern devolved British state: a situation in which the constituent kingdoms of Scotland and England (and, in different ways, Ireland too) were highly self-governing, though sovereignty lay ultimately with the crown. This was not unusual in early modern Europe - the Spanish monarchy was made up of a still larger array of semi-autonomous units - but the British case was perhaps notable for its asymmetry: the population ratio in the seventeenth century was more like five to one than ten to one, but it was still sufficient to ensure that the Scottish tail was not allowed to wag the English dog, not least when the ruling dynasty was based in London rather than Edinburgh. Moreover, although arguments for closer union were often couched in Protestant terms, it quickly became clear that Scots and English were as much divided as they were united by a common faith. It was attempts to impose on Scotland what were perceived as English forms of worship, and English norms of church government (bishops), that sparked the revolution against the authoritarianism of Charles I, plunging all three of his kingdoms into turmoil and leading to his execution at the hands of Oliver Cromwell in 1649.

Compared to today, what is striking about these events is that, however strained their relations with England became, the Scots never considered simply dissolving the union. The Scottish response to the English regicide was immediately to proclaim Charles II king of Great Britain and Ireland, a step that gave Cromwell no choice but to incorporate Scotland into an enlarged English republic by military force. If the Scots avoided the bloodbath that Cromwell inflicted on Ireland (they were at least Protestants, albeit of a dubious Presbyterian kind), they were nevertheless subject to English rule in a wholly unprecedented and repressive way. Yet still, acutely uncomfortable though the experience of living with the elephant had become, the Scots persisted in attempts to make union under the restored Stuart monarchy a workable partnership.

They were increasingly up against it. Never a particularly rich country, Scotland was by 1700 struggling economically. The rise of commercial empires, French, Spanish, Dutch, and English, all based on mercantilist principles, was gradually squeezing the life out of the Scottish economy. Still worse, the London-based government both excluded the Scots from England's colonial markets in the Americas and pursued foreign policies that disrupted Scotland's commercial relations with its traditional trading partners. The Scots may have hoped that acquiescence in the Revolution of 1688-1690 - the overthrow of the main Stuart line for their overt Catholicism - would pay economic as well as religious and political dividends. If so, they were sorely disappointed. The new king, William of Orange, and his successor Anne, plunged their British kingdoms into a series of wars from which Scotland gained nothing at all. The 'Glorious Revolution' secured for Scotland a free parliament and recognition of its distinctive Presbyterian church, but it worsened its economic woes.

These factors are critical to the parliamentary union of 1707. Against a backdrop of war with France, the English parliament passed an act designed to resolve future disputes over the royal succession by naming the House of Hanover as heirs to the childless Queen Anne. In doing so, it was simply assumed that the Scottish parliament would follow suit and recognize the Hanoverians as the future monarchs of both Scotland and England. The Scots, however, chose to use the issue as leverage to ensure that their economic and political grievances were addressed. Out of the grubby political wrangling that ensued emerged a Treaty of Union that, enshrining the Hanoverian succession, also nullified the Scottish parliament as a source of future political dissent by closing it down altogether, while appeasing Scottish economic grievances by allowing access to England's colonial markets.

Robert Burns, Scotland's national bard, subsequently described the Scottish political elite who negotiated the union as having been "bought and sold for English gold," and this has fed modern nationalist views of the union as a sell-out by a self-interested aristocracy.[4] But this is only a partial truth. Money certainly did change hands, and the political elite certainly did benefit disproportionately from the deal. Yet it is hard to see what alternatives were available given the London government's determination to have its way. In fact, so desperate was the government that, provided Scotland was politically and diplomatically neutered, it was pre-

ligious culture that still exists today.

The union of 1707 thus exposed - but signally failed to resolve - the paradox that had bedeviled Anglo-Scottish relations since 1603 and has continued to dog them ever since. Namely, despite Scottish protestations to the contrary, the union was not, and is not, a union of equals. It is as misleading to believe that the union was a treaty negotiated between two sovereign states as it is to pretend that the new parliament of the United Kingdom of Great Britain was anything other than an enlarged English one - a parliament that has subsequently ridden roughshod over almost every article enshrined in the Treaty. For some Scots the Treaty of Union is fundamental British constitutional law; but in England it has no status beyond that of an act of parliament, and, as

Whatever the result, the fact that [the referendum] is being held at all indicates how markedly attitudes toward the union have changed.

pared to make wholesale concessions to Scottish interests to seal the deal as quickly as possible. Crucially, therefore, the settlement allowed for the survival of key institutions which ensured that Scotland's distinct identity within the union remained intact. The Scottish parliament was gone, and with it the illusion of sovereignty (in reality it had followed the Stuart monarchy to London in 1603), but in its separate Presbyterian church, its own laws and legal institutions, and its own schools and universities, Scotland retained the foundations of the distinct civil and re-

such, may be overridden at parliament's will. In so far as sovereignty lies with parliament, how else could it be?

The modern Scottish answer is that sovereignty lies with the people - and it is the people who are being asked to exercise that sovereignty, and their right to self-determination, in next year's referendum. Whatever the result, the fact that it is being held at all indicates how markedly attitudes to the union have changed. The Scots did not immediately reap the promised economic rewards of the union of 1707, but gradually they carved out a lucrative niche in England's expanding commercial empire just as they recovered their self-esteem as Scots. In fact, the British Empire turned into a disproportionately Scottish project, and one from which Scotland benefitted immeasurably. So long as commerce and industry continued to thrive, Scots were generally content with their dual Scottish and British identities: both unionist and nationalist, they could have their cake and eat it too.

But commerce and industry now no longer thrive and, in post-industrial, post-colonial Britain, the constitutional fault-lines disguised for so long by imperial prosperity have come irresistibly to the fore. Recent decades have witnessed three key developments. First, the collapse of the established UK political parties in Scotland: the Conservatives' Scottish support was destroyed by Thatcherite condescension and insensitivity, while the 'New' Labour party that initially gained from the Tories' demise turned out to be ideologically indistinguishable from their conservative opponents and gradually discredited themselves in the eyes of both Scots and English voters. Second, parallel to these developments, the Scottish National Party (SNP) transformed itself from an irrelevant sideshow feeding off Scottish nostalgia into an effective political force that used the discovery of vast oil reserves in the North Sea to argue that an independent Scotland was economically sustainable for decades to come. Third, in response to the challenge posed by the SNP, and the rising tide of support for a greater degree of Scottish self-government, it was agreed to establish a representative assembly in Scotland (and others in Wales and

Northern Ireland) that wielded such powers as the UK Parliament deigned to devolve to it.

The Scottish Parliament first met in 1999 (the SNP prefer to say it was reconvened after a lapse of 300 years) and at first it seemed that it would work as Labour had envisaged, delivering them into power at regular electoral intervals. Yet so discredited had Labour become in Scotland, and so ineffective were the other unionist parties, that the SNP found themselves in a position to form a minority government after the election of 2007 and, having shown themselves to be competent in government, swept to a landslide victory in 2011 that gave them a sizable overall majority. A referendum on independence was central to their election manifesto and the UK government would have been hard put to stand in the way of what the SNP declared to be the Scots' right to national self-determination. By the terms of the Edinburgh Agreement of November 2012, the UK government (the coalition of Conservatives and Liberal Democrats led by David Cameron) and the Scottish government (the SNP led by Alex Salmond) agreed to a referendum and to respect the will of the people as expressed in a simple majority vote.

This is a long way from the force majeure of 1707. Moreover, the SNP have performed a remarkable feat, not only monopolizing the left-of-center political space left vacant by the rightward lurch of the UK parties, but also spinning a seductive narrative that embeds their social democratic values in the very fabric of Scottish history. Scotland, we are assured, is and always has been less hierarchical and deferential, more caring and communitarian, more egalitarian and populist than England, while the new Scottish Parliament is said to be the 'people's parliament,' founded, not on the reactionary English doctrine of parliamentary sovereignty, but on the progressive Scottish principle of popular sovereignty. In the process, it has exposed the strange anomalies of a ramshackle British constitution that, for example, prevents MPs elected to Westminster from Scottish constituencies through that the SNP needs to win the referendum.[5] On the other hand, the unionist parties, fighting under the 'Better Together' banner, have no grounds for complacency. The status quo - a flat-lining economy with austerity piled on austerity - makes it hard to project an attractive image of a prosperous British future. In contrast, the SNP's pitch is based on imagining the rosy future that will open up if only they have full control of Scotland's economy (includ-

The SNP answer to these constitutional conundrums is simple: independence.

from deliberating on matters of health and education relating to their own constituents (matters now devolved to the Scottish Parliament), but does allow them to vote on the same matters in relation to England. This absurd situation might be resolved by some form of federal constitution that formally separated an English Parliament from a UK one. Yet here again we are confronted by the UK's asymmetrical political geography. How can you make federalism work in a multi-national state so obviously dominated by one of its constituent parts?

The SNP answer to these constitutional conundrums is simple: independence. Yet they have still to convince a canny Scottish electorate of this. Polling data consistently show support for independence at around 30 to 35 percent and so far there is no sign of the break-

ing its oil revenues) and are able fully to develop the social democratic program that has thus far kept them in power. That program will be expensive, and its sustainability is debatable even at present levels in an independent Scotland. One can of course point to successful Scandinavian models, but when the price is a 60 percent personal tax rate, it is not an easy sell. Meanwhile, the unionists emphasize just how messy divorce will be: What about NATO and defense? What about the European Union? What about the Queen?

Ultimately, the complications as well as the cost of dissolving the union may make living with the elephant more attractive than living next door to it. But if a week is a long time in politics, fifteen months is an eternity. Scotland's future, and that of the UK, still hang in the balance.

NOTES

1 Pierre Trudeau, speech to the Washington Press Club, 25 March 1969: 'Living next to you is in some ways like sleeping with an elephant. No matter how friendly and even-tempered is the beast, if I can call it that, one is affected by every twitch and grunt' Internet, http://www.cbc.ca/player/Digital+Archives/Politics/Prime+Ministers/ID/1801879425/?page=12&sort=MostRecent (date accessed: 15 May 2013).

2 UK Office of National Statistics, "2011 Census: Population and Household Estimates for the United Kingdom," March 2011, Internet, http://www.ons.gov.uk/ons/rel/census/2011-census/ (date accessed: 15 May 2013).

3 *Braveheart*, Dir. Mel Gibson, Paramount Pictures and Twentieth Century Fox: 1995. Film.

4 Robert Burns in his poem, "A Parcel of Rogues in a Nation," 1791, Internet, http://www.bbc.co.uk/arts/robertburns/works/such_a_parcel_of_rogues_in_a_nation/ (date accessed: 15 May 2013).

5 See the data compiled by organizations such as: Ipsos MORI, http://www.ipsos-mori.com; and UK Polling Report, Internet, http://ukpollingreport.co.uk/scottish-independence (date accessed: 15 May 2013).

La Policía Comunitaria: Self-Defense Groups in Mexico
The Aftermath of a Poorly Designed Policy

Mauricio Merino and Jaime Hernández Colorado

On 4 January 2013, in the Mexican state of Guerrero, armed men calling themselves the "Ayutla de Los Libres Community Police Force" took self-defense into their own hands, sensing the inability of their government security forces to crack down on the violence of organized crime. In a total of nine states, the press has since documented additional community self-defense groups that have risen in response to the insecurity in Mexico, subsequently posing a challenge to the new government. This article examines the formation of community self-defense groups in light of the failures of the security policy implemented during the Felipe Calderón administration. This security policy resulted in the fragmentation of organized crime cartels and an increase in violence triggered by the diversification of criminal activities, leaving a trail of death, corruption, and human rights violations.[1] The rise of these self-defense groups lends credit to the idea that vigilantes themselves can serve as an antidote to insecurity, particularly in rural communities.

Across Mexico, groups seeking justice by their own hands have experienced widespread legitimacy, as exemplified by Javier Sicilia, who led the Movement for Peace with Justice and Dignity and demanded justice for the victims of Calderón's security policy; and Isabel Miranda, who became a Mex-

Mauricio Merino is a professor and researcher at Centro de Investigación y Docencia Económicas (CIDE) in Mexico City. His most recent book is *El Futuro que no Tuvimos. Crónica del Desencanto Democrático en México* (Editorial Planeta, 2012).

Jaime Hernández Colorado holds a BA in Political Science and Public Administration from El Colegio de México. He has published reviews in *Foro Internacional, Historia Mexicana, Estudios Sociológicos* and *Gestión y Política Pública*. His main interests are Federalism and Local Government.

ico City government PAN candidate in the 2012 elections after singlehandedly seeking and delivering her son's kidnappers to the authorities. These are just two cases of civilians who were victimized by organized crime and who therefore had to use every means necessary to mobilize society, highlighting the ineffective Mexican police force and the nation's judicial system. The leitmotif of urban social movements seeking for justice is not the same as that of the community police - but both are seeking justice and security because official security agencies have failed. Community self-defense groups are security corps composed by citizens working in their specific regions according to traditional rules and often recovering indigenous customs. These groups base their efforts upon civil society participation, solidarity, and other values that survive in rural Mexico, such as family relations, friendship, and social trust among the inhabitants of a town or region. It is important to state that these values as the basis of self-defense groups remain because members of these groups are members of the community too. The expansion of community groups is both old and new - these groups integrate romantic notions of justice with the more modern conception that society must participate in the fight against organized crime.[2] These two opposing dimensions are harmonized in the wake of an ineffective security policy, forcing society to reach beyond public protest so as to organize community police groups.

The Mexican State and Felipe Calderón's security policy. Calderón's security strategy exemplifies pub-

lic policy resulting from a circumstantial problem, without a causal basis or rigorous analysis of the circumstances.[3] This policy, designed after the increase in violence in Michoacán and Baja California in 2007, subsequently spread during Felipe Calderón's administration. The use of greater physical force available to the State was thought to be essential to counteracting organized crime.

Under the name "Operation Safe," this policy of violent confrontation based on military deployment was extended to seven states in just two years as the Calderón administration's main strategy for public safety, but killings in those states increased by 325 percent between 2007 and 2009.[4] Eduardo Guerrero notes that the rapid failure of the security policy was predictable: "the surprise element had disappeared and organizations were prepared to respond to the government's offensive. The authorities' capacity for response decreased as the focuses of attention multiplied."[5] Criminal groups adapted to their environments and mutated the nature of their crimes, limiting the response capacity of security agencies. As Guerrero argues, criminal groups were fragmented and their criminal activities multiplied. He argues that cartels now work in a decentralized manner with autonomous regional leaders. The fragmentation of criminal groups and the extinction of the 'big leaders' have therefore only triggered further violence.[6]

Although this policy was designed to recover the monopoly of physical violence by attempting to neutralize criminals through the State's physical force, its continued implementation was never accompanied by an objective assessment of the actual conditions of the security agencies, of the ability of the organized crime networks to adapt to circumstances, or of the societal effects of State-condoned violence. Later, in areas disturbed by violence, these effects manifested as changes in social behavior - such as mass hysteria in response to alleged shootings, self-imposed curfews, and the perception that violence had become an undeniable part of everyday life. Calderon's government fought violence with more violence, without analyzing either the variables its own decisions had altered or the subsequent substantive restrictions that would prevent its long-term success: the unpreparedness of local police, their infiltration by criminal groups, the flaws in the enforcement and administration of justice, and the ability of organized crime to adapt to new conditions.

To illustrate the significance of these variables, it is worth reviewing some data. At the end of Calderón's government, the Interior Ministry admitted that only 25 percent of the members of state and municipal security forces were properly qualified and only a quarter of police personnel had passed the trust controls.[8] The 2011 Institutional Survey on Public Safety (EISP) noted that three out of every ten public security institution employees had never undergone a polygraph test, while public safety personnel reported that they had never been comprehensively assessed by the "Skills Evaluations of Public Security Personnel."[9] The 2011 EISP revealed that even members of the police corps regarded municipal and state traffic police, federal police, and federal minis-

terial police as the most corrupt corps overall.[10]

During the Calderón administration, these diagnoses were regarded as confirmation that in the "War on Organized Crime," only the army and navy could be trusted, regardless of the effects of this strategy on Mexico's municipalities - particularly in traditional rural communities. The data proved that state and municipal security institutions were not only unable to fulfill their duties, but were also vulnerable to organized crime themselves, since a third of the population surveyed regarded their work as "jobs with no room for growth."[11]

It is important to state that "jobs with no room for growth" means those security employees will not have important wage increases in their whole working life and that there is not a consolidated civil service to improve policemen's career opportunities. Thus, organized crime could be an opportunity to earn extra money in a country where minimum daily wage is about 5.3 USD and the national average salary for state policemen is about 672 USD.[12]

Moreover, Calderón's policy fragmented the major criminal groups, which increased from six in 2006 to twelve in 2010, changing the nature of crimes committed from drug trafficking to abduction and extortion in a very short time, and increasing the turf wars between the new organized groups to control zones and illicit businesses.[13] The rate of homicides committed in 2008-2009 was 75.43 percent higher than it was in 2006-2007.[14] By the end of the Calderón administration, it was still impossible to calculate the exact number of fatalities or missing persons reported during his presidency.[15]

Illegal violence, which the government counteracted with legitimate state violence, led to a spiral of tragic effects and the perception that the State had actually enabled corruption, co-optation, and injustice to victims. According to Latinobarómetro measurements, this period witnessed the consolidation of low levels of trust in the State's security strategy.[16] Security agencies have fallen into this spiral of discredit, while citizens' confidence in the country's military forces has failed to increase.[17]

During these six years, several groups in society reacted against the Calderón government's strategy and, in several cases, those who took justice into their own hands or demanded it through social mobilization were socially rewarded. No one could predict, however, that the message generated by urban and modern citizens would result in the recovery and multiplication of traditionally legitimate community self-defense practices. The security policy of the Calderón government produced a maelstrom of violence; a growing lack of confidence in the State's ability to confront it; and a new social awareness of the need to react to the fragmentation, diversification, and impunity of organized crime by using one's own resources.

Self-defense groups. Self-defense groups emerged in tandem with the failures of the Calderón administration's security strategy. While attempting to win the war on organized crime, the State lost its ability to protect its citizens. Since the essence of community police is to ensure safety where other authorities have failed to do so,

Self defense groups represent a social response to the failures of the State security agency in ensuring peace and order.

self-defense groups represent a social response to the failures of the State security agency in ensuring peace and order in their communities.

The self-defense groups that have appeared are not the result of a single situation. Instead, they can be understood as a social response to the tragic consequences of the policy adopted to date, or as an adaptation by criminal groups to the new political conditions of the State. The armed social group that took Ayutla de los Libres in January 2013 declared that they "[would] continue their efforts until peace [was] restored in the municipality, because they [were] tired of the government doing nothing."[18] The same arguments have been wielded by the community police of Florencio Villarreal, as well as in the state of Guerrero, and also by the rest of the vigilante groups that have emerged to date. The most recent community police group took up arms on 14 March 2013 in Tlalixcoyan (Veracruz),[19] increasing the number of states experiencing this phenomenon to nine.[20]

Strictly speaking, self-defense groups are in essence not new to Mexico. There is a long tradition of community police related primarily to indigenous communities who selected their authorities on the basis of "uses and customs."[21] The very specific geographical features of nine states with community polices are important, because they all have diverse regional traditions, including indigenous customs. Furthermore, states like Guerrero, Michoacán, or Veracruz have very different topographic (mountainous) conditions within them that makes it difficult to ensure law and order. In addition, the nine states mentioned have many municipalities and huge disparities between them. For instance, Oaxaca has 570 municipalities, Veracruz has 212, Estado de México has 125, Michoacán has 113, and Guerrero has 81. The country has in total 2,440 municipalities.

It behooves us to note some similarities between Mexican community police and Peruvian "Rondas Campesinas." One significant converging points is the question of origin. Both corps have emerged as social responses to the inability of national security agencies to ensure peace in some - especially rural - regions. However, as we argue above, Mexican community police has features very specific to regional history, indigenous customs, and traditional political behavior. So, because of their circumstances, self-defense groups in Mexico should be considered a unique phenomenon.

Let us choose Guerrero to serve as an example. According to ancient tradition in this state, indigenous communities assert their own authorities. Traditional authorities organized life in their jurisdictions, intending primarily to ensure peace in their own communities.[22]

Community police operate within the framework of traditional authorities. We can trace their emergence back to the unsafe conditions in rural areas of Guerrero. Community police were thus the product of social organizational processes. Community police in Guerrero resulted from insecurity issues that these towns had never experienced before. Authorities that once focused on the proper functioning of their communities now needed to establish police corps.[23]

In order to organize the community police force, the "uses and customs" authorities relied on groups of agricultural

Self defense groups in Mexico should be considered a unique phenomenon.

producers and the Catholic Church. In 1995, organizations such as the Council of Indigenous Authorities, the Guerrero Council 500 Years of Resistance (CG-500), and the Regional Union of Ejidos and Communities formally created bodies of community police at a community assembly. At that meeting, none of the invited state authorities attended - nor had they attended any of the previous meetings. This grievance sparked the creation of community police grouped under the Regional Coordinator of Community Authorities (CRAC).[24]

Traditional community police corps worked with such existing authorities as judges to tackle major security problems in the 1990s. As the security situation within the country and the state of Guerrero was changing, however, community police corps were faced with other types of crime caused by criminal organizations.[25]

Modernizing this tradition is the body of community police who have updated their strategy and used previous institutional experience to redirect their actions, thus protecting the population from highly-structured crime organizations - a change since the 1990s, when community police dealt with

tal of the municipality. This group has also garnered significant social support, a key element in this analysis.[26]

The emergence of vigilante groups is linked to recent violence. This link becomes obvious when one compares the list of states with self-defense groups to the increase in homicide rate per 100,000 inhabitants. In Guerrero, self-defense groups have been created in twenty-two municipalities, where the homicide rate per 100,000 inhabitants for the period of 2008-2009 witnessed a 93.57 percent growth since the period of

The community police groups that emerged in 2012 can be seen as a traditional response to the crisis of violence in 2008-2009.

crimes committed largely by local offenders rather than criminal organizations. Recently established community police have followed the example of previous police corps, indicating a desire to recreate conditions of times past to restore peace in their communities. Notable features include their particular form of organization. Guerrero police corps, based on former community police organizations called coordinadoras, therefore derive a sense of institutional coherence and centrality to their actions.

We can observe a shift in how community police interpret the tradition of the past in the example of the Ayutla de los Libres group, which has always existed in the mountainous area of the municipality. They have now demonstrated a dramatic change of behavior by recently edging into the urban capi-

2006-2007.[29] Guerrero also has a strong tradition of self-defense dating back to the 1980s, as related to the problems of rural security at the time.[28] Therefore, the community police groups that emerged in 2012 can be seen as a traditional response to the crisis of violence in 2008-2009.

In Veracruz, the homicide rate per 100,000 inhabitants increased by 45.45 percent in 2008-2009 compared to 2006-2007.[29] This change is reflected in the creation of self-defense groups in three municipalities within that state alone. They are all systematically registered in the lists of municipalities most severely affected by criminal organizations.

Within Tierra Caliente, the municipality of Cherán, Michoacán - one of the areas that was most affected by violence - community police have replaced their municipality police, stressing that "community rounds" are "a self-defense movement that includes the whole town."[30]

The state and federal governments' response to these groups has been ambiguous. In Guerrero, the state government has offered material support.[31] In Veracruz, the state government has repeatedly denied their existence.[32] In Michoacán, the state government negotiated the release of twenty-one detainees with the community police of Buenavista Tomatlán. The community police agreed to hand them over, but only on condition that they would be taken into custody by the federal authority (the Attorney General's Office) rather than by the Michoacán security agencies.[33]

The response of state and federal governments to this phenomenon is a long way from reflecting the design of a new security strategy for the country. The complexity of the phenomenon is compounded by the fact that the Mexican Constitution enshrines respect for the traditional rights of indigenous peoples, while the nine states with self-defense groups also have local laws protecting the rights of indigenous communities to have their own authorities. It is important to note, however, that not all members of the community police are indigenous people. The composition of community police has been pluralistic in terms of ethnicity and class.[34] Thus, the response to these recently armed social groups should include a careful interpretation of these laws, and the freedom they grant citizens to organize and operate outside government intervention. Still, no one should rule out the fact that community police could also be a new form of local action by organized crime operating within their circumstances.

Conclusion. The rise of self-defense groups in Mexico reflects the need to redefine the security strategy adopted by the government over the past six years. Having originated in a climate of Calderón policy failures, the impotence of local police, and the deteriorating image of the armed forces, these community police forces have garnered significant social legitimacy along the way. These groups represent the natural exhaustion of a nation whose Army has engaged in police work totally outside of its jurisdiction since the Calderón administration began. The rise of self-defense groups reflects not only these failures, but also the increasing possibility that criminal organizations could permanently entrench violence in a social phenomenon much larger than themselves. This is compounded by the difficulty of distinguishing between cases where aggrieved communities are genuinely responding to the criminal groups that threaten them, and others where criminal organizations themselves occupy these territories under the guise of self-defense.

The response of the state and federal governments to this phenomenon - and especially their method of treatment - will determine the future course of violence in Mexico. We now face the imminent spread of social violence throughout the country, violence which not only pits criminals against the State, but also witnesses the emergence of self-defense groups. Given the lack of clarity regarding the outcome of this issue, we can only presume that some

Hobbesian state of nature is knocking | at our door.

NOTES

1 Eduardo Guerrero, "La estrategia fallida," Nexos, Internet, http://www.nexos.com.mx (date accessed: 14 March 2013).

2 Self-defense groups in Mexico are known as "community police."

3 Luis F. Aguilar, "Estudio introductorio" in *La implementación de las políticas*, Luis F. Aguilar Villanueva, ed. (México: Miguel Ángel Porrúa, 1993), 15-17.

4 Baja California, Guerrero, Nuevo León, Tamaulipas, Chihuahua, Durango and Sinaloa. Eduardo Guerrero, "La estrategia fallida," 2012.

5 Ibid.

6 Ibid.

7 Max Weber, Economía y Sociedad (México: FCE, 2012), 1056.

8 Verónica Macías, "Sólo uno de cada cinco policías pasan examen de confianza," *El Economista*, http://www.eleconomista.com.mx (date accessed: 14 March 2013).

9 The Institutional Survey on Public Safety is a measuring instrument conducted by Executive Secretariat of the National System of Public Security. The 2011 EISP was drawn up on the basis of the information received from 30 states. Veracruz and San Luis Potosí did not communicate their results of the survey implementation on time. Seventeen thousand, five hundred and seventy-six interviews were conducted with members of public security institutions. The State Public Security Councils or similar organizations executed the interviews. This survey assesses the perception of security agency members in the following areas: income, professionalization, training, personnel evaluation, equipment, working conditions, habits, and problems at work.

10 The survey does not state which of those corps is considered the most corrupt one. Secretaría de Gobernación, "Informe de Resultados de la Encuesta Institucional sobre Seguridad Pública," *Secretariado Ejecutivo del Sistema Nacional de Seguridad Pública*, Internet, http://www.secretariadoejecutivosnsp. gob.mx/en/SecretariadoEjecutivo/Informe_Nacional_Encuesta_Institucional_2011 (date accessed: 14 March 2013).

11 Secretaría de Gobernación.

12 According to Secretariado Ejecutivo del Sistema Nacional de Seguridad Pública, Internet, http://www. secretariadoejecutivosnsp.gob.mx (date accessed: 14 March 2013).

13 This fragmentation was obvious since, according to estimates by Eduardo Guerrero on the basis of an analysis of the printed media, the cartels at the start of the presidency of Felipe Calderon totaled six (Sinaloa, Juarez, Tijuana, Del Golfo, Familia Michoacana, Del Milenio). By the period from 2007 to 2009, there were eight (Sinaloa, Beltrán-Leyva, Juárez, Tijuana, Facción de "El Teo," Del Golfo-Zetas, Familia Michoacana, Del Milenio). In 2010, there were twelve (Sinaloa, Pacífico Sur, Independiente de Acapulco, "La Barbie," Juárez, Tijuana, Facción de "El Teo," Del Golfo, Zetas, Familia Michoacana, La Resistencia, Jalisco-Nueva Generación). Eduardo Guerrero, "La raíz de la violencia," *Nexos*, Internet, http://www.nexos.com.mx (date accessed: 14 March 2013).

14 The homicide rate refers to homicides per 100,000 inhabitants. Fernando Escalante, "Homicidios 2008-2009. La muerte tiene permiso," *Nexos*, Internet, http://www.nexos.com.mx (date accessed: 14 March 2013).

15 According to the Undersecretary of the Interior Lía Limón, the number of missing persons is 27,000 people. Antonio Baranda and Claudia Guerrero, "Ofrecen registro; lo critican panistas," *Reforma*, 22 February 2013, http://www.reforma.com (date accessed: 14 March 2013).

16 Latinobarómetro, "Banco de Datos," http://www.latinobarometro.org (date accessed: 14 March 2013).

17 Consulta Mitofsky, "México: Confianza en instituciones," Internet, http://ww.consulta.mx (date accessed: 14 March 2013).

18 "Ayutla de los Libres se levanta en armas por la ineficiencia del Guerrero Seguro", *Ágora Guerrero*, 8 January 2013, Internet, http://www.agoraguerrero2. com (date accessed: 14 March 2013).

19 Noé Zavaleta, "Ahora aparecen grupos de autodefensa en Veracruz; el gobierno niega su existencia," *Proceso*, 14 March 2013, Internet, http://ww.proceso. com.mx (date accessed: 15 March 2013).

20 That nine states are: Guerrero, Jalisco, Mexico, Michoacán, Morelos, Oaxaca, Sonora, Veracruz and Quintana Roo. List drawn up on the basis of the author's review of newspaper sources.

21 "Grupos de autodefensa en México. Un siglo de autodefensas mexicanas," *El Universal*, 28 February 2013.

22 Sergio Sarmiento Silva, "La policía comunitaria y la disminución de la delincuencia en la región Costa-Montaña de Guerrero," (paper presented at the First International Congress on Electoral Indigenous Uses and Costumes, Chihuahua, 2-3 October 2008).

23 Sarmiento, "La policía comunitaria."

24 In the Costal-Mountain region of Guerrero, there are two different "coordinadoras" of community police. The Coordinadora Regional de Autoridades Comunitarias (CRAC), founded in 1995, and the Unión de Pueblos y Organizaciones del estado de Guerrero (UPOEG), a subsidiary and an adversary of CRAC. Policía Comunitaria, "¿Quiénes somos?" http://www.policiacomunitaria.org (date accessed: 14 March 2013). Sarmiento, "La policía comunitaria." Ezequiel Flores, "Crece tensión en Ayutla; operan dos grupos de autodefensa civil,"

Proceso, 1 February 2013, Internet, http://www.proceso.com.mx (date accessed: 6 April 2013).

25 Citlali Giles, "La CRAC y no el estado, enfrentará al crimen organizado, acuerdan," *La Jornada de Guerrero*, 6 November 2011, Internet, http://www.lajornadaguerrero.com.mx (date accessed: 6 April 2013). Gloria Muñoz y Adazahira Chávez, "Enfrentando a una nueva delincuencia celebra la policía comunitaria de Guerrero sus 17 años," *Desinformémonos*, 26 November 2012, Internet, http://wwwdesinformemonos.org/ (date accessed: 6 April 2013).

26 "Marchan en apoyo a policías comunitarias en Guerrero," *24 Horas*, 2 March 2013, http://www.24-horas.mx (date accessed: 3 April 2013).

27 List drawn up on the basis of the author's review of newspaper sources. Escalante, 2011.

28 Policía Comunitaria, "¿Quiénes somos?," Internet, http://www.policiacomunitaria.org (date accessed: 14 March 2013).

29 Escalante, 2011.

30 Ariadne Díaz, "Denuncian campaña para difamar a policías comunitarias de Cherán", *La Jornada*, Internet, www.jornada.unam.mx (date accessed: 15 May, 2013).

31 "Aguirre entrega uniformes y un millón de pesos a la CRAC," *Guerrero al Día*, Internet, http://www.guerreroaldia.com (date accessed: 6 April 2013).

32 "No existen grupos de autodefensa en Veracruz: Buganza," *El Universal Veracruz*, Internet, http://www.eluniversalveracruz.com.mx (date accessed: 6 April 2013).

33 "Policía comunitaria de Tomatlán entrega a 21," *La Silla Rota*, Internet, http://www.lasillarota.com (date accessed: 15 March 2013).

34 Seven of the nine states with self-defense groups have laws on indigenous rights and culture. Quintana Roo has an "Indigenous Justice Act" and Michoacán has integrated the law regulating Article 2 of the Constitution of the United Mexican States into article 3 of its state constitution. "Entrevista sobre la policía comunitaria a Marciano, indígena mixteco," Praxis en América Latina, Internet, http://www.praxisenamericalatina.org (date accessed: 6 April 2013). Rosa Rojas and Sergio Ocampo, "Eligen autoridades comunitarias en Guerrero; la unidad, a salvo," *La Jornada*, 24 February 2013, Internet, http://www.jornada.unam.mx (date accessed: 6 April 2013).

Science&Technology Politics&Diploma
cy **Culture&Society** Business&Economi
cs Law&Ethics Conflict&Security Boo
ks **Science&Technology** Politics&Diplom
acy Culture&Society Business&Econom
ics Law&Ethics **Conflict&Security**
Books Science&Technology Politics&Dip
lomacy Culture&Society Business&Econ
omics **Law&Ethics** Conflict&Security Sc
ience&Technology **Politics&Diplomacy**
Culture&Society Business&Economics
Law&Ethics Conflict&Security Bo
oks **Business&Economics** Politics&Diplo
macy Culture&Society Business&Econ

Georgetown Journal

of International Affairs

Each Section. Every Issue. One Journal.
for more information or to subscribe
visit http://journal.georgetown.edu or email gjia@georgetown.edu

now featuring bi-weekly short essays, commentaries and analyses online

Law&Ethics

The Technologist's Dilemma
Ethical Challenges of Using Crowdsourcing Technology in Conflict and Disaster-Affected Regions

Charles Martin-Shields

The growth of mobile phone technology and Internet access globally has affected peoples' lives in various ways. For the field of governance and conflict management, this has meant unprecedented levels of information sharing from within conflict and crisis zones. As Internet access has expanded across Africa, entities like Kenya's Ushahidi—which build digital maps to publicly display real-time SMS text messages and social media feeds geographically—have been changing the way that citizens share their experiences of violence as they are happening. Probably the most important of these technologies—mobile phones—have expanded exponentially across the developing world; many countries in Africa, Asia and the Pacific have mobile phone market saturation rates of over 100 percent. The international development community has been actively developing tools and methods for using mobile phones for outreach and project monitoring for years; the governance and conflict management fields are beginning to find effective ways to use mobile phones and SMS text messaging.

While there has been excitement about the way these

Charles Martin-Shields is a doctoral student at George Mason University's School for Conflict Analysis and Resolution. His research focuses on the political economy of technology use in peacekeeping operations and quantitative methods. Special thanks to Rob Baker, Ushahidi's Operations Manager, for taking time to be interviewed for this article.

technologies can improve the work of conflict resolution and governance professionals, less popular attention has been paid to the unique risks and ethical challenges associated with using these tools in highly unstable political and social environments such as conflict zones. In these types of situations, crowdsourcing raises ethical issues of privacy, transparency of purpose and data protection. However, having secure technical data collection and storage procedures are not sufficient because most security failures are due to human error. To ethically run a crowdsourcing program in a conflict or disaster-affected environment, organizations need to ensure that their staffs and the "crowd" participating in the project have been trained to use the technologies and assess the unique risks of the digital information environment. This article will review the literature on digital information regulation, explore how the crisis response and crowdsourcing fields have evolved their data protection procedures and review the current state of practice for humanitarian crowdsourcing ethics and data security.

What is Crowdsourcing? Crowdsourcing is a data collection technique that encourages the "crowd" (the public) to provide answers to questions or content for consumption through open transmission systems like mobile phones, social media and websites.[1] It stems from the more formal methods associated with public opinion polling, deviating significantly in the way the sample is derived. Instead of using a traditional method, such as phone surveying that randomly selects the sample of respondents, crowdsourcing involves the voluntary sharing of preferences from the "crowd" on digital platforms such as Facebook or through mobile phone surveys. It was initially developed as a method for determining consumer preferences, but has expanded into the governance and international development arenas. Since the primary goal is to get reasonably reliable data from a large population sample using ubiquitous platforms like mobile phones, crowdsourcing is attractive to crisis responders, who are often dealing with a lack of data or are getting data slowly.

Why is Crowdsourcing an Ethical Issue? To date there is recognition that the modern information and communications technology (ICT) regulatory environment should include technical laws pertaining to the hardware, data ownership and storage. However, these laws will lag if they are solely technical in nature; the technologies will always outpace regulation. Therefore, an ethical component must be part of the regulatory framework. The European Commission has laid out a

Crowdsourcing involves the voluntary sharing of preferences from the "crowd" on digital platforms such as Facebook.

basic set of ethical expectations for digital information.[2] These expectations include respect for consent on the part of the individual sharing data, the ability to remove data or opt out of participation, and transparency regarding how data is used and stored.[3] Along with the legal ethics of ICT regulation, which are governmental, there are recommendations for how citizens can more effectively manage risks associated with using ICTs; Sembok highlights the fact that the volume and openness of data and information require that people and entities be aware of how the technologies work, as well as how to develop an awareness of the risks associated with using ICTs.[4]

The above citations deal with risks in the commercial ICT environment. In crisis response, the need for data protection, transparency of purpose and privacy is even more important. Criminal organizations and repressive regimes can benefit from the open data from crowdsourcing during crises and use it to enhance their level of repression.[5] Repressive regimes and criminal organizations will also adapt to an information environment and learn to take advantage of it. This is what makes data protection and participant privacy such a vexing challenge: the power of crowdsourcing in emergencies and crises is derived from the openness and timeliness of the data, and this openness is indeed what can be taken advantage of by a repressive government or criminal organization.

Ethical Issues of Crowdsourcing in Crisis Settings. Fortunately, the broad legal level of privacy, consent, and capacity outlined by the European

Union for commercial telecom use has in many ways translated to the crowdsourcing and disaster response environment. The adoption of professional standards and standardized processes for data collection and protection mirror many of the legal frameworks adopted at the European level. Nevertheless, there were challenges in the early stages of using crowdsourcing for disaster response.

The 2010 earthquake in Haiti was one of the first major examples of mobile phone-based crowdsourcing being used in disaster response. The challenges of privacy protection and data management, as well as managing expectations were first seen during the Haiti Ushahidi response. What do we do with massive amounts of digital data when there are no protocols for data storage? This problem was highlighted in an interview with Ushahidi's Robert Baker:

> There are two things that initially put us in a place where we find ourselves...looking at the potential for harm. Part this was because we didn't know what questions to ask and we weren't integrated with medical services and emergency services, government services...and on the other side of that, you have the rapid technological development. We spent the 72 hours before the mobile phone system came back online in Haiti monitoring Twitter and it became a digital "Times Square." People were putting up photos, date of birth, personal information...all that could be used to impersonate someone. We pushed this information into

Google Person Finder. By not knowing what to ask and who to coordinate with, we tried to solve the problem with transparency; we put all the information out there. When you think about all this information out in the open, it wouldn't be hard for someone with malicious intent to steal identities, or engage in human trafficking.[6]

Along with the risks associated with managing identifying information, there are also challenges meeting the expectations of the victims in a disaster zone. There were cases of misunderstanding how the Ushahidi deployment worked. People thought that texting was similar to calling 911: If you texted, there would be a response. There were many cases where there was indeed a response, but in many cases there was not. Offering a service to an at-risk or traumatized population means being responsible for either responding to calls for help, or making clear what the limits of a program like Ushahidi's Haiti response are. These challenges came up in Haiti because it was the first time crowdsourcing was used in a large-scale way for disaster response. In many ways the Ushahidi team and the volunteers cleaning and coding the data were learning as they went. These lessons became core to the ongoing discussion of ethics and responsibility in crowdsourcing during disaster response.

Data Management and Ethics: Organizational Response. Out of the Haiti experience came the recognition that protocols for responsible data collection and management was necessary when crowdsourcing during disaster response. Recognition of the need for a code of conduct when crowdsourcing using SMS text messaging, and guidelines for the effective and ethical use of SMS text messaging, emerged out of the lack of collection and response procedures in Haiti.[8] After Haiti, large organizations have had to figure out how their traditional standards for data management work in an increasingly digital environment. The International Organization for Migration (IOM) and the International Committee of the Red Cross (ICRC) now have a set of data collection and protection processes that include both technical and ethical guidelines for digital data collection and crowdsourcing.[9] One of the most productive meetings on this topic was covered in a meeting hosted by UNOCHA and World Vision after the Libyan civil way.

World Vision's meeting focused on UNOCHA's Libya map. Of concern was how publicly available the mapped information should be, and how it should be shared across United Nations entities.[10] The OCHA Libya map was a crowdsourced map that geocoded text messages and media related to the conflict; the data was collected and coded by trained volunteers who are part of the Standby Taskforce. While this crowdsourcing effort put many of the lessons learned from Haiti into practice, there were still challenges that came up outside of the core collection process. These included political questions about what to do with the crowdsourced data after the war ended. Libyan civilians who had contributed to UNOCHA's crisis map faced political risks as the data and their identities were publicized in the course of International Criminal Court prosecutions.[11] This case highlights the need for better rules for, or at a minimum discussion about, asking for and granting consent to crowdsourcing efforts in crisis situations. There should be an expectation that people submitting information know the risks of participating in a crowdsourcing program in a conflict-affected environment, as well as how the data they submit will be used during and after the conflict.[12] While the collection and data management process was well designed, the questions that emerged out of the UNOCHA Libya map started to focus on data use after the event.

people to subscribe to specific messages or to unsubscribe from receiving SMS texts.[13] These are basic, but are often overlooked. At a higher level, the IOM's guidelines for data collection and privacy protection are expansions of their traditional, non-digital methods.[14] Their basic guidelines focus on protecting privacy and confidentiality of respondents, and management of publicizing information so that confidential data is not shared inappropriately.[15] The ICRC's updated guidelines for data protection in the digital space have a similar focus. The ICRC's regulations include expectations of informed consent when crowdsourcing, but also go on to include issues about data use and bias in reporting,

The ethical responsibility for data protection goes beyond collection and storage procedures, and extends into the human capacity aspect of organizations using crowdsourcing techniques.

Therefore, the current state of the field in ethics and crowdsourcing can be looked at two ways: the first is well designed, safe collection processes, and the second is transparency about what will be done with the user-submitted data after the event.

Meier makes a few basic user level recommendations for effective crowdsourcing using SMS text messages; these include single streams of outgoing information messages for continuity, a complaint mechanism for subscribers, non-duplication of data collection efforts, and the ability for

and the protection of sensitive data in constrained political environments.[16] These processes for data collection and protection are not groundbreaking, but the challenge of maintaining these standards increases significantly when digital technology is used for collecting and storing data. This means that the ethical responsibility for data protection goes beyond collection and storage procedures, and extends into the human capacity aspect of organizations using crowdsourcing techniques.

Staff Training for Crowdsourcing: The Ethical Aspect of Institutional Capacity. None of the procedures and processes for protecting data in a crowdsourcing and digital collection program are unusual or beyond the standard scope of traditional data collection for humanitarian response. What makes ethical data collection and crowdsourcing using digital media unique is the technical risks associated with the medium. At this stage, with organizations recognizing the risks associated with the digital medium, the ethical part of the puzzle should focus on staff capacity. In general, information protection failures are not a technology problem; they are a human problem. With this in mind, how do organizations scale up technical ability of their staff?

A starting point is recognizing that doing crowdsourcing well involves investing in staff training. Organizations do not need all their staff members to be computer experts or software engineers, but as Robert Baker noted during my interview with him it is important for all team members to know what questions to ask.[17] Basic technical training that focuses on the limits of the technologies, and the ways that they work can help ensure that staff members are able to identify risks and ask the right questions when they reach out to software developers and engineers for technical support.

The second challenge is scaling this up. If the entire project staff needs to have basic technical knowledge of crowdsourcing software, it can be expensive and impractical to pull an entire team aside for a week of in-classroom training. The classroom model can also lead to insularity, where the only people sharing are the ones on the project team; this means that there is not an opportunity to learn from other people working in the field. There is a technical solution for this. Online training that leverages social software can provide a learning space for staff members from multiple organizations regardless of geography; the lessons are enhanced by the fact that participants are learning from each other, which is important in the crowdsourcing space where the technology changes quickly and lessons must be integrated in days and weeks instead of months or years.[18]

Conclusion. The use of crowdsourcing methodologies for data collection in crisis zones comes with unique ethical and technical challenges. Whether organizations can meet all the standards laid out by the IOM, ICRC and Searl and Wynn-Pope remains to be an open question.[19] The primary areas that are well within the control of organizations to address are training and risk analysis. Organizations that wish to engage in crowdsourcing should ethically be expected to secure staff competency in using the technology selected for the crowdsourcing project, and perform a technical and political risk analysis. If the project is particularly complex, entities such as the Standby Taskforce can provide expertise and technical support during a project. Crowdsourcing can be done ethically if organizations and individuals are properly prepared to handle the tangible risks and support research that continues to reveal more about the complex ICT environment in crisis-affected regions.

NOTES

1 Geoff Howe, "The Rise of Crowdsourcing," *WIRED* 14, no. 6 (June 2006), accessed 10 March 10 2013, Internet, http://www.wired.com/wired/archive/14.06/crowds.html.

2 European Commission, "Ethics of Information and Communication Technologies," Opinion 26 (2012), accessed 10 March 10 2013, Internet, http://ec.europa.eu/bepa/european-group-ethics/docs/publications/ict_final_22_february-adopted.pdf.

3 Ibid.

4 Tengku Mohd T. Sembok, "Ethics of Information Communication Technology," Internet, http://www.unescobkk.org/elib/publications/ethic_in_asia_pacific/239_325ETHICS.PDF (date accessed: 12 March 2013).

5 Nathaniel Raymond, Caitlin Howarth, and Jonathan Hutson. "Crisis Mapping Needs an Ethical Compass," Internet, http://globalbrief.ca/blog/2012/02/06/crisis-mapping-needs-an-ethical-compass (date accessed: 10 March 2013); Evgeny Morozov, *The Net Dellusion: The Dark Side of Internet Freedom* (New York: Public Affairs, 2011).

6 Robert Baker, personal interview by Charles Martin-Shields, 6 January 2013.

7 Charles Martin-Shields, "Power to the People: The Risk and Rewards of Mobile Technology in Governance Development," Internet, http://techchange.org/2011/04/21/power-to-the-people-the-risk-and-rewards-of-mobile-technology-in-governance-development (date accessed: 10 April 2013).

8 Patrick Meier, "Toward an SMS Code of Conduct for Disaster Response," Internet, http://irevolution.net/2010/03/06/sms-code-of-conduct (date accessed 15 April 2013); Patrick Meier and Robert Munro, "The Unprecedented Role of SMS in Disaster Response: Learning from Haiti," SAIS Review 30, no. 2 (2010): 91-103; Kyla Reid, Jacob Korenblum, and Patrick Meier, "Towards a Code of Conduct: Guidelines for the Use of SMS in Natural Disasters," Internet, http://irevolution.files.wordpress.com/2013/02/dr_sms_220213_spreads.pdf (date accessed: 16 March 2013).

9 International Organization for Migration, "IOM Data Protection Manual," Internet, http://publications.iom.int/bookstore/free/IOMdataprotection_web.pdf (date accessed: 10 March 2013); International Committee of the Red Cross, "Professional Standards for Protection Work," Internet, http://irevolution.files.wordpress.com/2013/04/icrc-prof-protection-standards-english-final-2013.pdf (date accessed 4 April 2013).

10 Louise Searle and Pheobe Wynn-Pope, "Crisis Mapping, Humanitarian Principles and the application of Protection Standards: A dialogue between Crisis mappers and Operational Humanitarian Agencies," Internet, http://irevolution.files.wordpress.com/2012/02/world-vision-geneva-report.pdf (date accessed: 10 March 2013).

11 Ibid.

12 Ibid.

13 Patrick Meier, "Toward an SMS Code of Conduct for Disaster Response," Internet, http://irevolution.net/2010/03/06/sms-code-of-conduct (date accessed 15 April 2013).

14 Ibid.

15 Ibid.

16 International Committee of the Red Cross, "Professional Standards for Protection Work," Internet, http://irevolution.files.wordpress.com/2013/04/icrc-prof-protection-standards-english-final-2013.pdf (date accessed 4 April 2013).

17 Robert Baker, personal interview by Charles Martin-Shields, 6 January 2013.

18 Charles Martin-Shields and Jordan Hosmer-Henner, "Dynamic Web-based Learning: Co-Creating Development Solutions Across Geographies," Internet, http://charlesmartinshields.files.wordpress.com/2012/04/dynamic-web-based-learning.pdf.

19 Louise Searle and Pheobe Wynn-Pope, "Crisis Mapping, Humanitarian Principles and the application of Protection Standards: A dialogue between Crisis mappers and Operational Humanitarian Agencies," Internet, http://irevolution.files.wordpress.com/2012/02/world-vision-geneva-report.pdf (date accessed: 10 March 2013).

Georgetown University
Institute for Law, Science, and Global Security

International Engagement
on Cyber

2013

Developing International Norms for a Safe, Stable & Predictable Cyber Environment

Georgetown Journal
of International Affairs

Business&Economics

Afghanistan in Transition:
Building the foundations for future economic growth and stability

Claudia Nassif

Afghanistan is facing uncertain times ahead. The withdrawal of most international military troops by 2014 will affect the country far beyond the hand-over of all security responsibilities. The operations of international troops were supported not just by a high level of military but also civilian aid that financed reconstruction efforts and the provision of public services. This has fueled fears that the security transition will also be followed by a reduction of aid with potentially devastating repercussions on Afghanistan's economy.

Based on analytical work that the World Bank conducted over the past two years, this article argues that while the transition process carries a number of risks for the country's economic outlook and the sustainability of the state, these risks can be managed to ensure continued growth and development.[1] In fact, the months leading up to the April 2014 presidential elections will be critical for the implementation of policy reforms that could move Afghanistan towards a more sustainable growth trajectory.

Demystifying the role of aid in Afghanistan's economy. Afghanistan's economic growth performance was

Claudia Nassif is a senior country economist for Afghanistan at the World Bank.

very strong over the past decade. Real GDP grew at an average annual rate of 9.2 percent between 2003 and 2012.[2] Part of this exceptional growth performance is explained by the high level of aid Afghanistan has received over the past decade. Official development aid and military assistance to Afghanistan grew continuously from $404 million in 2002 to more than $15.7 billion in 2010, the equivalent of 98 percent of GDP.[3] Around one-third of these aid flows went into the development of civilian infrastructure and services, such as education, health, electricity, and roads.[4] This has produced higher aggregate demand for good, services and construction (Fig. 1). And indeed, the growth decomposition in Figure 2 shows that public and private consumption, which captures aid agencies' demand for goods and services, has been the most important driver for growth over the past decade.[5] Private investment, on the other hand, has played a rather small role.

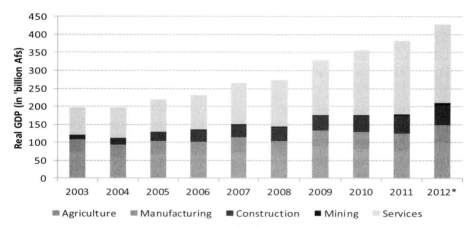

Figure 1: GDP (in constant prices). Source: Author's calculations based on data from the Afghan Central Statistics Office. Figures exclude opium.

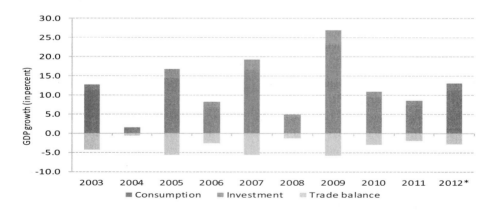

Figure 2: Growth Decomposition-Demand Side. Source: Author's calculations based on data from the Afghan Central Statistics Office. Figures exclude opium.

Experiences in countries such as Mozambique, Bosnia and Herzegovina, and Eritrea show that both military and civilian aid levels decline rapidly once international troops are withdrawn.[6] While these countries successfully absorbed the economic impact of large aid reduction, the exception-

produced goods and services; most of it flows out of the country in the form of imports, expatriated profits of contractors, and outward remittances. The public investments financed by aid projects increase the capital stock (e.g., by way of provision of health and education services) and improve

As long as the security situation continues to improve, Afghanistan will continue to grow.

ally high levels of aid that supported Afghanistan's development process and its anticipated rapid reduction have raised fears of a deep economic downturn.

But a 2012 World Bank study demonstrates that the impact of aid reduction might be less than what many expect; as long as the security situation continues to improve, Afghanistan will continue to grow at lower but still respectable rates of 4 to 6 percent on average between 2011 and 2018, even if aid declines by 50 percent from its 2010 levels.[7]

Indeed, economic developments over the past eighteen months support the results of the analysis. In spite of a reduction of troops by over 37,000[8] and military and civilian aid at only half of 2010 levels, Afghanistan grew by 11 percent in 2012 within a broadly stable macroeconomic environment.[9]

How can these results be explained? First, aid does not directly translate into domestic output for an economy. Only a small share of military and civilian aid is spent on locally

productivity (e.g., through improved infrastructure), but the impact of these investments on economic growth only materializes over time. This means that over the period of transition and beyond, Afghanistan will continue to benefit from investments made in the past.

Second, GDP growth relies strongly on agriculture developments. Between 2003 and 2011, aid flows grew continuously, but GDP growth exhibited strong volatility, echoing the volatility observed in agriculture output (Fig.3) caused by weather changes.[10] The high growth rate in 2012, for instance, was predominantly the result of an extraordinary harvest that year. On average, agriculture contributed 2.9 percentage points to real GDP between 2003 and 2012 and is, after services (4.1 percentage points), the most important source of growth (Fig. 4). Since changes in aid flows do not directly affect agriculture output, it is likely that agriculture will continue to drive growth throughout the transition process and beyond.

Figure 3: Real GDP growth in selected sectors. Source: Author's calculations based on data from the Afghan Central Statistics Office.

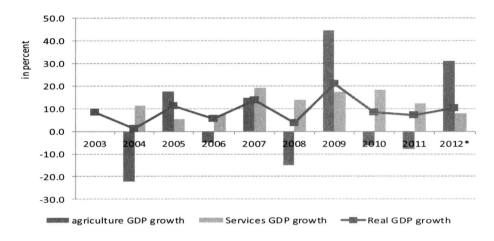

Figure 4: Growth Decomposition - Supply Side. Source: Author's calculations based on data from the Afghan Central Statistics Office.

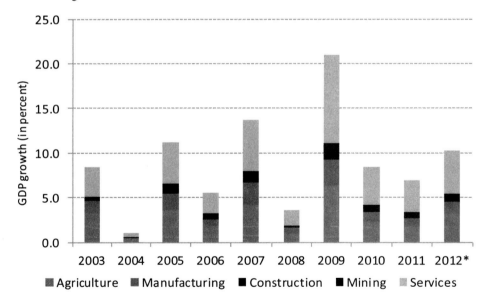

Third, Afghanistan has reasonable potential to develop its mining sector. Currently the mining sector is still very small at an estimated 1.8 percent of GDP in 2012.[11] But in the past two years, contracts for the construction and operation of two large-scale mines in Aynak and Hajigak have been successfully tendered. These investments and operations are expected contribute nearly 2.8 percentage points of GDP growth over the coming decade and could help to absorb some of the negative impact of aid reduction. Mining is expected to be a major source of fiscal revenue and could grow to compose 2.4 percent of GDP through the early 2020s.[12] While not completely impervious to security risks, investment in mining tends to be more robust in volatile environments than investment in other sectors.

Not all is good: Risks to the economic outlook and sustainability of the state. In spite of the relatively optimistic prospects, Afghanistan's economy is exposed to some serious medium-term risks which need to be carefully managed. The upcoming presidential elections in 2014 and the withdrawal of international troops create considerable uncertainty over Afghanistan's future among the local population, especially with respect to

the Aynak and Hajigak mines must be fulfilled and operations must start soon. This may prove difficult without improvements in the legal and regulatory environment which presently does not provide adequate provisions related to security of tenure, licensing, tendering, and mining obligations. This outlook also assumes the agriculture sector will grow at least the average annual rate of 4 percent achieved over the past decade.[13]

Even in the most conservative scenarios, both sectors will require large investments in infrastructure. According to World Bank estimates, $2 and $2.5 billion in investment will be needed until 2017 for hard infrastructure such as roads and power plants, to enable the exploitation of the mines and the transportation of goods and services.[14] In addition, the rehabilitation and development of irrigation systems and water resources for the agriculture sector will cost $1.4 billion.[15]

The ability of the country to achieve peace, stability, and reconciliation in the years to come will ultimately determine Afghanistan's development prospects.

the security situation. Crime, conflict and violence are currently the largest constraint to economic and social development in Afghanistan. The ability of the country to achieve peace, stability, and reconciliation in the years to come will ultimately determine Afghanistan's development prospects.

The medium-term outlook also hinges on some important assumptions; at a minimum, investments in

Much of this investment will need to be financed by public resources. Even more investment will be required to reform institutions, to create linkages and synergies to other sectors, and to properly train a growing labor force.

Another important risk relates to the fiscal sustainability of the government's budget. At the moment, domestic revenues cover only about 60 percent of the government's operational costs.[16] Over the next decade, public expenditures are expected to grow significantly as a result of the handover of security responsibilities and donor-built assets from foreign actors to the Afghan government. Higher expenditures are also required to further expand and improve the provision of public services that are still limited in coverage and quality. A recent fiscal sustainability analysis shows that government expenditure will increase dramatically, composing as much as 39 percent of GDP over the next decade. Over the same period, domestic revenues are only expected to increase to 16 percent of GDP by 2022—resulting in a financing gap of 21 percent of GDP and rendering the fiscal situation unsustainable.[17]

There are also risks arising from the uneven distribution of the impact of aid across the country. Over the past decade, in an attempt to foster stabilization, much more donor attention was given to conflict-affected provinces. Provincial reconstruction teams (PRT) of different sizes were established in twenty-six out of thirty-four provinces in Afghanistan and delivered direct assistance in the form of infrastructure development, creation of employment opportunities, humanitarian aid and governance support.[18] As a result, the per capita income of many conflict-affected provinces is often double that of the more peaceful provinces.[19] Thus, the reduction in aid is likely to be felt more strongly in the conflict-affected areas and in urban centers in which military and civilian aid activities were concentrated, for example, through a loss of job opportunities in military bases and PRTs

This will affect the severity of under-employment in Afghanistan, which is already very high at 48 percent.[20] The salaries of higher qualified people may also decline due to fewer employment opportunities in donor-financed projects. These factors are a serious risk to economic and political stability, but a lack of adequate data unfortunately makes it hard to conduct an analysis of the labor impact of the transition.

Managing the risks of transition. As demonstrated, Afghanistan will need to rely heavily on donor financing to ensure the continued provision of public services and investment over the transition period; the government will have special, significant and continuing fiscal requirements and development needs that cannot be met by domestic revenues. In 2012 the country secured pledges for funds for the security sector (roughly $4.1 billion annually) and for civilian aid ($16 billion until 2016).[21] The pledges could be sufficient to balance the budget throughout the transition period and to continue progress towards the achievement of Millennium Development Goals for a few years beyond. In return, the Government of Afghanistan committed to hold timely elections and to improve fiscal sustainability, government capacity, transparency, and accountability.

Achieving these commitments will require a strong effort by the government, which is already dealing with a dense reform agenda and competing priorities. The final year of this presidential term and preparations for the upcoming elections over the next twelve months could undercut incentives for reform. It is therefore vital that reform efforts in the coming year are selective, highly prioritized, and focused at measures that (i) promise the highest fiscal pay-off; (ii) increase the absorption capacity of the administration; and (iii) reduce opportunities for rent-seeking. These reforms include:

(1) Creation of a regulatory environment that encourages private investment in mining: A new minerals law is expected to improve security of tenure and strengthen social and environmental safeguards, measures that are critical to concluding the pending Hajigak contracts and to attracting

ally.[22] But because the VAT is costly to implement and rather difficult to understand, there is a risk that prolonged discussions in Parliament will delay the implementation of the new tax.

(3) Comprehensive reforms in the customs system: Making up 26 percent of total revenue, customs is one of the most important sources of revenue for the government.[23] Until now, customs reforms have largely been a success story; customs revenues have increased by an average of 25 percent annually.[24] But in spite of these reform efforts, the customs system in Afghanistan remains one of the institutions

Strong reform efforts will be required to prepare Afghanistan for the years after transition.

new investment. However, lengthy discussions within the government have delayed the timetable for passing the law and there is some uncertainty over further changes to the legislation that could undermine investor sentiment.

(2) Introduction of a value-added tax (VAT): The government is planning to introduce a VAT in 2014 that will collect a certain percentage of a commodity or service's value created at each stage of the production process. The VAT is expected to broaden the tax base, reduce tax evasion, and shift some of the tax burden away from the consumer. If effective, the tax could generate an estimated 2 percent of GDP in domestic revenue annu-

most vulnerable to corruption.[25] This implies that customs revenue collection is performing under potential—and that opportunities exist to raise domestic revenues by pushing reforms beyond current efforts to computerize the process. Reforms need to address the enabling environment for customs, including increasing oversight, strengthening enforcement, and offering incentives to trigger behavioral change among customs officials and traders. The change in the leadership of the customs administration in March 2012 indicates a strong reform desire. But more needs to be done; the agents of change within the customs administration need to be forcefully supported and empowered by higher levels of administration to implement the necessary reform measures and to oppose entrenched interests.

(4) Strengthening public financial management systems: in 2010/11 it was estimated that nearly 90 percent of total aid funds to Afghanistan were channeled and managed outside of government systems (e.g. by international organizations, NGOs, and PRTs).[26] While externally-funded aid projects are sometimes more effectively managed, they tend to be more costly because they create additional layers of administration and undermine country systems. In order to improve aid effectiveness in the medium and long term, donors agreed at the Tokyo Conference to channel at least 50 percent of aid through the national budget.[27] More aid on budget will increase spending pressures on public financial management and procurement systems whose absorption capacity is already low; only half of the development budget in 2011 and 2012 was executed.[28] Thus, more effort is needed to improve public financial management and procurement systems, as well as project management capacity in line ministries to ensure that execution does not fall below present levels. Emphasis should also be placed on improving transparency and accountability in the government. This could increase government effectiveness and provide more assurance to donors that money is being spent responsibly.

(5) Improving land management and acquisition processes: Difficulty in accessing land is a major constraint to investment across all sectors.

Afghanistan's land management system is governed by overlapping and conflicting legal systems, and the lack of tenure security and clear legal and policy frameworks has caused conflicts among individuals and between communities. These disputes exacerbate ethnic and religious tensions; slow the implementation of development and rehabilitation programs; and undermine public trust in the ability of government to promote development and protect citizens' rights. The government is currently considering revisions of land management and expropriation laws, but the experience of other countries show that land governance reforms are made difficult by the vested interests of various stakeholders. Moving land governance reforms forward will therefore require significant financial, technical, and political support, from the government and donors alike.

Conclusion. Afghanistan's government and the wider donor community face tremendous challenges ahead with navigating the transition process. The recent donor pledges for security and civilian aid at the 2012 Chicago and Tokyo conferences will help the government sustain its operations throughout the transition and beyond. However, strong reform efforts will be required to prepare Afghanistan for the years after transition. In particular, significant revenue must be mobilized to reduce aid dependency and ensure fiscal sustainability over time. Reforms with the largest pay-off in terms of fiscal revenue could include the creation of an enabling environment for private mining investment, the introduction of a value added tax, and deep reforms in customs to minimize opportunities for rent-seeking at borders. These reforms will show stronger impact if complemented by measures that aim to increase the absorption capacity of the administration through strengthening public financial management systems and improving land governance.

Notes

1 This article is an enhanced summary of previous World Bank publications to which the author contributed, in particular *Afghanistan in Transition: Looking beyond 2014* (2013) and *Afghanistan Economic Update* (April, 2013).

2 Author's own calculation based on national account data from the Afghanistan Central Statistics Organisation.

3 Hogg, Richard, Claudia Nassif, Camilo Gomez Osorio, Willam Byrd, and Andrew Beath, *Afghanistan in Transition: Looking beyond 2014:* 47-48; *Directions in Development,* Washington, DC, 47-48.

4 Ibid.

5 Official development aid enters in two ways into the Afghan national accounts: private consumption (demand for goods and services by aid agencies) and public consumption and investment (for the portion of aid channeled through the government's budget).

6 Hogg et al., *Afghanistan in Transition: Looking beyond 2014:* 10.

7 Ibid. Appendix 1. For this analysis, the World Bank used a Computable Equilibrium Model (CGE) to simulate the likely impact of declining aid on economic growth under different scenarios.

8 International Security Assistance Force (ISAF): Key Facts and Figures, Internet, http://www.isaf.nato.int/images/stories/File/Placemats/ISAF-ANA%20Troops%20Placemat-Feb19%202013.pdf.

9 World Bank, *Afghanistan Economic Update,* (Washington, D.C., April 2013): 3.

10 More than 30 percent of Afghanistan's agriculture is rain-fed; agricultural output is therefore strongly exposed to weather fluctuation. Source: Author's calculation based on data from the Ministry of Agriculture, Irrigation and Lifestock.

11 World Bank, *Afghanistan Economic Update:* 4.

12 Hogg et al., *Afghanistan in Transition: Looking beyond 2014:* 27.

13 Hogg et al., *Afghanistan in Transition: Looking Beyond 2014:* Appendix 1.

14 World Bank, *Resource Corridor Initiative - Technical Summary,* (Washington, D.C., forthcoming May 2013), 11 (figures extrapolated from underlying analysis by author), Internet, http://siteresources.worldbank.org/SOUTHASIAEXT/Resources/223546-1328913542665/8436738-1341156360475/Afghanistan-Resource-Corridors-Technical-Summary.pdf.

15 Government of Islamic Republic of Afghanistan, Agriculture and Rural Development Cluster National Priority Program 1: National Water and Natural Resources Development, (Kabul, Afghanistan, December 2012), 127-28.

16 Authors own calculation based on data from Afghanistan's Ministry of Finance.

17 World Bank, *Afghanistan Economic Update:* 17.

18 PRTs are joint civilian-military diplomatic outposts at the provincial level established to improve security, to extend the authority of the Afghan central government, and to facilitate reconstruction.

19 Hogg et al., *Afghanistan in Transition:* 40.

20 World Bank and the Islamic Republic of Afghanistan, Poverty Status in Afghanistan, (Washington, D.C., 2010): 44, Internet, http://go.worldbank.org/WD88TOSCB0.

21 Derived from the Chicago Summit Declaration, Internet, http://www.nato.int/cps/en/natolive/official_texts_87595.htm and the Tokyo Declaration, http://president.gov.af/Content/files/Tokyo%20Declaration%20-%20Final%20English.pdf.

22 International Monetary Fund, *Islamic Republic of Afghanistan: Joint World Bank/IMF Debt Sustainability Analysis Update,* IMF Country Report No. 12/245, (Washington, D.C., 2012): 2.

23 Afghanistan Ministry of Finance, Quarterly Fiscal Bulletin, 3Q1391, (Kabul, 2013).

24 Author's calculation based on data from the Afghanistan Ministry of Finance.

25 United Nations Office on Drugs and Crime, *Corruption in Afghanistan: Recent Patterns and Trends,* (Vienna, 2012), 11.

26 Hogg et al., *Afghanistan in Transition:* 28.

27 Calculation based on information from Hogg et al., *Afghanistan in Transition.*

28 World Bank, *Afghanistan Economic Update:* 14.

The Link Between Oil Prices and the U.S. Macroeconomy

Blake Clayton

For the United States and other net importers of oil, the last two years have the dubious distinction of featuring the highest average annual crude oil prices, in both real and nominal terms, since the beginnings of the modern oil industry in the 1860s.[1] Such elevated prices for oil, marked by extreme volatility at times, pose risks to the still-anemic U.S. and global economies, though they have proven a boon to the domestic oil industry and the regions of the country where oil and gas are produced. Still, the U.S. economy is much less affected by changes in oil prices today than it was in the 1970s, for instance, when the first modern oil crises wreaked havoc on the national economy.

Understanding how oil prices affect the economy of the United States is crucial to sensible domestic policymaking. The consequences of today's relatively high oil prices, for instance, vary tremendously across the country's geographic regions, economic sectors, and population segments. Pinpointing the exact dynamics at play, as well as measuring their magnitudes, is difficult to do with precision. But several decades of research have yielded critical insights. These findings can help inform policy decisions in realms as diverse as economic sanctions, strategic petroleum reserve

Blake Clayton is the fellow for energy and national security at the Council on Foreign Relations. His publications include *Commodity Markets and the Global Economy* and *Fear, Greed, and Oil: A Century of Panics in the World Oil Market* (both forthcoming in 2014.) He received his DPhil at Oxford University and holds dual master's degrees from the University of Chicago and Cambridge University.

releases, and gasoline taxes, limiting any negative implications their effects on oil prices might cause to the broader economy and maximizing their potential benefits.

How do oil prices affect the U.S. economy? The primary channel through which higher oil prices reduce U.S. economic activity is by squeezing consumers, taking away discretionary income. Higher oil prices, which result in higher bills for essential goods like gasoline, heating oil, and to a much smaller extent, food, function like a tax on U.S. households. Because demand for oil is highly inelastic (i.e., even a large increase in the price does little to discourage consumption), particularly over the short term, more costly oil means that Americans tend to put more of their income towards it. Consumers, rather than businesses, bear the brunt of this income effect. The outflow of wealth from the United States overseas to pay for imported oil, only a fraction of which is eventually recycled back by net oil-exporting countries, means less spending on domestic goods and services, thereby reducing U.S. purchasing power and aggregate demand.

Less significantly, a change in oil prices affects aggregate output and labor productivity, so-called supply-side mechanisms. Oil is a vital input to production. The more expensive oil is, the more costly it is for firms to produce goods and services. This dampening effect on productivity puts downward pressure on real growth rates and tends to increase the unemployment rate. Moreover, if consumers expect the oil price increase to be temporary, they will save less and borrow more, which

also puts upward pressure on real interest rates and prices. This effect is partially offset by the fact that, thanks to a rise in revenues, greater savings in oil-exporting countries tend, in theory, to lower global interest rates and boost demand in the United States for interest-rate-sensitive assets, like housing, during the boom years.

But the effects of higher oil prices extend beyond the constraints on the physical process of production or on national income.[2] There are several reasons for this. Higher prices carry adjustment costs for firms and consumers as they struggle to reallocate their capital, which can weigh on short-term aggregate demand and thus retard growth. Consumers shy away from purchasing durable goods complementary with oil usage, particularly automobiles, almost immediately after a significant oil price rise. Labor and capital will tend to flow out of relatively oil-intensive sectors into more fuel-efficient ones, but this switch is costly.[3] In the meantime, capital equipment can go idle or be retired prematurely, and workers must find jobs in new companies or industries. As a result, sudden oil price increases tend to cause a rise in frictional unemployment. Jobs in energy-intensive industries like manufacturing are hit especially hard, with the least-skilled and least-experienced members of the workforce bearing the brunt of the change. Employment opportunities for skilled workers can actually rise following oil price increases, as managers substitute their productivity for more energy-intensive production inputs.[4]

There are other amplifying mechanisms as well. Oil price increases can cause uncertainty about the future, leading to a rise in precautionary saving among consumers and lower capital investment by firms as they wait to see how prices play out.[5] Higher oil prices also risk harming consumer sentiment. According to James Hamilton of the University of California at San Diego, an increase in energy prices that reduces consumer spending power by as little

asymmetry.[9] This nonlinearity has also been shown to apply when it comes to the effects of changes in oil prices on domestic employment levels and industrial production.[10]

Moreover, volatile oil prices, even when they move downward, are not ideal for economic growth. Oil price volatility has been shown to predict

Oil price volatility thas been shown to predict slower U.S. GDP growth, implying that even falling prices can have contractionary consequences.

as 1 percent can prompt a dramatic decline in consumer sentiment.[6] Oil price changes may also lead to coordination problems among firms. Competing firms, lacking information about how their peers' output and pricing decisions will be affected, may be more hesitant about expanding their operations, causing a drag on aggregate output. Threshold effects may also come into play. When prices rise to very high or very low levels, relative to the historical norm, they may pass a critical limit whereby their influence on areas like consumer confidence and spending or capital investment far exceeds the usual impact at milder price levels.[7]

A jump in oil prices tends to do the U.S. economy more harm than a drop in prices of the same magnitude does it good. A drop in oil prices may lead to small gains in economic growth, but the response tends to be a fraction of the size of the losses that tend to follow an equal rise in prices.[8] The macroeconomic frictions associated with rising energy costs, such as consumer uncertainty and the reallocation of resources across sectors, appear to be behind this

slower U.S. GDP growth, implying that even falling prices can have contractionary consequences.[11] Predictability in oil price changes allows consumers to shift their decision making in order to prepare themselves for what the future might hold. When prices swing wildly, defying forecasts, their bounce can stymie attempts by affected businesses and households to adjust as seamlessly as possible, whether through reducing their consumption, increasing the efficiency of their consumption, or hedging their exposure.

It is also important to note that various parts of the country experience the economic consequences of changing oil prices very differently. The benefits of high prices in terms of employment, output, and public revenues overwhelmingly accrue to the producing regions (though the lattermost blessing also applies to the federal government); for other regions, such prices hinder economic activity more than help it, on the net. The sensitivity of a net-producing state's economy to oil prices depends largely on share of the total economy consisting of the energy sector and related areas like petrochemicals. For Texas, a hub of domestic oil-related industry, research by the Federal Reserve Bank of Dallas found that a 10 percent increase in oil prices led to a 0.5 percent rise in GDP and a 0.36 percent rise in employment between 1997 and 2010.[12] However, prolonged periods of low oil prices also weigh disproportionately on economic activity in these regions. The oil crash in 1986 caused a recession in Texas, though the state's economy appears less sensitive to prices now than it was then.[13] Public revenues in states like Alaska, which derives 64 percent

their products. In theory, this could result in an uptick in inflation and tighter monetary policy, which could weaken growth.[15] This effect is likely less applicable under current economic conditions, where low resource utilization means that upward pressure on wages from rising oil prices is limited. Perhaps more relevant, though, is the risk that an increase in energy prices could spill over into the prices of other goods and thus filter into core inflation, with similar implications for central bankers.

In practice, however, the relationship between oil prices, core inflation,

In practice...the relations between oil prices, core inflation, and monetary policy is less straightforward.

of its state tax revenue from severance taxes, and Oklahoma, which takes in 19 percent of its labor income from the oil and natural gas industry, are also affected by changes in oil prices.[14]

Oil prices and U.S. monetary policy. Fluctuations in oil prices carry important ramifications for the Federal Reserve. In a robust economy—unlike the one today—a rise in oil prices can distort wages and prices and discourage growth. Wages and prices can be inflexible in the face of changes to energy prices, which can weigh on the demand for capital and labor in the short run. Higher oil prices can put upward pressure on labor costs, as the workforce tries to maintain purchasing power, and labor productivity can temporarily fall. Firms then pass on these higher costs to consumers by raising prices for

and monetary policy is less straightforward. Jumps in oil prices did appear to contribute to higher core inflation in the case of the 1970s oil price shocks but little since then, as suggested by empirical research based on backward-looking Philips curves.[16] This change in core inflationary effects speaks in part to the progress that increasingly technocratic central bankers have made in credibly keeping market expectations of long-term inflation in check. Global core and headline inflation were stable through 2006 despite rising oil prices, though they did turn upwards in 2007-08. That uptick was likely partly due to robust global resource utilization rates, though it may also have been the delayed, cumulative effect of several years of rising oil prices. Still, the U.S. experience since the recession demonstrates that consecutive years of high oil prices need not necessarily translate into materially higher core inflation, though their impact on headline inflation is definitional. This change is fortunate, given that it reduces the likelihood that higher oil prices force central bankers to raise short-term rates, which weighs on economic activity. High inflation can generate uncertainty in an economy that drag down capital investment and add an inflation risk premium to interest rates. Ultimately, conditions in the broader economy as well as public policy decisions influence the degree of pass-through.[17] In the case of the United States, long-term inflation expectations appear capable of remaining firmly anchored in spite of increasing energy costs due to an increase in the Federal Reserve'santi-inflation credibility since the 1970s, as well as due to structural changes in the domestic economy.[18]

How much do higher oil prices matter to the U.S. economy? How large and long-lasting are these effects on important economic outcomes such as gross domestic product, employment, and inflation? And how might broader economic conditions, as well as the drivers and contours of the oil price change, offset or amplify these effects?

There is little question that structural changes to the U.S. economy have made the effects of oil prices on growth, inflation, and employment much less pronounced than they were prior to the mid-1980s, for several reasons. For one thing, oil's value share in domestic production and consumption has fallen, reducing the effect of a price change on spending patterns. Labor markets have become more flexible. Lower wage rigidity has mitigated the tradeoff between stabilizing inflation versus a gap in output. Monetary policymaking has also improved. Central bankers have gained greater credibility in inflation targeting, which has enabled them to anchor inflation expectations in the face of a commodity price increase without the same risks to output growth.[19] The U.S. economy is also less energy intensive than it was decades ago, reducing the sensitivity of output to an unforeseen change in oil prices.[20] Moreover, rationing may have magnified the ill effects of oil price changes on the U.S. economy during the 1970s.[21] As a result of these altered conditions in the domestic economy, according to one estimate, a change in oil prices may bring about roughly one-third the impact on output and price levels after 1984 as they did prior to that time.[22]

Various studies have been done over the last decade aiming to quantitatively relate real GDP growth, employment growth, and changes in consumer price levels to oil prices.[23] Some of these studies employ disaggregated models of the U.S. economy; others rely on regression analysis to try to isolate the effect of oil price volatility on another facet of the economy. Six recent studies of the effects of an oil price increase on U.S. GDP and the GDP price deflator (a measure of inflation) appear in the appendix.[24] These studies do not offer a perfect apples-to-apples comparison, given their differences in methodology and reference year.[25] Nevertheless, there is some degree of cohesion across the results—if not in the magnitude of the effects, then at least in their direction and size.

Recent model-based analyses imply that a ten-dollar per barrel increase in the price of oil sustained over one or two years generally reduces real GDP by somewhere between -0.2 and -0.3 percent relative to the baseline over the first year and between -0.3 and -0.6 percent the following year. As for inflation, the impact is estimated at between +0.2 and +0.5 percent over the first year and then +0.3 and +0.5 percent in the second year relative to the baseline. In terms of unemployment (not included in the table), the Global Insight's 2005 study and the 1999 U.S. Federal Reserve study both estimate a departure from the baseline of +0.1 percent in year one and +0.2 percent in year two for a ten-dollar per barrel oil price increase. The lone time-series study surveyed, by Jimenez-Rodriguez and Sanchez in 2004, implies that a 10 percent increase in prices would cause real GDP to fall by roughly -0.5 percent in year one then again in year two. It judges the effects of a drop in prices of the same magnitude to be only roughly a quarter of that size, in line with the asymmetric dynamic explained earlier. Other dynamics can partially offset these economic impacts. Feedbacks between the U.S. current account deficit and the value of the dollar can increase demand for U.S. exports and thus moderate the drag on aggregate output. Similarly, a rise in external receipts to the United States from net oil exporters enjoying higher incomes and savings are partially recycled into demand for U.S. goods, though emerging-market countries have received the lion's share of these funds.[26] Additionally, other macroeconomic events well outside the oil market can mask the effects of exceptional oil market conditions, as occurred during the Asian financial crisis in the late 1990s and the

onset of the global recession in 2007.

The suddenness, unexpectedness, persistence, and historical context of the price change also influence its macroeconomic effects. All things equal, the more jarring and unforeseen the volatility, the more pronounced its implications, which can be much stronger or milder than the estimates provided. When businesses and consumers do anticipate a change in prices, they may begin to undertake precautionary saving, leading to an especially protracted economic pullback that can predate the actual market disruption. Additionally, an increase in oil prices that consumers expect to persist tends to be more disruptive to the broader economy than a jump they believe will fade fast, even a large one.[27]

When oil prices jump, the broader economic consequences depends in part on whether they have broken new ground, rising higher than any time in the recent past, or whether they stay in familiar territory. Econometric modeling suggests that net oil price increases only have a significant effect when they exceed their level over the last three years.[28] An increase that simply reverses a previous trend tends to be mostly ineffectual, as consumers have likely already adjusted their behavior. The public also becomes accustomed to sudden price fluctuations and takes steps to reduce their vulnerability, which mitigate the implications of a future change.[29] These dynamics are likely partly why the triple-digit oil prices appear to have had a milder impact on the economy over the last few years than they would have had in previous eras.

The source of an increase in oil prices—whether it is caused by swelling demand or interruptions to supply—makes a critical difference to its larger effects on the economy. Not all oil price changes are alike in their implications. This is intuitive: oil prices are not exogenously determined but are in part a function of economic growth, on which they then feed back. A jump in oil prices that comes about as a result of a rise in aggregate demand actually tends to correspond to no change or even an increase in net economic output over the short term. The same economic growth that lifts oil prices also lifts the economy in other ways, such as by stimulating demand for U.S. exports, which can entirely offset the negative shock of greater energy costs for a stretch. Yet over time these effects appear to wear off, and more expensive oil begins to take its toll on aggregate demand. This dynamic may help partly explain why the U.S. economy weathered rising oil prices so well for much of the 2000s, given that the bull market was mostly a result of global demand growth. On the other hand, when higher oil prices are sparked by an unanticipated supply interruption, real GDP tends to fall immediately. It remains negatively impacted at statistically significant levels for two years. Consumer prices, however, are not significantly affected.[30]

Domestic economic conditions at the time of the price change, as well as the response by monetary authorities, also affect the magnitude of the economic impacts. If inflationary pressures prior to the shock are running high, the Federal Reserve may face constraints in allowing money supply to expand, which will make it more difficult to offset the drag on output. The monetary response to rising oil prices is an important determinant of the economic impact. For example, the oil price shocks of the 1970s were followed by recessions partly because they coincided with tightening monetary policy, another negative shock.[31] High unemployment can also tie central bankers' hands. Like inflation, it heightens the tradeoff they face in attempting to navigate their dual mandate between inflation and output. Price trends in other commodity markets besides oil also matter; rising prices for other raw materials compound the challenge for monetary authorities to keep inflation expectations well anchored without resorting to raising benchmark rates.

What next for the U.S. oil economy? The links between the U.S. macroeconomy and the price of oil are complex and multifaceted. Often, these ties are ambiguous in nature: The picture is never of a change in oil prices being uniformly good or bad, but rather of a diverse set of trade-offs as well as winners and losers. Much of the country might cheer on declining oil prices, but for some parts of the country (and, pointedly, for some other countries in the world) they can be devastating. The linkages are also dynamic. The magnitude of the effects of a change in oil prices on subsections of the country, whether demographic or geographic, vary over time as technology, the location of oil production, and other aspects of the national economy evolve.

The U.S. oil landscape is undergoing a period of profound change, in terms of supply patterns as well as demand. Tight oil production is ramping up in places far beyond the traditional epicenter of domestic oil production, like

North Dakota, which has widened the geographic locus of economic growth associated with more drilling sparked by higher oil prices. This evolving geography expands the economic pie in new production centers, but also exposes their economy to new vulnerabilities caused by downturns in prices or disappointed expectations of future abundance. The same trend is playing out even more dramatically in natural gas, with booming production in Pennsylvania and other states that were previously far removed from the action. Meanwhile, a combination of high prices at the pump, increasingly fuel efficient cars and trucks, a weak economy, and an aging population, which tends to drive less, has led to a secular downshift in U.S. oil consumption.

Many of these factors are likely to persist for some time, given the tepid outlook for the American economy over the next decade, and some will be here to stay even after the recovery gains traction. The evolution that has occurred since the 1970s—of a national economy less sensitive to unexpected changes in oil prices since that tumultuous decade—continues to this day. No better evidence of that fact exists than that today's triple-digit oil prices, which once would have been unthinkable, are not the economic Armageddon that many analysts would have predicted a decade ago. With such tectonic changes in the country's oil economy, the nature of the domestic economy's ties to oil prices will no doubt continue to evolve.

Much of the country might cheer on declining oil prices, but for some parts of the country they can be devastating.

NOTES

1 BP, *BP Statistical Review of World Energy 2012* (London: BP, June 2012).

2 Christopher L. Foote and Jane S. Little, "Oil and the Macroeconomy in a Changing World: A Conference Summary," Federal Reserve Bank of Boston Public Policy Discussion Paper No. 11-3 (June 2011): 44, Internet, http://www.bostonfed.org/economic/ppdp/index.htm. (date accessed 11 December 2012).

3 During the 2007-08 oil price run-up, for instance, spending on domestic cars and trucks suffered quickly in response to rising prices, though sales of small foreign cars went up. Had the U.S. auto industry not suffered this drop in demand, one study finds, the domestic economy would have actually grown 1.2 percent in the first year of the recession, rather than shrunk. See James D. Hamilton, "Oil Prices, Exhaustible Resources, and Economic Growth," (18 October, 2011, updated 1 October 2012), 27. Chapter prepared for Roger Fouquet, ed., Handbook on Energy and Climate Change (Northampton: Edward Elgar Publishing, forthcoming 2013), Internet, http://dss.ucsd.edu/~jhamilto/handbook_climate.pdf. (date accessed: 11 December 2012).

4 Michael P. Keane and Eswar S. Prasad, "The Employment and Wage Effects of Oil Price Changes: A Sectoral Analysis," *The Review of Economics and Statistics* 78 no. 3 (August 1996), 389-400; James D. Hamilton, "Causes and Consequences of the Oil Shock of 2007-08," Brookings Papers on Economic Activity (Spring 2009), 215-282.

5 Lutz Killian, "Oil Price Volatility: Origins and Effects," World Bank Staff Working Paper ERSD-2010-02, World Bank (1 December 2009): 8.

6 Foote and Little, "Oil and the Macroeconomy in a Changing World," 44.

7 Hillard G. Huntington, "The Economic Consequences of Higher Crude Oil Prices," EMF SR 9, Energy Modeling Forum (3 October 2005): 20.

8 For a review of the literature on the asymmetric response of economic activity to oil price changes, see James D. Hamilton, "Nonlinearities and the Macroeconomic Effects of Oil Prices," Working Paper, (9 December 2009; Revised 15 November 2010), Internet, http://dss.ucsd.edu/~jhamilto/oil_nonlinear_macro_dyn.pdf, 1-6 (accessed 11 December 2012).

9 James D. Hamilton, "This is What Happened to the Oil Price-Macroeconomy Relationship," *Journal of Monetary Economics* 38 no. 2 (October 1996): 215-220.

10 Steven J. Davis and John Haltiwanger, "Sectoral Job Creation and Destruction Responses to Oil Price Changes," Journal of Monetary Economics 48 (2001): 465-512; Ana María Herrera, Latika Gupta Lagalo, and Tatsuma Wada, "Oil Price Shocks and Industrial Production: Is the Relationship Linear?," Macroeconomic Dynamics 15, S3 (November 2011): 472-497.

11 J. Peter Ferderer, "Oil Price Volatility and the Macroeconomy: A Solution to the Asymmetry Puzzle," *Journal of Macroeconomics* 18 no. 1 (Winter 1996): 1-16; John Elder and Apostolos Serletis, 2010. "Oil Price Uncertainty," Journal of Money, Credit and Banking 42, no. 6 (2010): 1137-1159.

12 Mine K. Yücel and Jackson Thies, "Oil and Gas Rises Again in a Diversified Texas," *Southwest Economy* (First Quarter 2011): 10-13.

13 This more muted relationship is a result of greater diversification of the state's industrial base and oilfield activity more immune to price fluctuations. See Steven P.A. Brown and Mine Yücel, "Do High Oil Prices Still Benefit Texas?," *Face of Texas* (October 2005): 33-36, Internet, https://www.dallasfed.org/assets/documents/research/pubs/fotexas/fotexas_brown.pdf (date accessed 11 December 2012).

14 Sean O'Leary, "Investing in the Future: Making Severance Tax Stronger for West Virginia," West Virginia Center on Budget and Policy (December 2011), Internet, http://www.wvpolicy.org/downloads/SeveranceTax022812.pdf; and PricewaterhouseCoopers, "The Economic Impacts of the Oil and Natural Gas Industry on the U.S. Economy in 2009: Employment, Labor, Income, and Value Added," Prepared for the American Petroleum Institute (May 2011), Internet, http://www.api.org/policy/americatowork/upload/economicimpacts_of_industry_on_us_economy_in_2009.pdf.

15 Hillard G. Huntington, "The Economic Consequences of Higher Crude Oil Prices," EMF SR 9, Energy Modeling Forum (3 October 2005): 28.

16 James D. Hamilton, "Oil and the Macroeconomy," Working Paper (August 24, 2005), 10. Chapter prepared for Steven N. Durlauf and Lawrence E. Blume, eds., *The New Palgrave Dictionary of Economics,* Second Edition (U.S. and UK: Palgrave Macmillan, 2008), Internet, http://dss.ucsd.edu/~jhamilto/JDH_palgrave_oil.pdf (date accessed 11 December 2012); Ethan S. Harris, Bruce C. Kasman, Matthew D. Shapiro, and Kenneth D. West, "Oil and the Macroeconomy: Lessons for Monetary Policy, Proceedings of the U.S. Monetary Policy Forum," The Initiative on Global Markets at The University of Chicago Booth School of Business and The Rosenberg Institute of Global Finance at the Brandeis University International Business School (February 2009, revised November 2009): 13. http://research.chicagobooth.edu/igm/docs/2009USMPFReport.pdf (date accessed 12 December 2012).

17 Ethan S. Harris, Bruce C. Kasman, Matthew D. Shapiro, and Kenneth D. West, "Oil and the Macroeconomy: Lessons for Monetary Policy, Proceedings of the U.S. Monetary Policy Forum," The Initiative on Global Markets at The University of Chicago Booth School of Business and The Rosenberg Institute of Global Finance at the Brandeis University International Business School (February 2009, revised November 2009): 13.

18 Ibid.

19 Olivier J. Blanchard and Jordi Gali, "The Macroeconomic Effects of Oil Shocks: Why are the 2000s

So Different from the 1970s?," NBER Working Paper No. 13368, National Bureau of Economic Research (September 2007): 1-5. http://www.nber.org/papers/w13368 (date accessed 12 December 2012).

20 Jorg Decressin, "Global Economy Learns to Absorb Oil Price Hikes," *International Monetary Fund Survey* (25 May 2012). http://www.imf.org/external/pubs/ft/survey/so/2012/num052512a.htm (date accessed 12 December 2012).

21 Valerie A. Ramey and Daniel J. Vine, "Oil, Automobiles, and the U.S. Economy: How Much Have Things Really Changed?," in Daron Acemoglu and Michael Woodford, eds., *NBER Macroeconomics Annual 2010* (Chicago: University of Chicago Press, 2010): 333-367.

22 Olivier J. Blanchard and Marianna Rigg, "The Oil Price and the Macroeconomy: What's Going on?," *VoxEU.org*, (7 December 2009), Internet, http://voxeu.org/article/price-oil-and-macroeconomy (date accessed 11 December 2012).

23 These studies generally utilize one of two approaches. The first type uses complex, disaggregated macroeconomic models of the U.S. economy. These models try to dynamically replicate the interrelationships among important macroeconomic variables, drawing on historical data to estimate the strength of these relationships. The second approach uses time-series analysis. Typically the simpler method, it tries to isolate the effect of a change in crude oil prices on another economic outcome, like changes in GDP or inflation, based on historical experience.

24 Table 1 below. Effect of an oil price increase on U.S. GDP and the GDP price deflator (inflation): A survey of recent estimates

25 Of these six, all but one rely on some form of macroeconomic model, with the outlier being the 2004 European Central Bank study. Most of the model-based studies report broadly similar findings with regard to the economic effects of an oil price increase.

26 Between 2002 and 2007, exports from emerging market countries to OPC rose by $186 billion, $5 billion more than the increase in imports, for a ratio of 103 percent in new imports to exports. Developed countries, where this ratio was only 52 percent, saw far less money flowing back from OPEC. See Ethan S. Harris, Bruce C. Kasman, Matthew D. Shapiro, and Kenneth D. West, "Oil and the Macroeconomy,"13-15.

27 Ray Barrell and Olga Pomerantz, "Oil Prices and the World Economy," National Institute of Economic and Social Research Discussion Paper 242 (December 2004), Internet, http://goo.gl/H09FN (date accessed 24 April 2013).

28 James D. Hamilton, "What is an Oil Shock?," *Journal of Econometrics* 113, no. 2 (2003): 363-398.

29 Kiseok Lee, Shawn Ni, and Ronald A. Ratti, "Oil Shocks and the Macroeconomy: The Role of Price Variability," *The Energy Journal* 16 no. 4 (September 1995): 39-56; Hillard G. Huntington, "The Economic Consequences of Higher Crude Oil Prices," Energy Modeling Forum, EMF SR 9 (3 October 2005): 8-9.

30 Lutz Killian, "Not All Oil Price Shocks Are Alike: Disentangling Demand and Supply Shocks in the Crude Oil Market," *The American Economic Review* 99, no. 3 (June 2009): 1053-1069.

31 James D. Hamilton, "Will Gas Prices Trigger Another Recession?," *CNN.com*, May 5, 2011, Internet, http://edition.cnn.com/2011/OPINION/05/05/hamilton.oil.recessions/index.html (date accessed 11 December 2012).

Study	Approach	Type of Price Increase	Impact on real GDP		Impact on inflation	
			Year 1	Year 2	Year 1	Year 2
Carabenciov et al. (2008), IMF	Macro- econometric model	(Permanent) 10 % increase		-0.20		0.27
Barrell and Pomerantz (2004), NIESR	NiGEM Macro-econometric model	(Permanent) $10 increase	-0.2	-0.48	0.3	0.52
OECD Global Model, Hervé et al. (2010)	Macro- econometric model	(Permanent) $10 increase		-0.31		0.41
Jimenez-Rodriguez and Sanchez (2004), ECB	Vector autoregression (VAR)	Impulse response to a 1% oil price shock^	-0.05	-0.05	—	—
Global Insight, Inc. (2005)	Macro-econometric model	(Permanent) $10 increase	-0.3	-0.6	0.2	0.5
U.S. Federal Reserve Bank (1999)	FRB/US macroeconomic model	(Permanent) $10 increase	-.02	-0.4	0.5	0.3

^ Accumulated response of GDP growth to a 1% oil price shock, asymmetric case
Source: OECD, U.S. EIA

Science&Technology

While We Watched: Assessing the Impact of the Satellite Sentinel Project

Nathaniel A. Raymond, Benjamin I. Davies, Brittany L. Card, Ziad Al Achkar, and Isaac L. Baker

When mass atrocities occur in conflict zones, corroborated, publicly available information about events happening in near-real time is often in short supply, if available at all. The difficulty of obtaining credible information during mass atrocities may impede international response to these complex events and, as a result, can increase the vulnerability of at risk populations. The recent, public deployment of remote sensing and data collection technologies during the alleged mass atrocities in Sudan provides insight into what potential impact and challenges these platforms may have in these scenarios.

The experience of the Satellite Sentinel Project (SSP) suggests that attempting to enhance the situational awareness of policymakers and the public does not appear by itself, at least in the case of Sudan, to directly affect whether, and to what degree, governments respond to mass atrocities as they occur. This article offers an overview of the relationship between the SSP reports published by the Harvard Humanitarian Initiative (HHI)[1] and international policy makers. It also explores SSP's use of technology and the development

The authors are currently the staff of the Harvard Humanitarian Initiative's (HHI) Signal Program on Human Security and Technology. Between December 2010 and June 2012, the authors were the operations staff and analysts of the Satellite Sentinel Project and were based at HHI.

of its methodology, identifying possible lessons to guide future mass atrocity response operations.

A Radical Proposition. When SSP publicly launched in December 2010,[2] the ensuing headlines ostensibly focused on two things: the application of technology (satellites), and its cofounder and patron, actor George Clooney. SSP's stated mission was to help prevent a return to full-scale war between Sudan and then-southern Sudan through satellite monitoring of threats to civilians along the contested border.[3] Implicit in the ambitious objective of preventing the civil war was the aspiration that the surveillance would affect the policies of the international community in ways that benefited vulnerable populations.

For SSP to become operational, two obstacles had to first be overcome: Regular access to the necessary volume of satellite imagery over the right locations and the means to immediately analyze relevant imagery and non-imagery data. The necessary imagery access and analysis support was provided by DigitalGlobe, a high-resolution satellite imagery provider. However, HHI, initially with the support of UN satellite imagery analysts, was responsible for solving the second challenge: collecting and interpreting high volumes of satellite and non-satellite data in twenty-four hour cycles.

SSP's radical proposition was that persistent near-real time remote surveillance could prevent or curtail the risks to vulnerable populations in Sudan and southern Sudan from gross human rights abuses.[4] SSP thought that achieving this effect could provide a blueprint for scaling this approach to other, future mass atrocity scenarios. If SSP did not have that effect, at the very least, evidence of alleged atrocities would be captured and documented to a degree previously impossible. No civilian platform similar to SSP had been built before due to high costs of satellite imagery and the absence of the methodology required for managing vast streams of relevant data.

Satellites, traditionally used by governments, provide otherwise unattainable, contemporaneous information about events occurring in non-permissive environments. Orbiting hundreds of miles above the Earth, their sensors collect unique data about certain observable objects (i.e. tanks, planes, burned buildings, etc.) from places not easily accessible from the ground.

At the time SSP was launched, approximately two weeks before the January 2011 referendum deciding southern Sudan's secession from Sudan, credible data about events on-the-ground were scant. Violence was escalating. Specific ethnic groups in Abyei, Blue Nile, and South Kordofan were seen by analysts as potential targets for atrocities by the government of Sudan. The information available about the events in these areas was often second-hand and largely impossible to confirm. The international community had minimal capacities for collecting impartial information and freely assisting civilians inside critical areas of Sudan due to restrictions on their freedom of movement.

United Nations Mission in Sudan (UNMIS) peacekeepers operated in Abyei and South Kordofan only until their mandate expired on 9 July 2011. Some international humanitarian groups were allowed by the Government of Sudan to stay in parts of the region until August that year, though heavy restrictions were placed on their activities. Because of these limitations, satellite monitoring was, at the time, SSP's most optimal option for collecting better corroborated information.

A New Methodology for a Costly Technology. SSP represents a substantial paradigm shift from traditional, often retrospective, collection of evidence corroborating alleged human rights violations. Instead, unprecedented access to recently captured imagery allowed SSP analysts to proactively anticipate some of these events. Evidence of enhanced fortifications or the presence of heavy equipment necessary to transport armored vehicles, for example, became harbingers of potential threats to specific civilian populations.

Unlike government geospatial analysts, HHI researchers began their work with limited precedents and pedagogy for guiding this tempo and volume of analysis in a humanitarian setting. A new methodology was needed for SSP's operations. The resulting approach is a hybrid of tactics for assessing military movements, humanitarian indicators, and melding together different streams of data into a more fused view of crisis events.

DigitalGlobe's constellation of satellites travels each day around the Earth in a geosynchronous trajectory, passing over the north and south poles as they orbit. The amount of images collected by SSP in such short periods of time allowed for a level and tempo of "refresh" (i.e. collection of new imagery) over key locations that made the observation of micro-changes in a village or a military base possible. HHI also had to collect, geo-code and sometimes translate non-imagery data. This data is essential for making sense of imagery. To address this issue, HHI staff geo-coded all relevant data in English, Arabic, and other languages by time stamps and geographic coordinates.

HHI researchers then fused together these two independent streams of data. The result is a previously unavailable, non-classified tool for situational awareness during alleged atrocity events. However, HHI analysts faced numerous challenges employing this new capacity.

The most important issue was the inherent limitations on analyzing remote sensing data without reliable ground confirmation. Satellites could offer a rare glimpse into the highly non-permissive Sudan-South Sudan border areas. However, imagery still represents only a single source of data about alleged events within a dynamic conflict zone. Though the HHI team strove to draw definitive conclusions about the conflict, remote sensing analysis alone could not result in conclusive knowledge of a situation, only interpretations.

HHI researchers recognized that remotely monitoring the conflict meant that reaching a consistent threshold of certainty about events on the ground was impossible. Reflecting this reality, HHI wrote all SSP reports in caveated language. For example, an image of a main battle tank was never simply reported as "a tank." That "tank" was always reported as an object "consistent" with a specific type of tank. Each specific type of tank had to be identified by measuring the object and comparing it to public databases about what vehicles or weapons are reportedly in the armed actors' arsenal.

As a result, HHI developed its own standards for what constituted appropriate levels of certainty to first reach and then release analytic conclusions. These standards enabled the HHI team to produce an experimental body of work that was both rich with retrospective data and of potential value to policymakers and the public. As the scope of reports collected and the archive of relevant imagery grew, HHI improved these systems for identifying and assessing intersections between imagery and geo-coded data.

Soon, HHI analysts were able to detect and corroborate evidence of abuses in a highly non-permissive environment. This approach allowed HHI to identify repeating patterns of behavior derived from public reports. Overlaid on recent imagery, these intersecting clusters of interrelated, digital information were critical in deciding where satellites should collect imagery.

This approach enabled SSP to become increasingly predictive. SSP moved from a traditional "documentation posture" into a more predictive "detection posture." Analysts were thus able to better target their collection of imagery to be more relevant to the real time security of vulnerable populations. This move towards prediction forced HHI researchers to weigh the unintended consequences of publicizing information and images about vulnerable populations when the audience included the parties to the conflict themselves. This task was especially difficult given SSP's access to near-real time satellite imagery and the ability

to rapidly share those images globally through the international and Sudanese domestic media.

As SSP worked to minimize the risk associated with these near-real time products, the challenge for the project was neither an absence of reports presenting compelling evidence of apparent mass atrocities, nor media exposure for its findings. Instead, the primary challenge was leveraging SSP's unique information to motivate international response to the alleged abuses in Sudan.

Barriers to Impact. Analysis of SSP's eighteen month pilot phase identifies multiple factors that may have limited the impact of SSP's reports in affecting the policy response of the U.S. government and others towards the crisis. One key factor that may have significantly limited SSP's ability to bring about policy changes was the perception of the project as being biased against the Government of Sudan and sympathetic towards South Sudan. Arguments concerning bias or the equal coverage of armed actors in SSP's reports are not without merit. They are actually critical to take into account when assessing the SSP model.

The SSP partner responsible for the project's communications and advocacy strategy, the Enough Project, and its funding source, Not On Our Watch, both had clearly stated positions against the Bashir regime. While HHI produced SSP's reports, SSP's founders, George Clooney and John Prendergast, a co-founder of the Enough Project, engaged in a high-profile advocacy campaign against the policies and leadership of the Government of Sudan. This included a March 2012 trip to Sudan's

Nuba Mountains region, as well as the subsequent arrest of George Clooney and other public figures, including Members of Congress, at the Sudanese Embassy in Washington, DC. Looking back on the first eighteen months of SSP, the public attention primarily centered either on the SSP's technological uniqueness or the involvement of its famous founder, George Clooney. SSP's novelty and its association with a celebrity often received more focus than the ramifications of its analysis for foreign policy.

Although all SSP reports during the pilot phase were independently produced by HHI, they were published under the SSP brand. The Enough Project acted as the delivery mechanism for SSP research products while simultaneously advocating its own policy recommendations on Sudan. Despite efforts to differentiate roles within the consortium, this structural reality reinforced the perception that SSP was an advocacy non-governmental organization (NGO) targeting President Bashir and the Sudanese leadership. For the high profile nature of the project, public questions or criticism concerning these core operational dynamics were rare.

Another factor that may have hindered the ability of SSP products to influence policy decisions was that policymakers possessed independent sources of information about events in Sudan. This information includes intelligence analysis and more advanced, routine satellite access to the region. If this information provided more comprehensive conclusions different to those reached by SSP, it could cast doubt on the SSP's findings.

Due to the classified nature of government intelligence, SSP analysts were not able to compare the outcomes of their analysis with the totality of information available to policymakers. Compounding this issue, even if SSP's reporting was timely and accurate, the true calculus of what was necessary at the policy level for any type of intervention in Sudan was and remains unknown. These extremely significant blind spots made it impossible for SSP to know what credibility or relevance their reports would have when they reached those in a decisive position to act.

SSP's Contribution. SSP confronted the reality that regardless of the publicity resulting from its reports, it was unable to catalyze timely or robust action within policy communities. As a consequence, the impact of SSP was an indirect but critical one: it generated public attention and made it necessary for policymakers to pay attention.

The project's published reports became recognized as an otherwise unavailable, contemporaneous source of information about the conflict in Sudan. SSP's ability to collect, analyze and release information in near-real time about potential threats to civilians, as much as the findings themselves, made its reporting more relevant and timely than other available information. To enhance this effect, SSP initially publicized each report through international news bureaus in East Africa, releasing them around 7am East Africa Time, in an attempt to better inform populations in danger. SSP's reports became a widely cited resource on the evolving situation in Sudan by a range of policy actors, including the International

Criminal Court,[7] the U.S. Congress, UN agencies, and others.

The project represents a critical step towards ascertaining what is required to transform the remote surveillance act into a means of better protecting civilians inside atrocity producing settings. For example, in the case of Kadugli, South Kordofan, during the summer of 2011, SSP conducted the first ever non-governmental, remote collection of alleged evidence of mass grave sites in a non-permissive environment. This occurred while reported systematic killings were ongoing.[8] SSP also visually confirmed the looting of the World Food Program facility in Abyei[9] and detected SAF forces moving to attack civilian areas in Blue Nile.[10] These successes resulted from unique insights that only remote-sensing technologies could deliver; improving the speed, agility and tempo with which evidence could be collected and presented for the benefit of vulnerable populations.

Through the use of a robust methodology and advanced technology, SSP hoped to change the balance of consequences for both armed actors in Sudan and policymakers around the world. So far, the evidence does not show that SSP met that objective. However, by advancing the practice of near-real time monitoring and documentation of alleged mass atrocities, SSP did help ensure that when policymakers and the public will not serve as rescuers, they will at least become witnesses.

NOTES

1 HHI led SSP's data collection, analysis, and report production during SSP's eighteen months pilot phase from December 2010 until June 2012. HHI withdrew from SSP to found the Signal Program on Human Security and Technology to conduct research on the emerging operational and ethical issues related to the use of information communication technologies during complex humanitarian disasters.

2 Mark Benjamin, "Clooney's 'Antigenocide Paparazzi': Watching Sudan," *Time Magazine*, December 28, 2010, Internet, http://www.time.com/time/magazine/article/0%2C9171%2C2040211%2C00.html

3 *Satellite Sentinel Project,* "Our Story", n.d., http://satsentinel.org/our-story.

4 Patrick Meier, "Will Using 'Live' Satellite Imagery to Prevent War in the Sudan Actually Work?" *iRevolution*, 20 December 2010, Internet, http://irevolution.net/2010/12/30/sat-sentinel-project/.

5 Larisa Epatko, "George Clooney on Sudan: 'It Gets in Your Bloodstream.'" *PBS Newshour*, 14 March 2012, Internet, http://www.pbs.org/newshour/rundown/2012/03/george-clooney-on-sudan.html.

6 Dana Hughes, "George Clooney Arrested at Sudanese Embassy," *ABC News*, 16 March 2012, Internet, "http://abcnews.go.com/Politics/OTUS/george-clooney-arrested-sudan-embassy-washington-dc/story?id=15936415#.UW2YYyuG0bo.

7 Mark Benjamin, "George Clooney's Satellites Build a War Crimes Case Against an Alleged War Criminal," *Time Magazine*, 3 December 2011, Internet, http://www.time.com/time/world/article/0,8599,2101425,00.html.

8 Satellite Sentinel Project, *Crime Scene: Evidence of Mass Graves in Kadugli*, July 14, 2011, Internet, http://satsentinel.org/sites/default/files/SSP%20 16%20Final%20Smaller.pdf.

9 *Satellite Sentinel Project*, Burned to the Ground, May 28, 2011, Internet, http://hhi.harvard.edu/sites/default/files/publications/burned to the ground.pdf.

10 *Satellite Sentinel Project, State of Emergency: Threat of Imminent SAF Attack on Kurmuk, Blue Nile*, September 23, 2011, Internet, http://www.satsentinel.org/sites/default/files/Satellite Sentinel Project report 092311.pdf.

How is NATO Dealing with Emerging Security Challenges?

Jamie Shea

For most of human history, states have seen their primary role in the field of security as the defence of their borders and their territories against the predations of other states. Though populations faced other threats, such as famine, major epidemics or starvation, governments felt no need to intervene unless there was an immediate threat to the state or social order.

Today, states have taken on the responsibility to cope with a much broader spectrum of threats because of voters' increased expectations of protection and the impact of globalization, which has made states much more vulnerable to non-traditional security threats. These can be easily transmitted across borders and can originate virtually everywhere: local and international terrorism, cyber threats to public and private networks, the spread of diseases and pandemics, vulnerabilities to critical infrastructure and energy grids, dependency on globalized supply chains, extreme weather conditions, uncontrolled immigration, organized criminal networks, and the proliferation of chemical, biological, radiological and nuclear (CBRN) devices with greater use of delivery vehicles such as missiles. The national security strategies of most NATO countries today prioritize these non-traditional threats before the more traditional

Jamie Shea is NATO's Deputy Assistant Secretary General for Emerging Security Challenges. He has previously held a number of high NATO positions, including Deputy Assistant Secretary General for External Relations, Public Diplomacy Division and Spokesman of NATO and Deputy Director of Information and Press. He holds a PhD in Modern History from Oxford University and has held a number of academic positions, int. al. Associate Professor of International Relations, American University, Washington DC.

The views expressed in this article are those of the author alone. They do not represent an official position of NATO.

threats from rising and rival powers or collapsing states. Although most of these non-traditional threats have existed for some time, NATO has only recently focused its attention on them.[1]

However, the Alliance is still associated with more classical military operations that take place outside its territory and emphasize flexible and deployable forces capable of cooperating with non-governmental organizations (NGOs), election observers, police trainers and democratic institution builders.

The "Responsibility to Protect" is partly responsible for NATO's shift away from the defence of states to the defence of populations. Simultaneously, NATO linked its interventions to traditional security interests.[2] Thus, despite

malware, drones, robotics and bioengineering), giving them the disruptive power that used to be the preserve of states. We could live in a future in which anyone could be targeted, anywhere, and at any time. These non-conventional threats cannot be deterred by the threat of military retaliation in the way that nuclear weapons could maintain a balance of power and peace, albeit uneasy, throughout the Cold War. Cyber attacks, for instance, have been a daily occurrence almost everywhere and most can still be carried out with relative impunity. The gain from espionage or financial crime greatly outweighs the risk of being caught or even the current legal penalties. Thus there is yet no significant incentives for the attackers to

Too much protection would constrain people's liberties and freedom of movement and seriously undermine the way of life that NATO defends.

the frequent portrayal of interventions as part and parcel of a new international morality to uphold human rights in foreign lands, in reality NATO has not strayed far from its traditional focus on the security of its member states.

Given this focus on defending and protecting interests, NATO has recently had to consider the new spectrum of threats which are not classically military in nature but which will undoubtedly be frequent sources of disruption in the years ahead. Moreover, these threats can originate just as easily from within our borders as from outside. Malicious individuals may easily gain access to modern technologies (int. al.

desist other than that they may damage and degrade information and communications infrastructure on which they also depend. It would be good if this "deterrence through interdependence" would eventually take hold, but we are clearly still a long way from it.

Deterrence or Prevention. Similarly, regarding terrorism, an attack by suicidal fanatics is difficult to pinpoint in advance or to stop, as we do not have the means or even the social ambition to permanently defend every conceivable vulnerability to our economies and societies. Too much protection would constrain people's liberties and freedom of movement and seriously undermine the way of life that NATO defends. Furthermore, a terrorist who accepts death as the inevitable outcome of his mission is not amenable to deterrence but only prevention. Consequently the early warning systems and methodologies that NATO relies upon to underpin deterrence or even to mobilize its own resources in anticipation of an attack no longer work. The best it can do is to achieve some early warning of an attack, calculate how to best limit the damage and recover as quickly as possible.

Attribution and Retaliation. Another problem is attribution. Actors come in ever smaller groups or use modern technologies, such as encryption, to cover their tracks. A cyber attack can be routed through so many countries that it is difficult to trace and can be started by an individual in a location remote from himself. A terrorist cell can operate thousands of miles away from its directing headquarters (HQ). Establishing proof of culpability, especially in the event of cyber or terrorist attacks, can take a long time. In some cases, such as cyber attacks, a response has to come within nano seconds to prevent further penetration of a network and major damage. This rapidity of response does not always fit organizations such as NATO, which is best at orchestrating military responses and often needs lengthy consultations to build consensus and to approve detailed operational plans and rules of engagement before acting. A military response may also not be the right response; for instance after an energy cut-off or a terrorist attack. If we have clear

evidence that a state and a single leader is responsible, then a military operation is appropriate, but most modern attacks do not fit this "single aggressor" paradigm.

What level of solidarity can we expect and can we offer? These threats are not existential in the way that a Soviet tank thrust through the Fulda Gap or a rocket strike would have been for all Allies during the Cold War. No lives were lost or critical infrastructure damaged when Estonia suffered a devastating eleven-day distributed denial of service (DDoS) attack in 2007. The situation in the twenty-five other NATO member states at the time remained quite normal. What is the threshold for a collective response? Some Allies believe that a response should be collective and multinational from the outset. Others believe that the nation is primarily responsible, for instance in the protection of critical information or energy infrastructure. NATO's entire history has been dedicated to fostering a collective approach to security and promoting the primacy of collective responses. But cyber defence is an area where we have largely gone back to national policies and programmes; nations are still very secretive even vis-à-vis their Allies regarding their cyber vulnerabilities or cyber capabilities and reluctant to share information beyond the very small trusted communities in which their intelligence services and private-public partnerships operate. It would thus take some time and effort to raise cyber defence within NATO to the same level of collective engagement as traditional force planning or force generation for operations. It took NATO many decades to persuade its members to adopt a collective approach and to share their capabilities and defence plans, recognizing that in this way they would ultimately have more security. In dealing with new challenges like cyber threats, however, we cannot afford the luxury of several more decades before we arrive at the same collective approach.

The proliferation of actors. A final challenge is the fact that most of the non-traditional threats require responses by various actors and here NATO is rarely in the lead - a culture change for the Alliance, which for sixty years has been a leader in its field. NATO is not accustomed to sharing leadership and decision-making responsibilities with a range of different civilian actors outside the conventional military chain of command. Cyber issues require links with interior ministries, intelligence services, the police and cabinet offices that are not NATO's normal interlocutors and have no permanent bureaucratic links with NATO HQ of the sort that foreign and defence ministries have long enjoyed. Moreover, as over ninety per cent of information networks are owned by the private sector, the ability to bring private companies in to everyday cyber defence management is crucial to success. NATO no longer defines the terms. Allies may be reluctant to be told by private industry what the threat is and to have to share daily management after decades of seeing industry purely as the deliverer of a capability decided uniquely by governments. But this is already happening at the national level in the cyber area and in information and intelligence sharing, and it will have to be elevated to the international level as well.

NATO's Responses. Consequently, NATO's traditional toolbox of political consultation processes and military means can be useful in addressing the new security challenges but it is certainly insufficient for serious action. To have a real impact rather than simply raising awareness about the new threats NATO has to be willing to adopt measures that fall outside the traditional mould of high-end conventional military conflicts. The nature of the challenges has to define the responses. Also, NATO has to be honest in admitting that it has no "silver bullet" and that in some areas its role will be subjugated to other actors. For instance, missile defence is an exclusively military programme where only one Ally, the United States, has the radars, missile interceptors and overall systems architecture to provide the capability to the Alliance. The other Allies may have elements that they can add on (for instance, Patriot air defence missiles or satellite and reconnaissance assets) but they cannot replace the US in this area. Other issues, such as cyber, terrorism and energy security are very different. Here the non-US Allies have very important capabilities but many of these are in the civilian area (for instance intelligence). NATO would thus not be the only or even the principal forum of activity. Consequently the Alliance has to define carefully the areas where it can add value to the existing international efforts to contain and counter these new threats. The overall challenge is to avoid promising more than it can deliver; but, at the same time, not to become so reductionist or minimalist that NATO ends up leaving its member states vulnerable in areas where it is perfectly capable of protecting them.

What does this mean in practice?
The first step is to create a clear mandate for the Alliance to deal with these challenges. This was accomplished in the new NATO Strategic Concept[3] and Lisbon Summit Declaration of 2010,[4] which placed cyber, terrorism, energy security and CBRN threats on the same priority level as more traditional threats such as state aggression. Certainly the eloquent language of these high-level political statements does not in itself guarantee full consensus among the Allies on its interpretation, nor the implementation. But it is the necessary beginning.

The second step is to create a firm bureaucratic foothold in the NATO organization. The recently established Emerging Security Challenges Division (ESC) within NATO today brings the following threats under one roof: Cyber Defence, Counter-Terrorism, Energy Security, WMD Proliferation and Nuclear Policy, Strategic and Defence Economic Analysis and Scientific and Technological Cooperation with NATO's multiple partner countries. The new unified division facilitates tackling the crosscutting nature of the challenges. They are frequently most ominous in a combination thus achieving a critical destructive or disruptive mass; for instance terrorist attacks on critical infrastructure, cyber attacks on supervisory control and data acquisition systems (SCADAs) that control energy pipelines and electricity grids or terrorist access to weapons of mass destruction and associated missile technologies. Given NATO's continuing preoccupation with its operation in

Afghanistan and the consequences of defence budget cuts in North America and in Europe for the future levels and interoperability of its armed forces, a single ESC Division helps to keep these issues on NATO's agenda. It supports Allies in focusing on cost-effective prevention and resilience measures, even if there has not been (thankfully) a major terrorist strike or a paralyzing cyber attack in many NATO countries for some years to galvanize political attention and mobilize resources.

The third step is to develop coherent policies in all these areas with a common denominator that the Allies are all willing to support. This establishes the political and technical basis needed for the Allies to be more willing to agree to concrete actions in the subsequent implementation plan. Since its establishment two years ago the ESC Division has updated NATO's policy documents in all the key areas. It has developed a cyber policy and action plan; new counter-terrorism policy guidelines and work is on-going on an associated action plan. After difficult debates, Allies now have a clearer view on how NATO can contribute to energy security, particularly in the realm of critical infrastructure protection and a sharing of best practices among government and industry experts. NATO has also reviewed its WMD arms control and nuclear policies and has developed a new doctrine for defence against CRBN devices. Its Science for Peace and Security Programme (SPS) is now more focused on key priorities which link science and technology to NATO's core activities making it more relevant to Allies. One example is a project involving the emplacement of scanners at the borders of Central Asian countries and Afghanistan. These scanners improve the customs of our partner countries and facilitates the transit of military equipment coming in and out of Afghanistan in support of NATO's ISAF mission. NATO has also come to the conclusion that it has to be able to identify threats more in advance and be less reactive. This can be done by establishing the link between threats at an earlier stage (for instance, weapons, transfers, organized crime and terrorism in the Sahel region) and identifying the triggers that can mark their evolution from a local problem to a real security threat to NATO. This also generates periodical attention by identifying various scenarios and the pros and cons of different courses of action by NATO – from early to late. A Strategic Analysis Capability and an Economics Assessment Unit are helping to spark discussion and inform decisions regarding these future crisis areas and the means NATO has to respond. This type of staff work unfortunately does not guarantee political attention but without it political consultations would not happen or produce any actionable conclusions.

The challenge now is to build capabilities. NATO has always been an organization based on physical capabilities, such as integrated command structures, common communications and planning mechanisms, and forces. Thus, the new challenges will be more effectively anchored in the Alliance if they also have a hard capability dimension. In cyber defence, this currently means upgrading the NATO Computer Incident Response Capability[5] to allow it to protect NATO's civilian as well as military networks and to have the most advanced assets for detecting intrusions, freezing data for analysis and evidence, and sending rapid response teams to assist Allies facing cyber attacks on their NATO and military-related networks. For the first time this year, cyber defence will become part of NATO's defence planning process and nations will accept Capability Targets to create more effective national cyber defence organizations and national Computer Emergency Response Teams (CERTs) to centralize cyber defence management and responses. In the field of terrorism, NATO is developing technologies to detect suicide bombers (the Stand-off Detection of Explosives - STANDEX project) and counter improvised explosive devices (IEDs). These may have originated from operational requirements in Afghanistan but they will be useful in other operations and also in civil defence at home. In energy security, NATO has developed best practices on protecting critical infrastructure and has a project to enhance the more efficient use of energy in the military, given our recent experience of having to transport fuel to Afghanistan at very high cost.

Building on these activities, NATO has been trying to factor the emerging challenges into its exercises. Handling a cyber crisis is not the same as handling a conventional or WMD attack. Exercises are useful to identify and fix the weaker spots in NATO's political procedures and military capabilities and to discern issues that may not always surface in normal political consultations. They not only pinpoint institutional weaknesses but also expose national positions and disagreements, which can be hidden in more theoretical debates. Exercises are also a good way of obliging nations to clarify, which capabilities they are prepared to make available to NATO in a crisis and how ready for use those capabilities are.

Highly networked challenges require highly networked responses. We have long spoken of the need for a comprehensive approach to military operations, where military and civilian efforts are integrated from the outset, but we need this comprehensive approach just as much in dealing with cyber attacks, terrorism or energy cutoffs. As we know in this field, many branches of government as well as the private sector are involved. The Dutch Cyber Defence Information Centre has no fewer than fourteen government agencies permanently participating, all of whom would be expected to be involved in managing a major cyber attack. So it is important to have clear procedures, validated through exercises to determine the respective roles of all key actors, thereby avoiding duplication, gaps or mutual blockages once a crisis occurs. As NATO lacks early warning regarding specific attacks, it also becomes all the more important to improve the overall understanding how these threats originate and to chart their evolution, both geographically and functionally. NATO needs to determine at which point of the threat chain a NATO response is both justified and effective. The challenge is to identify the right point for counter-measures against threats such as cyber or terrorist attacks. This also includes summoning the political will to act timely and decisively against these threats before it

is too late and our societies are severely harmed.

It does not have to be a choice between a full-scale NATO military intervention or no involvement at all. To be successful, NATO must appeal to and build closer ties with other international organizations, NGOs, think-tanks and the private sector. For the first time in its history, NATO is dealing with challenges that cannot be understood and responded to within the narrow confines of its own twenty-eight members. NATO must also embrace its partner countries that share the urgency of the threat and have as much to contribute as to receive in terms of intelligence sharing and experience. Post-ISAF, partners may well become less involved in NATO's operations; thus it becomes all the more important to sustain these partnerships by anchoring them also in the emerging security challenges. The Alliance will have to become as good at leveraging the contributions of others as in inducing its own members to act. If the future of security for the Western countries is to do less themselves and rely more on the local actors, then organisations like NATO will have to improve their political dialogue with the new African, Asian and Arab security actors in order to foster more genuine trust.

Conclusion. Dealing with the new challenges requires NATO to take a less reactive and more anticipatory approach. We cannot restrict our discussions only to the immediate crises. NATO will have to consider a much broader intellectual landscape and identify multiple niche opportunities where NATO can make a difference. This will require a change of mind-set and more focus on what other actors are doing in the field of international security so that NATO has a better understanding of the strengths and weaknesses of their operations should it be called upon to support them. Modern security challenges are much more multifaceted and complicated than what we have seen in the past. Complexity could in itself become a form of self-deterrence if we start to believe that we should not try to influence regional conflicts or crises because we do not sufficiently understand the actors on the ground or the dynamics at play. Our publics might be

curity environment around it, particularly in an age where defence budgets will be subject to the same stringency as every other government spending programme and the margin for policy errors or waste of precious resources is far narrower.

In sum, addressing the new security threats is a daunting challenge for the Alliance. It will have to become a hub of political dialogue and security services rather than a monolithic structure focussing only on one security issue at any given time. As this article has demonstrated, some significant cultural and intellectual changes are re-

Modern security challenges are much more multifaceted and complicated than what we have seen in the past.

relieved that less engagement means less cost or risk, particularly after Iraq, Afghanistan and Libya; but to let the rest of the world go its own way and to remain on the side-lines looking outwards cautiously is not a long-term recipe for stability in the 21st Century. Therefore NATO will have to ensure that its actions are based on the best and most detailed knowledge of the se-

quired but the Alliance has also many of the standard ingredients for success: a record of adaptability, a large range of willing and able partners, legitimacy in the UN and more broadly and, last but not least, its proven military planning and capability development structures. So although the challenge to remain relevant is daunting, it is also entirely manageable.

NOTES

1 Even the first cyber attack (allegedly against a Soviet pipeline in Siberia) goes back to 1983.

2 For instance, the interventions in the Balkans in 1995 and 1999 were justified by the need to prevent a spill over of the conflict onto NATO territory. The overall objective of the International Security Assistance Force (ISAF) in Afghanistan remains the stabilization of Afghanistan in order to prevent the country from re-emerging as a base for terrorist attacks again NATO Allies. For reference see, The North Atlantic Treaty Organization, The North Atlantic Treaty, 4 April 1949.

3 NATO's New Strategic Concept, North Atlantic Treaty Organization, accessed 17 March 2013, Internet, http://www.nato.int/strategic-concept/index.html.

4 North Atlantic Treaty Organization, "Lisbon Summit Declaration", 20 November 2010, Internet, Internet, http://www.nato.int/cps/en/natolive/official_texts_68828.htm.

5 North Atlantic Treaty Organization, *NATO and Cyber Defence*, Internet, http://www.nato.int/cps/en/natolive/topics_78170.htm.

Science&Technology Politics&Diplomacy Culture&Society Business&Economics Law&Ethics Conflict&Security Books Science&Technology Politics&Diplomacy Culture&Society Business&Economics Law&Ethics Conflict&Security Books Science&Technology Politics&Diplomacy Culture&Society Business&Economics Law&Ethics Conflict&Security Science&Technology Politics&Diplomacy Culture&Society Business&Economics Law&Ethics Conflict&Security Books Business&Economics Politics&Diplomacy macy Culture&Society Business&Econ

Georgetown Journal

of International Affairs

Each Section. Every Issue. One Journal.

for more information or to subscribe

visit http://journal.georgetown.edu or email gjia@georgetown.edu

now featuring bi-weekly short essays, commentaries and analyses online

Books

The Killing Zone: The United States Wages Cold War in Latin America

Review by John McNeill

Stephen G. Rabe, *The Killing Zone: The United States Wages Cold War in Latin America*. New York and Oxford: Oxford University Press, 2012. 247 pp. $19.95.

Stephen Rabe is an academic historian with an ax to grind, and he grinds it well. He begins this book by explaining that he is under no illusions about the character of the Soviet Union during the Cold War. He visited former KGB prisons in Latvia, befriended Czechs persecuted for showing insufficient enthusiasm for the Red Army invasion of Prague in 1968, and educated himself about the many nefarious aspects of the Soviet empire in Eastern Europe. But his point here is to draw attention to the nasty Cold War conduct of the United States in its own backyard, Latin America.

Rabe finds American Cold War triumphalism objectionable in general and specifically because it overlooks the election-rigging, *coups d'état*, and massacres to which the U.S. government contributed in Latin America. He does not claim that these deeds were equally as evil as those perpetrated by the Kremlin. But he vigorously argues that they were unnecessary in every sense and did nothing to

Dr. John McNeill is a professor in the School of Foreign Service and History Department at Georgetown where he teaches courses in World History, Environmental History, and International History. His publications include *Mosquito Empires: Ecology and War in the Greater Caribbean, 1640-1914*, *The Human Web: A Bird's-eye View of World History*, and *Something New Under the Sun: A Environmental History of the 20th-Century World*.

advance the American cause in the Cold War. He maintains that U.S. Cold War policy in Latin America "helped perpetuate and spread violence, poverty, and despair within the region."[1]

The many U.S. interventions – to use a gentle term – in Cold War Latin America were first presented [within the bureaucratic and political organs of the U.S. government] as helpful or even necessary measures to secure the American hemisphere from communist or Soviet power. When they were not kept secret, the interventions were then marketed to the American public with the same Cold War *raison d'état*. Rabe argues that these efforts at justification were at best based on ignorance and at worst on calculated dishonesty. U.S. officials consistently overestimated, and sometimes deliberately

informed U.S. policymaker, such as Viron ("Pete") Vaky, a career diplomat, often a lonely dissenting voice (and at times a professor in the School of Foreign Service). But more often Rabe detects a "patronizing, condescending attitude" among U.S. officials, who "often implicitly judged Latin Americans as marked at birth for lives of wickedness and degeneracy."[2] Prominent policymakers who come in for particular condemnation include George Kennan, Henry Kissinger, and Jeanne Kirkpatrick (another former professor at Georgetown). Their bosses, secretaries of state and presidents of both parties come off little better. All followed in the tradition of Theodore Roosevelt, who regarded the population of Colombia as "crazy Dagos."[3] William Jennings Bryan, Secretary of

To borrow a phrase from Talleyrand, the interventions were worse than crimes, they were blunders.

exaggerated, Soviet activities in Latin America, which were modest indeed compared to Soviet engagements in other world regions. Moreover, the ill-advised U.S. interventions alienated Latin American populations and contributed to anti-American popular and political sentiment throughout the region. To borrow a phrase from Talleyrand, the interventions were worse than crimes, they were blunders.

Rabe finds that U.S. Cold War policy towards Latin America was based on pervasive ignorance and disdain, and often on outright racism. He finds an occasional thoughtful and

State for Woodrow Wilson, encapsulated ignorance, disdain and racism pithily when, after a briefing about Haiti, he said: "Dear me, think of it. Niggers speaking French."[4]

Rabe begins with a survey of U.S. involvement in Latin America before the Cold War, starting with the aftermath of the Spanish-American War of 1898. The U.S. undertook 30 armed expeditions in the Caribbean and Central America between 1900 and 1933, and at various times occupied Cuba, Haiti, the Dominican Republic, Honduras and Nicaragua. Motivations included improving the position of various U.S. corporations involved in Latin America and trying to create stable societies. The latter ambition often began with instruction in the virtues of U.S. institutions and ended in support for brutal thugs such as Rafael Trujillo in the Dominican Republic, Fulgencio Batista in Cuba, or Anastasio Somoza in Nicaragua, all of whom attained power through careers in security forces created with the support of the U.S. Marine Corps. Although Rabe applauds Franklin Roosevelt for treating Latin Americans with respect, Roosevelt's Good Neighbor Policy appears here as simply a softer version of previous policies. The pattern of U.S. involvement in Latin America set early in the twentieth century, according to Rabe, prefigured U.S. Cold War policy in the region, although after 1950 Washington was likelier to send in the CIA rather than the Marines.

Rabe begins his account of the Cold War with the most influential American diplomat of the age, George Kennan. By 1950 Kennan's interpretations of Soviet conduct had acquired a wide following in Washington. He was at the height of his powers at age 46 and among the foremost architects of U.S. foreign policy. In February of that year he visited Latin America, stopping in seven countries. His diary reveals that he found the experience a tiresome ordeal. The long memorandum he produced upon his return found Latin America offered a "hopeless background for the conduct of human life...."[5] He saw the region as having no significance of its own, existing as a source of raw materials for the U.S. economy and military. U.S. policy towards Latin America should serve to keep it in Washington's orbit without undue regard for the feelings of Latin Americans, relying as needed on "harsh governmental measures of repression." Kennan's report was too undiplomatic for distribution even among U.S. officialdom and gathered dust until its declassification in 1976. It had no political importance, but for Rabe it is important because it reveals the attitudes and approach of U.S. mandarins, no more generous towards Latin America in 1950 than in 1900.

Rabe devotes a chapter to the toppling of Guatemala's President Jacobo Arbenz Guzmán in 1954. Arbenz initiated land reform by breaking up big estates and distributing land to poor peasants. This allowed his enemies to paint him as a communist and a tool of Moscow. (Arbenz did have an interest in Marxist theories of history, but had no links to the Kremlin). In the early 1950s anxieties about communist infiltration within the U.S. and the Americas were so feverish that the CIA met little resistance in the corridors of power in Washington when it proposed to finance and arm a Guatemalan colonel, a graduate of training courses in Ft. Leavenworth, to overthrow Arbenz. President Truman's Secretary of State, Dean Acheson, temporarily delayed the scheme, feeling that U.S. prestige ought not be gambled on something as trivial as a Central American state. But under President Eisenhower the deed was done. The CIA concluded that such interventions could serve as a useful tool of U.S. policy, even if post-Arbenz Guatemala degenerated into a seething cesspool of class warfare, repression, and violence. The chapter inevitably reminds one of the 2003 invasion of Iraq: U.S. policy-makers convinced themselves of a falsehood, dismissed all conflicting evidence, and launched an operation that succeeded

cies as a result.

The foreign policy of Nixon and Kissinger merits another chapter, devoted mainly to Chile. Nixon had long come to the view that Latin Americans pre-

Rabe presents Castro as a deep obsession of John F. Kennedy's.

in its short-term goals at great political cost to the U.S. and human cost to the targeted countries. Arbenz's communist ties were as imaginary as Saddam's weapons of mass destruction.

Rabe allots two chapters to the U.S. struggle to overturn the Cuban revolution of Fidel Castro and to prevent any imitations elsewhere in the region. He presents Castro as a deep obsession of John F. Kennedy's and details the clumsy failure of the CIA in the Bay of Pigs operation of 1961, in which a handful of Cuban exiles landed on a beach hoping to provoke an uprising and overthrow Castro. They were killed or captured, and the CIA's bumbling provided Castro with his greatest victory over the colossus to the North. Kennedy appears irrational over Cuba, and Lyndon Johnson little better. The U.S. invasion in the Dominican Republic (1965) and support for the authoritarian military regime that seized power in 1964 in Brazil arose from irrational anxieties about communist potential in those countries and Latin America in general – anxieties that Castro's success inflated. Democrats as well as Republicans could deceive themselves about the level of communist threat in Latin America and commit the U.S. to bloody and counter-productive poli-

ferred dictatorship to democracy, and in 1970 he and Kissinger concluded that Chile's elected president, Salvador Allende (a Marxist and friend of Castro), was an intolerable presence. Kissinger said that the U.S. ought not "let a country go Marxist just because its people are irresponsible."[6] Through the CIA, Nixon actively encouraged a Chilean general to mount a coup, which took place in 1973. The overthrow of Allende ushered in an era of energetic state repression in which several thousand Chileans were murdered by their new government, a military dictatorship. Several tens of thousands were tortured. Kissinger, in a transcript of a telephone call with Nixon, complained that the U.S. press did not see this in the proper light, and that "in the "Eisenhower period we would be heroes."[7] Kissinger would be no more pleased if he were to read Rabe's account.

The final chapter concerns U.S. efforts to undo the 1979 Sandinista revolution in Nicaragua and the Reagan administration's approach to Central America in the 1980s. Rabe emphasizes the illegal aspects of Reagan's policies, the use of death squads in El Salvador and Reagan's enthusiastic embrace of a genocidal general in

Guatemala, Efraín Ríos Montt, whom he described as "a man of great personal integrity."[8] Here Rabe attributes great importance to Jeanne Kirkpatrick, who not long earlier had written a defense of authoritarian government and admired the generals who were then in the process of murdering about 30,000 Argentinian citizens for political reasons. Kirkpatrick provided an intellectual patina for U.S. support of a new generation of brutal thugs in Central America and the Southern cone, men who never tired of reminding U.S. officials that they were on the same side in the struggle against communism. General Ríos Montt was

issues out of his book. His afterword, a narrative of post-Cold War U.S.-Latin American relations, does not mention the NAFTA accords, a major departure in Mexican-U.S. diplomacy. The effort to stress human rights in U.S. foreign policy, associated above all with President Carter, gets two pages. In order to earn extended discussion in Rabe's book, it seems, sordid misdeeds are required.

Rabe chose not to offer much Cold War context for his story. Rabe writes that Latin America "would become 'the killing zone' of the Cold War."[9] Latin America was indeed a killing zone during the Cold War, but it was

Rabe is right that U.S. policy in Latin America was often morally indefensible.

the worst of the lot, responsible for the death of a minimum of 200,000 Guatemalans. He is currently on trial for genocide and crimes against humanity.

Rabe is right that U.S. policy in Latin America was often morally indefensible, based on ignorance and disdain of the sort exemplified by Kennan, Kissinger, and Kirkpatrick. But he has almost nothing to say about those components of U.S. policy that do not merit such condemnation. For example, the most important country in Latin America for the U.S. was and remains the one with which it shares a border, Mexico. Rabe mentions it in passing three times. U.S.-Mexican relations during the Cold War included several important issues, not least the migration of upwards of ten million Mexicans to the U.S. Rabe leaves these

one of many and far from the most murderous. U.S. hot wars in Korea and Vietnam were far more deadly, and so were several proxy wars in places such as Angola. Readers without a sense of the urgency and variety of U.S. commitments during those years will have trouble assessing Rabe's arguments and understanding the pattern of neglect and haste that characterized Washington's approach to Latin America. The Chinese Revolution and Soviet acquisition of nuclear weapons in 1949, the Suez Crisis and Hungarian uprising of 1956, the escalation in Vietnam in 1965 and the Iranian revolution of 1979 were justifiably foremost in the minds of presidents and their cabinets. While the U.S. bureaucracies had no shortage of full-time specialists on Latin America, those holding the levers of power could rarely afford to give much attention to the region – which is not to say that if they had done so their choices would have been wiser. It is still important to recognize that aside from the immediate aftermath of the Cuban Revolution, at no time did Latin America command top priority in U.S. policy circles. Rabe's book would have been a bit longer had he sketched in the overall contours of the Cold War more regularly, and perhaps that is reason enough not to have done it. But Rabe's intended audience, undergraduate students, probably would benefit from a fuller sense of the competing priorities in U.S. foreign policy formation.

Rabe has taken pains to make his book student-friendly. At the outset it has a timeline of events in U.S.-Latin American relations extending from 1945 to 2010. At the end it has a detailed and thorough set of recommended readings, book, articles, and websites. And, uniquely as far as I know, he includes his address and email address, inviting readers to ask for further bibliographic advice. He assures readers that he does not regard inquiries as an imposition but as part of his job. He can't be faulted for lack of public-spiritedness.

He and his publisher can be faulted for some sloppy presentation. Early in the book Rabe repeatedly refers to the "United Kingdom" in the nineteenth century (it was created in 1922). On occasion it is unclear where a quotation begins or ends. Apostrophes sometimes appear where they don't belong and are missing where they do belong. Oxford University Press can do better than that.

In sum, Rabe's book should not be mistaken for a general history of U.S. policy toward Latin America during the Cold War. It is a spirited indictment of a series of sordid misdeeds committed by the U.S. government in Latin America before and during the Cold War. Rabe's book will help a new generation of Americans face that grim record.

Notes

1 Rabe, *The Killing Zone: The United States Wages Cold War in Latin America*, New York and Oxford: Oxford University Press, 2012: 29.

2 Ibid, 31.

3 Ibid, 31.

4 Ibid, 12.

5 Ibid, 23

6 Ibid, 134.

7 Ibid, 137.

8 Ibid, 34

9 Ibid, 36.

Understanding Iran

Review by John McNeill

William R. Polk. *Understanding Iran: Everything You Need to Know, From Persia to the Islamic Republic, from Cyrus to Ahmadinejad.* New York: Palgrave Macmillan, 2009. 247 pp. $17.

William Polk, born in 1929, is one of the more successful scholar-diplomats in American life. He has written more than a dozen books, mainly on the modern Arab world, some for trade publishers and some for university presses. He taught Middle East and Islamic history at Harvard and the University of Chicago. He also served in the Kennedy and Johnson administrations, on the State Department's Policy Planning staff and later as an adviser to McGeorge Bundy, President Johnson's National Security Adviser, charged with handling the aftermath of 1967's Six-Day War between Israel and its Arab neighbors.

His latest book is his first on Iran. He has visited the country from time to time since 1956, and in the 1960s met the Shah, Mohammed Reza Pahlavi and some of the Iranian political elite.

Aware of the stalemate that bedevils U.S.-Iranian relations, and frustrated by what he sees as the narrowness of war-game exercises and the field of international relations,

Dr. John McNeill is a professor in the School of Foreign Service and History Department at Georgetown where he teaches courses in World History, Environmental History, and International History. His publications include *Mosquito Empires: Ecology and War in the Greater Caribbean, 1640-1914, The Human Web: A Bird's-eye View of World History,* and *Something New Under the Sun: A Environmental History of the 20th-Century World.*

Polk wrote this book "to bring forward what war games omit: in short, what it means when we speak of Iran and Iranians."[1] He feels American policy-makers pay insufficient heed to the history and culture of Iran and Iranians, and are thereby baffled by what seems to them illogical behavior. If they had adequate grounding in things Iranian, he believes, they would better understand Iran, its government, its policies, and its people.

Adequate grounding, in Polk's view, extends back 2,500 years. He maintains that even if the majority of Iranians alive have scant knowledge of the Achaemenid dynasty they are nonetheless influenced by it. Indeed, he writes, "I am certain that the inhabitants of Iran today are largely governed by their past regardless of whether they consciously

as a "national intelligence survey" of the kind produced by the CIA. Given Herodotus' fanciful imagination and weakness for tall tales, one hopes the CIA does rather better. His initial chapter continues through the conquests of Alexander, the Seleucid, Parthian, and Sassanid empires, the advent of Islam, the influx of Turkic nomads, and the Mongol invasion and formation of the Il-Khanid (Mongol) state in the thirteenth century C.E. It is all rather breathless, a bit in the Iranian nationalist vein, but clear and lively throughout.

The second chapter carries the narrative from the thirteenth century through the reign of Shah Abbas in the seventeenth century. It focuses on the rise and rule of the Safavid dynasty, in power from 1501, and the force that made most of Iran Shi'a. Here Polk

> **He maintains that** even if the majority of Iranians alive have scant knowledge of the Achaemenid dynasty…they are nonetheless influenced by it.

remember it."[2] He appeals to Carl Jung's notion of "collective unconscious" and Jean-Jacques Rousseau's "social contract" to make his case.

Polk starts his first chapter with the Indo-European forebears of modern Iranians. He narrates the (rather murky) rise of Zoroastrian religion, one of ancient Iran's gifts to the world that lives on to this day among the Parsis of India, before settling in for a discussion of Cyrus, Darius, and the Achaemenid dynasty. The Achaemenids are known to us mainly through the pages of Herodotus, whose work Polk describes

helpfully provides something more than political history touching on the social structure of Safavid Persia and themes such as urbanization and trade. He emphasizes the crueler aspects of the autocracy of Shah Abbas, who brought Safavid Iran to the apex of its power while wantonly murdering opponents real and imagined, and blinding all his brothers lest they conceive designs on the throne. Polk finds him a fine example of the axiom that power corrupts and absolute power corrupts absolutely – which he (or perhaps his spellcheck) attributes to Lord Action rather than Lord Acton.[3]

Polk's third chapter mixes the political sociology of Ibn Khaldun with narrative of the Iranian state through the turn of the twentieth century. Polk finds the insights of the fourteenth century Tunisian useful in seeking to understand the relationship between the Safavid monarchs and the various pastoral peoples who moved through and across Iran. He understands the rise of the Qajar dynasty, for example, as the conquest of a decrepit state by a vigorous outsider. In truth, he stretches Ibn Khaldun's theories here applying them to individuals (dissipated shahs and their ambitious overthrowers) rather than to peoples. Polk also squeezes in a discussion of Shi'a theology and its resemblances to Zoroastrianism, as well as a discussion of the relations between the ulama and the monarchy. The chapter concludes with a narrative of the incursions of Russian and British merchants and military men into Iran especially in the nineteenth century.

Chapter Four covers the decades between Iran's 1905 revolution that brought constitutional rule and the 1979 revolution that ended the Pahlavi dynasty. In the early part of the twentieth century Iran was one of several states that underwent self-strengthening, modernizing reforms in hopes of competing economically and militarily with its neighbors and more distant European powers. The Qajar dynasty showed little talent for this undertaking, and was overthrown by Reza Shah, founder of the Pahlavi dynasty, in 1921-25. He and his son, Mohammed Reza Pahlavi, ruled as autocrats, committed to their own power as well as the modernization of Iran. Polk's main theme

in this chapter is Iran's struggles with foreign powers. Russian and British forces struggled for influence in Iran, and indeed Cossacks helped put Reza Shah in power. Oil deals signed with the Anglo-Persian Oil Company (the forerunner of British Petroleum) surrendered Iran's only significant natural resource for tiny royalties. In 1941, Britain forced the abdication of Reza Shah, who sought neutrality in World War Two, which was inconvenient to Britain and the USSR, then fighting for survival. After 1945, Iran became more or less a Cold War client state of the United States, which kept the Shah well-armed in return for reliable supplies of oil and vehement anti-communism.

It is a good chapter, perhaps Polk's best, although a bit credulous in some respects (such as the claim that a quarter of the Iranian population died in upheavals in 1919).[4] Polk does a good job of explaining the growing alienation between the monarchy and the religious establishment, which did not share much of the Shah's modernizing agenda, resented American influence, feared the erosion of Iranian and Shi'a culture, and played upon the population's economic plight to political advantage. He claims that American diplomats, spies, and analysts failed to foresee the revolution of 1979 because they were insufficiently versed in Iranian history and culture.[5] He does not say whether or not he saw it coming. (The events of the Arab Spring of 2011 serve as a reminder that even well-informed analysts can fail – indeed usually do faiL – to foresee popular uprisings).

Polk's next chapter treats the career of the revolutionary regime from 1979 to 2009, beginning with the hostage crisis of

1979-80, vividly remembered by most Americans over age forty-five, and recently brought back to popular attention by the movie Argo. The Iran-Iraq War figures prominently, as it should, as does the rough revolutionary justice meted out by the Ayatollah Khomeini and his followers in the first years of the regime. He provides a narrative of Iranian politics in recent decades, dwelling on the role of the current president, Mahmoud Ahmadinejad.

Polk devotes his final chapter to U.S.-Iranian relations from the 1940s onward. He recounts the CIA's involvement in the coup that ended the parliamentary rule of Prime Minister Muhammad Mossadegh, and the oil deals that the U.S. subsequently negotiated with the Shah. He maintains the United States was taken in by reports of creeping communism, including some put about by British diplomats. The most curious feature of this chapter is what Polk presents as a verbatim account of a meeting between himself

moment it ended and believes it to be accurate. One wonders whether Polk is among the very few humans who can remember extended conversations verbatim, or whether one should take the words written here as a general indication of what the Shah had to say. The chapter ends with a withering critique of the neo-conservative approach to Iran and the Middle East, whose hostility towards Iran strengthened Teheran's resolve to acquire nuclear weapons.

Polk's book is intended for the general reader. Specialists will learn little they don't know already. His sources are English-language published works, including some diplomatic documents, press accounts, and in the final chapters, the occasional personal communication from participants in the events he describes. He has not delved deeply into the existing literature on Iranian history, especially for the earlier periods, and leaves many social and economic themes unexplored. But the premise of the book is that it provides

He claims that American diplomats, spies, and analysts failed to foresee the revolution of 1979 because they were insufficiently versed in Iranian history and culture.

and the Shah in 1967. It concerns distrust between the Shah and the Americans, and suggests remarkable candor on the part of the Shah (185-89), who apparently bridled at American condescension – except when speaking with Polk. In a footnote Polk says he wrote up his account of the conversation the

what Americans interested in U.S.-Iranian relations need to know about Iran. On that measure, it probably succeeds as well as any other single book.

His attention to 2,500 years of Iranian history raises the question of how much history education is enough for the practical purposes that Polk has in mind. Should people trying to deal with Iran today know about the Achaemenids and Sassanians? Should they know about the Safavids and Qajars? About the Anglo-Persian Oil Company and the forced abdication of Reza Shah? Or is all this "ancient history," in the dismissive phrase of the American vernacular? How much does one need to know about Zoroastrianism or the struggles among Muhammad's successors that divided the house of Islam between Sunni and Shi'a? An easy answer would be: the more the better. But that neglects the opportunity cost of time spent studying history at the expense of time spent mastering other skills. If one cannot learn everything, is studying international trade theory or international relations theory more useful than the history of centuries long ago?

Polk is convinced that few other skills are as important as the insight developed by studying history. He would include language and culture among worthy subjects. But the more theoretical arenas, such as formal international relations, economics, and especially war-gaming strike him as fool's gold -- approaches that create misplaced confidence in one's own understanding. Others of course will disagree with Polk, and will find his attachment to the long sweep of history a pedantic distraction from the more pertinent issues. Just what education is most useful for people responsible for foreign affairs, whether with respect to Iran or anywhere else, is an open question and should be of interest to students, teachers, and practitioners.

Notes

1 William R. Polk, *Understanding Iran: Everything you Need to Know, From Persia to the Islamic Republic, from Cyrus to Ahmadinejad*, New York: Palgrave Macmillan, 2009: 14.

2 Ibid, 16.
3 Ibid, 56.
4 Ibid, 100.
5 Ibid, 124.

Lee Kuan Yew: The Grand Master's Insights on China,the United States and the World

Review by Pamela Sodhy

Graham Allison, Robert D. Blackwill, and Ali Wayne. *Lee Kuan Yew: The Grand Master's Insights on China, the United States and the World.* Massachusets: The MIT Press, 2012. 232 pp. $17.95.

This book, a compilation of Lee Kuan Yew's views and insights on foreign policy matters, is unique in that its contents are pulled from interviews with Lee and from his speeches and writings. The compilation is the work of three scholars: Graham Allison, the Douglas Dillion Professor of Government and the Director of the Belfer Center for Science and International Affairs at the Harvard Kennedy School; Robert D. Blackwill, the Henry Kissinger Senior Fellow for U.S. Foreign Policy at the Council on Foreign Relations; and Ali Wyne, a researcher at Harvard's Belfer Center. They use a question and answer format, starting each chapter with a list of specific questions and then providing Lee's answers.[1] Their aim, as stated in the Preface, is "not to look back on the past 50 years, remarkable as Lee's contributions to them have been. Rather our focus is the future and the specific challenges that the United States will face during the next quarter century."[2] To them, Lee's answers are meant to be "of

Pamela Sodhy is an Adjunct Professor in the Asian Studies program at Georgetown University where she teaches courses about Southeast Asian History, U.S.- Southeast Asian relations, and the Association of Southeast Asian Nations. Prior to this she was an Associate Professor in the History Department at the National University of Malaysia. She earned her Ph.D from Cornell University and her publications include *The U.S.-Malaysian Nexus: Themes in Superpower-Small State Relations, The United States and Malaysia: The Socio-Cultural and Legal Experience,* and *US-ASEAN Trade: Current Issues and Future Strategies* value not only to those shaping U.S. foreign policy, but also to leaders of businesses and civil society in the United States."[3]

The book spans Lee's insights over a half century, covering different periods: as Prime Minister of Singapore; Senior Minister under his successor, Goh Chok Tong; Minister Mentor under his son, Lee Hsien Loong; and, since 2011, as Senior Advisor and Emeritus Senior Minister. In terms of content, the book is very comprehensive as it deals with Lee's views on numerous foreign policy topics. As for the book's organization, its first part is unusual in that a Foreword, by former U.S. Secretary of State Henry A. Kissinger, is followed by a short section with a title in the form of a question: "Who is Lee Kuan Yew?" Next is another short section, also with a question, this time entitled "When Lee Kuan Yew Talks, Who Listens?" After that is the Preface, followed by ten chapters, with the first eight providing Lee's views about the future.

tion. Moreover, his achievements serve as concrete proof that he is a master politician. Lee personifies leadership, determination, discipline, and vision. This book, named after him, can thus be considered a timely tribute to a great leader in the twilight of his life, as he is now eighty-nine years old and in poor health.

Another strength of the book is that it provides, in one relatively slim volume, Lee's most valuable insights on a wide array of topics on international relations. These insights reflect his deep knowledge of the world, international relations, history, and human nature. Since these insights are very useful, the book has, to a large extent, met the aim of its authors that it be of "value" to U.S. leaders in politics, business, and civil society regarding specific future challenges. Lee's insights can also serve as a guide to non-U.S. leaders or to readers in general about current events.

An example of Lee's valuable insight can be found in Chapter One, "The Fu-

Another strength of the book is that it provides...Lee's most valuable insights on a wide array of topics on international relations.

Overall, the book has several strengths. Lee is a fascinating, brilliant, and very complex man who merits attention, not only as Singapore's premier for thirty-one years but also as a statesman on the regional and global stage, courted by leaders around the world. He is most well known for his vital role in transforming a tiny island without resources into a first-world na-

ture of China," when he is asked "Are Chinese leaders serious about displacing the United States as the number one power in Asia? In the world?[4] He replies "Of course. Why not? They have transformed a poor society by an economic miracle to become now the second-largest economy in the world – on track ... to become the world's largest economy in the next 20 years."[5] His words shows that he is attuned to China's ambitious plans for he adds that "[t]he Chinese will want to share this century as co-equals with the U.S." and that "It is China's intention to be the greatest power in the world".[6]

At the same time, Lee shares his view that China will not overtake America as the world's biggest economic power until after a few decades. This is because China needs to overcome major hurdles before it can reach its ultimate goal. Lee lists some of these obstacles when he is asked "What are the major hurdles in executing that strategy?" and he replies "[i]nternally, the chief challenges are culture, language, an inability to attract and integrate talent from other countries, and, in time, governance."[7] He then explains that "The biggest single fear that China's leaders have is the corrosive effect of graft and the revulsion that it evokes in people."[8] With much discernment, he notes too that although "China will inevitably catch up to the U.S. in absolute GDP" its "creativity may never match America's, because its culture does not permit a free exchange and contest of ideas."[9]

In the case of the United States, Lee also offers deep insights in Chapter Two on "The Future of the United States". For instance, in reply to "Is the United States in systemic decline?," his answer is "Absolutely not" as he believes in its "great capacity for renewal and revival."[10] He is correct as the United States has bounced back from previous economic crises, such as the Panic of 1819, the Panic of 1873, and the Great Depression in the 1930s. Lee also notes perceptively, when asked "What are America's primary strengths?", that "Americans have a can-do approach to

life" and that "Whether it can or it cannot, Americans believe it can be solved, given enough money, research, and effort."[11] To Lee, "What has made the U.S. economy preeminent is its entrepreneurial culture."[12] He is right again, as borne out by the biographies of American entrepreneurs like Henry Ford, John D. Rockefeller, and Andrew Carnegie. They all took risks, persisted despite setbacks, and eventually achieved great success.

In Chapter Three, on "The Future of U.S.-China Relations", Lee has useful insights into this relationship, seen by many foreign policy experts, including Kishore Mahbubani, Dean of the Lee Kuan Yew School of Public Policy at the National University of Singapore, as one of the most critical bilateral relationships of the 21st century. For instance, Lee is right on mark when he points out that "[u]nlike U.S.-Soviet relations during the Cold War, there is no irreconcilable ideological conflict between the U.S. and a China that has enthusiastically embraced the market."[13] In his opinion, "Sino-U.S. relations are both cooperative and competitive. Competition between them is inevitable, but conflict is not."[14] He also believes, rightly, that "A stabilizing factor in their relationship...is that each nation requires cooperation from and healthy competition with the other."[15] Furthermore, "Chinese leaders know that U.S. military superiority is overwhelming, and will remain so for the next few decades."[16]

Lee is also very perceptive about India in Chapter Four, on "The Future of India." For example, he notes correctly that "India is such a diverse country – it is not one nation but thirty-two different nations speaking 330 different dialects."[17] He then sharpens this description of India by adding that "In China, it is 90 [percent] Han Chinese all speaking the same language, with different accents, but reading the same script."[18] Lee also has noteworthy views about the constraints that India's system of democratic governance imposes on the nation's long-term prospects. He highlights constraints like "bureaucracy and corruption", the "caste system", and the "limitations in the Indian constitutional system and the Indian political system."[19]

In addition to the solid subject matter of the book in Lee Kuan Yew, a third strength is the examples of Lee's wisdom gained from his experience as a politician and leader. This wisdom has possibly been accumulated by him through decades of first-hand experience in handling problems on the political, security, economic, and socio-cultural fronts. A sample of Lee's wisdom can be found in his following reply to

tory as having a crucial role in guiding a nation in policy formulation as history helps to explain the past. History thus links a nation's past, present, and future. Lee implies that history has lessons to teach and that these lessons can prepare a nation to meet its many challenges.

Another sample of Lee's wisdom is his reply to the question "What are the most common public policy mistakes that leaders make?"[21] He says "Sometimes they succumb to hubris and overconfidence, and other times they miss a transformative opportunity when it arrives."[22] These remarks reveal that Lee is an astute judge of character and keenly aware of the faults of leaders, weaknesses usually associated with their egos. Yet another sample of Lee's wisdom can be seen in his comments on the late Goh Keng Swee, one of his former cabinet ministers, whom Lee praised for being a "troubleshooter" by challenging some of Lee's decisions.[23] This disclosure shows that Lee, with his keen foresight and strategic vision,

Lee is an astute judge of character and keenly aware of the faults of leaders.

the question "What role should history play in strategic thinking and policy-making?"

To understand the present and anticipate the future, one must know enough of the past, enough to have a sense of the history of a people. One must appreciate not merely what took place, but, more especially, why it took place and in that particular way. This is true of individuals, as it is for nations.[20]

Lee's reply shows that he regards his-

has not been afraid of opposition to his policies. Instead, he has been wise enough to appreciate dissenting views for the value that they hold, as they have enabled him to avoid mistakes and to implement better and more carefully crafted policies.

A fourth strength of the book is that it brings out very clearly the controversial and provocative nature of some of Lee's insights. This can be considered a strength as it allows for dialogue and for the exchange of different views. In the book's Preface, in reference to Lee's answers, the authors acknowledge that "Many of those answers have an edge, since he has congenitally pushed back against 'political correctness' and never shrunk from controversy."[24] An example of a controversial and provocative insight by Lee can be found in Chapter Five on "The Future of Islamic Extremism." When asked "What are the roots of Islamic extremism?," Lee replied: "The Israeli-Palestinian conflict is not the cause of Islamic terrorism."[25] This answer marks Lee's rejection of what many scholars believe is one of the main reasons for Islamic terrorism. To these scholars, this conflict is a major cause as it has been building up and festering between the two sides for decades, ever since the creation of Israel in 1948.

Among the scholars subscribing to the Israeli-Palestinian conflict as a main cause for Islamic terrorism is Kumar Ramakrishna. In an article entitled "Terrorism in Southeast Asia: The Ideological and Political Dimensions" in Southeast Asian Affairs 2004, he points out that a Singapore Jemaah Islamiyah (JI) leader, Ibrahim Maidin, "declared that the 'U.S. had to change its policy towards the Middle East', and that 'as long as the U.S. hits Islam, JI would have to attack the U.S.'"[26] In another article, "Delegitimizing Global Jihadi Ideology in Southeast Asia" in *Contemporary Southeast Asia*, (2005), Ramakrishna is more vehement about the Israeli–Palestinian conflict being the major cause of Islamic terrorism. He stresses that "[i]t must be understood that generalized Muslim antipathy towards America stems from one single issue in particular: the plight of

the Palestinians and the status of Jerusalem."[27] He explains that Jerusalem, as the site of the Al Aqsa mosque, is the third holiest place in Islam after Mecca and Medina and adds, "the suffering of the stateless Palestinians has served as a metaphor for the suffering of Muslims as a whole in the face of a supposed Zionist-Crusader conspiracy."[28]

Another example of Lee's controversial and provocative insights is found in his comments about U.S. culture in Chapter Two. When asked "What worries you about U.S. culture?", he replies "The ideas of individual supremacy...when carried to excess, have not worked. They have made it difficult to keep American society cohesive. Asia can see that it is not working."[29] In this connection, he also says "The top 3 to 5 [percent] of a society can handle this free-for-all, this clash of ideas. If you do this for the whole mass, you will have a mess."[30]

Lee's words are controversial because America's emphasis on individual rights can also be viewed as encouraging the creativity, innovation, and genius of its people. One could argue also that individual rights have allowed some Americans minds to soar to new heights, resulting in many new inventions and technological breakthroughs as intellectual and entrepreneurial growth have been promoted, not inhibited or stifled. Americans face fewer restrictions than Singaporeans, who have to deal with media control, censorship of the press, and fines for even failing to flush public toilets. Perhaps Lee's views on individual rights have been unduly influenced by Singapore's experience as a small island sandwiched between two much larger Islamic nations. Under such circumstances, the need to ensure national security at all times can make the rights of the community seem far more important than those of the individual. In any case, Lee's controversial and provocative insights on various topics foster discussion as well as a healthy exchange of different views.

While the book has many strengths, there are also a few shortcomings. One inherent shortcoming is that it deals mainly with the future, which is difficult to prognosticate as there are many variables that can affect it, such as leadership changes, wars, natural disasters, and the state of the economy. Making a forecast of a nation, like making a forecast of the weather, is never easy nor foolproof. Another inbuilt shortcoming is that the book uses Lee's insights by arranging them in such a way that they serve as answers to the questions that the authors of the book have drawn up. This means that some views, originally intended for other purposes, now represent Lee's answers to specific questions for which they might not have been intended. While this can be considered an ingenious method to author a book, it can also be seen as a contrived way to do so.

Yet another shortcoming is that the book deals predominantly with praise for Lee Kuan Yew. Praise for Lee is found throughout the book, starting with the Foreword, where Kissinger commends Lee as "a man of unmatched intelligence and judgment" and as "Singapore's first premier and its guiding spirit ever since."[31] Kissinger also claims that although he has met many world leaders, "none, however, has taught me more than Lee Kuan Yew."[32] Praise of Lee continues in the next section, "Who is Lee Kuan Yew?" with its three pro-

Lee subtitles: "A Strategist's Strategist", "A Leader's Leader", and "A Mentor's Mentor". More praise follows in "When Lee Kuan Yew Talks, Who Listens?" as it contains glowing comments in subsections entitled "Presidents"; "Chinese Leaders"; "Other Heads of State"; "Heads of Global Corporations and Economic Institutions"; "Senior Policy Makers"; and "Commentators". The U.S presidents who laud Lee are Barack Obama, Bill Clinton, and George H.W. Bush. In these sections, praise for Lee revolves around his "judgment"; "vision"; "analysis"; "public service"; "leadership"; "brilliant intellect"; "geopolitical understanding"; "grasp of regional issues"; and "depth...understanding of the world."[33]

Thus, there is hardly any criticism of Lee in the book. One attempt, by Nicholas Kristof, an opinion columnist for the New York Times listed under "Commentators", is that under Lee "intolerance and authoritarianism have never had so articulate or stimulating a spokesman."[34] But Kristof does not elaborate on his comments while Lee himself only hints at some misdeeds. He says in Chapter Nine, in reply to "How do you wish to be remembered?": "I am not saying that everything I did was right, but everything I did was for an honorable purpose. I had to do some nasty things."[35]

The "nasty things" that Lee alludes to can stand for his harassment and imprisonment of his political opponents. These opponents included Chia Thye Poh, Lim Chin Siong, and Chee Soon Juan, who were all imprisoned for long periods. In the case of two other political opponents, JB Jeyaretnam and Gopalan Nair, both lawyers, they were disbarred from practicing law in Singapore due to their criticisms of Lee's government. At times, Lee sued his enemies, as in the case of Devan Nair, former President of Singapore. He also brought defamation lawsuits against some journalists with the then Far Eastern Economic Review and with the International Herald Tribune for criticisms against him. Lee's ill-treatment of his opponents paints a negative picture of his leadership in Singapore and also shows the price he had to pay for his success. One could also argue that his attacks on his political opponents eventually made Singapore a one-party state, without an effective opposition.

Another drawback of the book is that there are some gaps in its content. For example, in Chapter One, there is no mention of China's claims to all of the Spratly islands or to China's insistence on holding bilateral talks, rather than multilateral talks, with the other claimants. In Chapter Two, President Obama's use of clandestine drone strikes and the criticism of this policy are not touched upon. Also missing is Obama's new Asia-Pacific policy, described as a "pivot" to Asia. Discussion of this policy is also missing in Chapter Three, about U.S.-China relations. Some mention should be made of the "pivot" policy and of the Trans-Pacific Partnership because they have become stumbling blocks in U.S.-China ties, as China suspects that they are aimed at curbing its rise. America's concern with commercial cyber-espionage by China could also be mentioned. In Chapter Four, the answer to "What is the forecast for U.S.-India Relations" is incomplete as it leaves out other pertinent issues, such as India's engagement with Iran, India's wariness about the U.S., and America's disappointment with the U.S.-India Strategic Partnership as India has not yet signed two key defense agreements. The United States is also not sure if India can be a trusted ally in its "pivot" to Asia.

In conclusion, despite any shortcomings with the book or of its subject matter as a leader, the book represents a significant contribution to the scholarship on Lee Kuan Yew, complementing and supplementing the many other books already written about him, including some that Lee himself authored, like *The Singapore Story*, *From Third World to First*, and *Keeping my Mandarin Alive*. The most important aspect of the book's contribution lies in Lee's keen insights on international relations. These insights also reveal something more – his character. They disclose his tenacity, single mindedness, courage, and perseverance in pursuing his goals. Since Lee's life is so closely intertwined with developments in Singapore, the book serves also as a valuable contribution to the history of Singapore over a very long period, from 1959 when Lee, its most illustrious son, became his nation's first premier.

1 Graham Allison, Robert Blackwill, and Ali Wyne, *Lee Kuan Yew: The Grand Master's Insights on China, the United States, and the World*. (The MIT Press, 2013), xxvii.

2 Ibid, xxvi.

3 Ibid, xxvi.

4 Ibid, 2.

5 Ibid, 2.

6 Ibid, 3.

7 Ibid, 7.

8 Ibid, 8.

9 Ibid, 8.

10 Ibid, 20.

11 Ibid, 22.

12 Ibid, 22.

13 Ibid, 38.

14 Ibid, 38.

15 Ibid, 39.

16 Ibid, 39.

17 Ibid, 54.

18 Ibid, 54.

19 Ibid, 52.

20 Ibid, 137.

21 Ibid, 147.

22 Ibid, 147.

23 Ibid, 148.

24 Ibid, xxvii.

25 Ibid, 69.

26 Kumar Ramakrishna, "Terrorism in Southeast Asia: The Ideological and Political Dimensions," *Southeast Asian Affairs* (2004): 58.

27 Kumar Ramakrishna, "Delegitimizing Global Jihadi Ideology in Southeast Asia," *Contemporary Southeast Asia* 27, no. 3 (2005): 360.

28 Ibid, 360.

29 Allison et al., 29.

30 Ibid, 29.

31 Ibid, vii.

32 Ibid, vii.

33 Ibid, vii-xxiii.

34 Ibid, xxiii.

35 Ibid, 149.

The Decline and Fall of the United States Information Agency

Review by Juliet Antunes Sablosky

Cull, Nicholas J. *The Decline and Fall of the United States Information Agency: American Public Diplomacy,* 1989-2001. New York: Palgrave Macmillian, 2012. 276 pp. $85.00.

To the second volume of his history of the U. S. Information Agency, Nicholas Cull brings a similarly skillful survey of the institution and the role it played in furthering American foreign policy goals.[1] This time he concentrates on the changes wrought by the end of the Cold War and the impact they had on the Agency, its programs, and its people. Throughout the book major attention is given to the Voice of America and to the policy advocacy aspects of USIA's work. Professor Cull gives less attention to the other three "core components" of public diplomacy, which he identifies as listening, cultural diplomacy, and exchange diplomacy. This meticulously documented book, based on archival research, private papers, and interviews, helps fill a long-standing gap in the literature and sets the stage for further research on American public diplomacy. It will be much appreciated by those teaching and researching the public diplomacy dimension of international relations.

The Decline and Fall of the U.S. Information Agency com-

Juliet Antunes Sablosky, Ph.D. is Adjunct Professor of Liberal Studies at Georgetown where she has taught courses in Cultural Diplomacy & American Foreign Policy and European Politics. Prior to this she was a Foreign Service Officer with the U.S. Information Agency, serving in Western Europe and Mexico as a cultural affairs officer. Her Washington assignments have included Deputy Director of the Fulbright Academic Exchange program and Director of the Arts America program.

plements nicely a number of books written over the years by practitioners of public diplomacy that are important for the understanding they provide of its possibilities and constraints, as well as for the vivid pictures they paint of how it was carried out overseas.[2] But the Cull book provides a different perspective, coming from an established academic observer and concentrating on the domestic side of policy-making. While primarily of interest to the foreign policy and public diplomacy communities, students and researchers of public policy will find grist for their mills here as well. The political machinations that accompanied the death of the USIA as an independent agency and its integration (or re-integration, if one considers its early history) into the Department of State make for lively reading and provide an excellent case study.

of all Agency elements, made the best adjustment to the challenges of the post-1989 world. He praises the policy advocacy work done by many USIA departments in connection with the First Gulf War and post-Dayton Bosnia. He also gives USIA high marks for its use of new technology. Throughout the book the focus is on the policy and decision-making of the last three directors and their impact on the agency's future. Cull assesses a number of factors accounting for USIA's demise, some of them long term in nature. The political climate of the moment was key, he believes, especially the tug of war between the Clinton administration and Senator Jesse Helms, then chairman of the Senate Foreign Relations Committee, over the Chemical Weapons Convention and the consolidation of the foreign affairs agencies in the Department of State. Cull concludes that "it is plain that the

Cull concludes that "it is plain that the Agency suffered in part because of the coincidence between new challenges and a weakness at the top."

Professor Cull traces developments through four narratives describing the path to amalgamation with the State Department. These include: the political battles within the Agency and with Congress and the Executive; how the USIA carried out its work in the post-Cold War period; how it reacted to the changed communications and technology environment of the "new public diplomacy" and its efforts in the Middle East prior to 9/11. In assessing USIA's work, Cull concludes that the VOA,

Agency suffered in part because of the coincidence between new challenges and a weakness at the top."[3] The profiles of USIA's leaders and the inside look provided on the Agency's last years provide a unique window into the decision-making and politics involved. For some, the detail will prove excessive, for others, fascinating. But at the end of the day what *The Decline and Fall* documents is the failure of an institution and its leadership to rise to the challenges of a changed environment post-1989 and make a persuasive case to Congress and the administration that it could play a significant role in meeting those challenges.

There was a case to be made for USIA, it seems to me. It had years of experience, for example, in promoting democratic ideas and processes abroad. It had years of experience teaching English as a foreign language abroad. It had networks of former grantees holding significant positions in government, academia and the media. Yet when it was decided to emphasize support for democratization and English teaching in post-1989 Eastern Europe, the Peace Corps was given the lead and the money for English Language Teaching and the Agency for International Development, the budget for democratization projects, many of which it then subcontracted to USIA. What sort of leadership might have made a difference? Or could it have? These are interesting questions which merit further discussion. Some input from leaders of the private sector organizations with which USIA worked or from Congressional staff or Department of State officials at the time would have contributed yet another dimension.

Among the long term factors mentioned in the book is the role played by our political culture with its underlying current of isolationism, not only in USIA's history, but also in that of its predecessors. Distrust of the federal government's role in matters of education, culture, and communications has been a constant. As Cull notes, it has contributed to the stop and start nature of our national efforts in public diplomacy. Start in times of war or crisis; stop once they are over. This underlying distrust, I would add, applies domestically as well. The battles over the establishment of a cabinet level department of education and the legislation authorizing the National Endowments for the Arts and Humanities, bear vivid witness to the impact of these factors. Perhaps then, it is not surprising that the USIA sank with little public debate or outcry on Capitol Hill.

For all its merits, there are two areas in *The Decline and Fall* where further analysis would have been welcome: the overseas dimension of public diplomacy and the evaluation of USIA's role in foreign policy. While the political drama played out in Washington, there were serious implications for the overseas posts. USIA was first and foremost a foreign affairs agency. It was designed to engage audiences abroad and to promote a better understanding of the United States, its people, its history, and its values in support of the country's foreign policy objectives. To be sure, there are some examples of overseas projects given in the book such as efforts to support conflict resolution and intercommunal understanding in Cyprus. Given the thrust of the book, however, it would have been even more interesting an analysis had it dealt at greater length with some of the effects the Washington manipulations had on the practice of public diplomacy. What was the impact of steady staff and budget cuts? How has our capacity to interact with other people and cultures been affected by the closing of so many cultural centers, libraries, and consulates? How have the overseas posts compensated for this – and with what results? Cull may have felt that the overseas aspects were covered sufficiently in some of the first-hand accounts referred to earlier. But to be truly useful for the academic study and research of public diplomacy, the overseas dimension needs the same rigorous, scholarly attention given to the Washington institution.

Secondly, some additional evaluation of USIA's role would have benefitted the analysis. Had the USIA outlived its usefulness as critics charged? What were its lasting accomplishments? What lessons might be learned from its successes -- and failures? As Professor Cull has demonstrated, there are rich sources available and they continue to grow. In recent years, for example, the Association for Diplomatic Studies and

Training has put its collection of some 2,300 oral histories of Foreign Service Officers on line. These first hand accounts as well as the many reports by government and non-government organizations and Congressional committees over the years should provide plentiful material for interested researchers.

One hopes that Nicholas Cull's fine work *In The Decline and Fall of the United States Information Agency* will stimulate further discussion not only of the past, but also of the contours that our twenty-first century public diplomacy ought to take in the challenging overseas environment of today.

NOTES

1 Nicholas J. Cull, *The Cold War and the United States Information Agency: American Propaganda and Public Diplomacy, 1945-1989* (Cambridge: Cambridge University Press, 2008).

2 Among the many available accounts: William P. Kiehl, ed., *The Last Three Feet: Case Studies in Public Diplomacy* (Washington, D.C.: Public Diplomacy Council, 2012); William A. Rugh, *American Encounters with Arabs: The "Soft Power" of U.S. Public Diplomacy in the Middle East* (Westport, CT:

Praeger Security International, 2006); Richard T. Arndt, *The First Resort of Kings: American Cultural Diplomacy in the Twentieth Century* (Washington, D.C.: Potomac Books, Inc., 2005); Alan L. Heil Jr., *Voice of America: A History* (New York: Columbia University Press, 2003); Yale Richmond, *Cultural Exchange & The Cold War: Raising the Iron Curtain* (University Park: The Pennsylvania State University Press, 2003).

3 Cull 2012, 181.

A Look Back

Global Women's Issues

Ambassador Melanne Verveer

GJIA: What were the challenges implicit in becoming the first U.S. Ambassador-at-Large for Global Women's Issues? Did the nature of your role change over time?

Verveer: Secretary Clinton and I were not new to these issues, nor was the State Department. Secretary Albright actually established the first Office for Global Women's Issues in 1996 and it was she who issued an important cable to the State Department staff, including those engaged in our operations around the world, to report on the situation of women and girls (from education to economic participation). In some ways, we had been flying blind due to the lack of reporting on these issues - an omission concerning half the population of the world - that really was important to the conduct of our foreign policy. Secretaries Powell and Rice continued the office.

Secretary Clinton clearly understood this approach must become a cornerstone of U.S. Diplomacy. My appointment by President Obama was consistent with her broader efforts on U.S. foreign policy, as was evidenced in the Quadrennial Diplomacy and Development Review and other initiatives. At the outset, some perhaps regarded the focus

Ambassador Melanne Verveer is the first U.S. Ambassador-at-Large for Global Women's Issues. She is also the inaugural director of the Georgetown Institute of Women, Peace and Security.

on women's issues as marginal, but the relevance of these issues in enabling us to more effectively achieve our foreign policy goals became clear.

The agenda in this area was advanced in many ways, certainly through an integrative approach throughout the Department, but also through multilateral forums in which the US participated, through bilateral strategic dialogues, through development, and so on.

For me, establishing America's leadership on these issues mattered, both symbolically and practically. As the Secretary often said, "[t]his is not just the right thing to do, but also the smart thing."

GJIA: What remain your issues of most outstanding concern?

Verveer: Violence against women and girls remains a global epidemic. From the kinds of brutal violence in the Democratic Republic of Congo, for example, where rape is used as a

in their reproductive years. Feticide and infanticide solely because of son preference has begun to skew the demographics of countries like India and China. It is also not a problem confined to the poor. We are already seeing that when millions of young men outnumber women, additional violence occurs in the form of trafficking, child marriage and the kidnapping of girls. At the root of much of this is the lack of value placed on girls.

The situation of women in Afghanistan and preserving the gains they have made there in the last decade must be a priority for the United States. Moreover, if women are marginalized or silenced, any potential for a sustainable peace will be jeopardized. They are more than half the population of the country and have demonstrated leadership at all levels of society and in politics, the economy and civil society.

We have seen progress too. We are better attuned to addressing some of the deeply entrenched practices that

Violence against women and girls remains a global epidemic.

tool of war to the everyday impunity against prosecution of domestic abuse. Governments have an obligation to enforce laws and bring all perpetrators of violence to justice.

The World Bank has written evocatively about, "the Missing" – some four million girls and women who are more likely to die, relative to males, either through infanticide and feticide, deaths in early childhood and deaths

take a toll on women and girls. In our development policies, we have invested in girls' education because we know it is one of the most effective development investments for a girl's future employment, the nutrition for her children, positive health impacts and more. Programs like conditional cash transfers put in the hands of mothers to invest in their children have had a transformational impact in countries like Brazil and Mexico. In addressing deeply entrenched cultural practices with harmful health impacts, working at the grassroots level has helped to shift norms from the practice of FGM, for example, to primary concern for the health of women and girls. There is greater progress being made to confront violence against women in post conflict societies like Guatemala where government has made ending impuni-

violence against women globally.

I also think significant advances have been made in promoting women's economic participation. In the Asia Pacific region, perhaps the most economically dynamic, potential GDP remains constrained by the under-representation of women in the economic sphere. APEC, through US leadership, now has a strong focus on women and the economy and lifting the barriers

Today we know from volumes of data that no nation can grow the economy and create jobs without engaging women.

ty a priority. So there is much progress to note, but it is uneven.

GJIA: Which instruments of statecraft proved most useful in advancing your agenda as Ambassador?

Verveer: Women's issues have been integrated into diplomacy and development and this integration also extends to the training of our diplomats, to budgeting to elevating responsibility for these issues, as well as infusing them across all the operations of the Department - human rights, economics, political military, etc - to achieve more effective outcomes. The President also issued an Executive Order and National Action Plan on Women, Peace and Security, something we are focusing on here at Georgetown at the new institute. The President also issued a Presidential Memo to make the position of Ambassador for Global Women's Issues permanent, as well as an Executive Order on preventing

that confine women's entrepreneurship.

Today we know from volumes of data that no nation can grow the economy and create jobs without engaging women.

GJIA: Perhaps your most important theme has been the importance of education. Could you reflect on your own experiences at Georgetown University?

Verveer: Without education our horizons are limited. Education is critical to effecting change and protecting human dignity around the world.

When I consider the impact of my Georgetown education, I reflect on three themes. First, the formal content of my studies considerably broadened my outlook and intellectual development. Second, even many years ago when I was a student, Georgetown had strong international representation in its student body. Foreign students provided a perspective that stretched far beyond Washington, DC. Long before email and the Internet made the world more accessible, it was here on the doorstep of GU. Studying in the Nation's Capital was also stimulating because some of the most prominent leaders and thinkers debated key issues on foreign policy on the campus. Finally, Georgetown and its Jesuit tradition imbued in me a strong set of values and service. We were called to serve something bigger than ourselves, to make a difference and create change in the world. These three attributes – scholastic accomplishment, the international environment and a call to service – all had a profound impact on me.

Ambassador Verveer was interviewed by Christopher Johnston on 21 March 2013.